KU-741-110

# THE · MACDONALD · ENCYCLOPEDIA · OF
# Alpine Flowers

# THE · MACDONALD · ENCYCLOPEDIA · OF
# Alpine
# Flowers

## Guido Moggi

LITTLE, BROWN AND COMPANY

## A LITTLE, BROWN BOOK

©1984 Arnoldo Mondadori Editore S.p.A., Milan
©1985 in the English translation
  Arnoldo Mondadori Editore S.p.A., Milan

English translation by Sylvia Mulcahy

First published in Great Britain in 1985
by Macdonald & Co (Publishers) Ltd

First reprint 1990.
This Little, Brown edition published 1995

*All rights reserved*
No part of this publication may be reproduced,
stored in a retrieval system, or transmitted,
in any form or by any means without the prior
permission in writing of the publisher, nor be
otherwise circulated in any form of binding or cover
other than that in which it is published and without
a similar condition including this condition being
imposed on the subsequent purchaser.

British Library Cataloguing in Publication Data

Moggi, Guido
  The Macdonald encyclopedia of
  alpine flowers.
  1. Alpine flora
  I. Title
  582.13    QK937

  ISBN 0-316-878391

Printed in Spain by Artes Gráficas Toledo, S.A.
D.L.TO:1147-1995

Little, Brown and Company (UK)
Brettenham House
Lancaster Place
London WC2E 7EN

# CONTENTS

# ABOUT THIS BOOK

Species are listed in alphabetical order according to scientific name. The specific binomial for each species is in bold capital letters, followed by the abbreviation or full name of its botanical author, i.e. the person who first described the species. In certain cases the synonym by which the plant is known is included in italics. Any English common name follows the author.

The following information is also given for each species: the family to which it belongs, a short description of the plant, its size, flowering period, the environment in which it grows, and geographical distribution. The indications of size, flowering period and altimetric distribution sometimes include one or two figures in brackets; these indicate the extreme specifications while the numbers outside the brackets refer to the average, i.e. most frequently recurring, figures. In some cases, notes have been added regarding principles of classification of the species, its eventual utilization, rarity, and status as a protected species. A detailed map of alpine areas can be found on page 28.

## KEY TO SYMBOLS
### Plant habits

Erect or ascending, isolated or in groups

Acaulescent with leafless (or nearly so) stalk

Tufted

Mat-, carpet- or cushion-forming

Diffuse, creeping or prostrate

Branched or tree-like with woody stem

Shrub-like or low-growing

## Geographical distribution

Black dots on maps indicate the geographical distribution areas of plants.

## Environment and subsoil

High altitude woods and clearings: grey base, on any subsoil; red base, on a mainly calcareous subsoil; blue base, on a mainly siliceous subsoil.

High altitude moorlands and scrub: grey base, on any subsoil; red base, on a mainly calcareous subsoil; blue base, on a mainly siliceous subsoil.

Fields, pasturelands and grassy places in general: grey base, on any subsoil; red base, on a mainly calcareous subsoil; blue base, on a mainly siliceous subsoil.

Marshlands, streams, upland bogs and other damp areas: grey base, on any subsoil; red base, on a mainly calcareous subsoil; blue base, on a mainly siliceous subsoil.

Screes, moraines, stony and pebbly ground: grey base, on any subsoil; red base, on a mainly calcareous subsoil; blue base, on a mainly siliceous subsoil.

Rock faces, crags and fissures in the rocks: grey base, on any subsoil; red base, on a mainly calcareous subsoil; blue base, on a mainly siliceous subsoil.

## Altimetric distribution

The altimetric distribution of the plant. A strip of colour at the base indicates that the plant is also distributed in the Arctic and sub-Arctic at low altitudes down to sea level. The altitude is marked in metres. The exact equivalent in feet is provided in the accompanying text.

*Altimetric succession of alpine vegetation in the Rocky Mountains.*

## Foreword

Mountains will always thrill and fascinate. Their mystery is indefinable, and for many irresistible. They constitute a world apart, and those who have experienced this magical attraction know only too well how they are drawn back, time and again, to explore the exceptional beauty of the mountain environment. Part of the fascination of the great heights lies in the wealth of mountain flowers, which totally transform what might otherwise be arid wastes.

It is hoped that the photographs and descriptions of this selection of mountain plants will convey to the reader something of the outstanding beauty, range of colours and habits of alpine flowers from every continent.

A comprehensive description of all the world's mountain plants, could not be attempted in a book of this size. We have decided accordingly to choose the most attractive and better-known alpine plants and those which, although less well known, are interesting for their beauty, rarity or other unique qualities. Hence the juxtaposition of such common and well-known species as the edelweiss and martagon (Turk's-cap) lily with the rare adonis (Pheasant's Eye) of the Pyrenees, and the Balkan ramonda, the curious American lysichiton and the New Zealand Raoulia.

Preference has been given, however, to those plants that

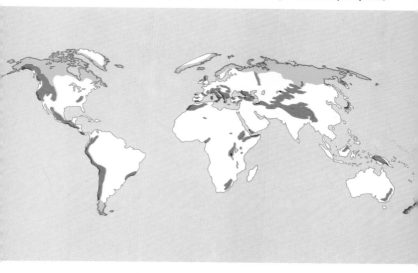

inhabit European mountain ranges. The best-known is probably the Alps, and some of the species illustrated are only to be found in that area, although those that occur in the mountains of Great Britain have not been neglected.

Throughout the book the terms 'alpine', 'mountain' (or 'montane') and 'high mountain' are used interchangeably, although botanists prefer a more precise definition; *Alpine flora* includes plant species that inhabit mountains, or the Alps in particular, above the tree-line, that is, 6,560–7,220 ft (2,000–2,200 m), while *mountain flora* or *montane flora* refers to plants whose natural home is the montane zone (see pp. 20–21). Specialists, however, tend to use the term *high mountain flora* when referring to plant species that grow at very high altitudes on any mountain, reserving the term *Alpine flora* solely for plants native to the Alps; these plants are also frequently referred to as *alpines*.

The terms 'flora' and 'vegetation' both occur frequently throughout the book and are often confused by the layman. *Flora* refers to all the plant species that may be found in a particular area. *Vegetation*, on the other hand, covers all aspects of the plant life of a particular area, including the various forms of association between the plants, their habit, and so forth.

*Association* is the grouping of plants which occupy any definite, uniform area of land. For example, wet meadows in

11

*A larch wood with green alders in the upper montane zone of the Alps (see page 21). Opposite: the most characteristic environment of mountain plants is among rocks, crags and on stony slopes.*

England usually show an *association* between buttercups, meadowsweet, marsh thistles and meadow grasses; none of these would be found in a heath *association* containing heather, ling, dwarf furze, harebell, bilberries, etc.

*Habit* is the external appearance of a plant, not to be confused with *habitat* which is its natural location.

Thus, *Alpine flora* embraces all plants native to mountainous regions and includes such familiar names as saxifrage, gentian and primula, while *Alpine vegetation* includes the high alpine pastures, heathlands and upland moors.

## Where alpine plants live

Every continent has mountains: the great ranges such as the Rocky Mountains of North America, the Andes of South America, the Karakoram and the Himalayas of Asia are well known, as are the Alps, Pyrenees, Scottish Highlands and Carpathians of Europe. Equally famous isolated mountains include Africa's Mt. Kilimanjaro and Mt. Kenya, Japan's Mt. Fuji and Alaska's Mt. McKinley; famous volcanoes include Mt. Etna in Sicily and Popocatepetl in Mexico.

In geological terms, all these mountains are of relatively recent origin, the greater part of such ranges as the Andes, Himalayas, Alps and Rockies having been formed during the

so-called Alpine orogeny, the vast convulsions of the Earth which spawned them during the Tertiary period – about 30–60 million years ago. These mountains, subjected as they have been to only a few million years of erosion, conserve their original rugged form to a large extent. The highest altitudes in the world are to be found in these young mountains, typified by Mt. Everest which rises to a height of 29,025 ft (8,847 m).

Towards the end of the Palaeozoic era, during the Carboniferous and Permian periods – about 250 million years ago – the Hercynian orogeny took place. The most important mountains which were then formed were those of central Europe, notably the Jura (Switzerland/France) and the Vosges in eastern France; these are not particularly rugged and rise to a height of only 4,890 ft (1,490 m).

During the earlier periods of the Palaeozoic era, in the course of the Silurian and Devonian – about 400 million years ago – the Caledonian orogeny occurred, when the mountains of Scotland, Ireland, Scandinavia and other northern European countries were formed.

Although the most important and spectacular mountain ranges are to be found in Asia and America, alpine flora occurs in every continent, sometimes even at quite low altitudes.

The most extensive chain in the world is the Rocky Mountains of North America. Covering an area from northern Alaska to central New Mexico, the range extends along almost the

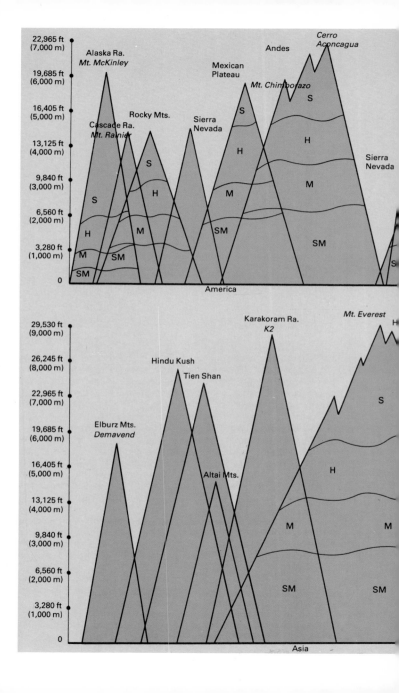

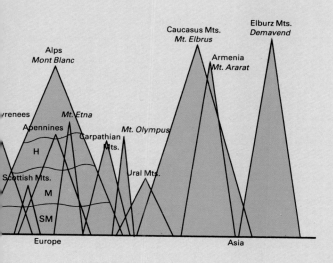

Alps
*Mont Blanc*

Caucasus Mts.
*Mt. Elbrus*

Elburz Mts.
*Demavend*

Armenia
*Mt. Ararat*

Pyrenees

*Mt. Etna*

Apennines

Carpathian
Mts.

*Mt. Olympus*

H

Scottish Mts.

Ural Mts.

M

SM

Europe

Asia

as
*henjunga*

S   snow zone
H   high alpine zone
M   montane zone
SM  sub-montane zone

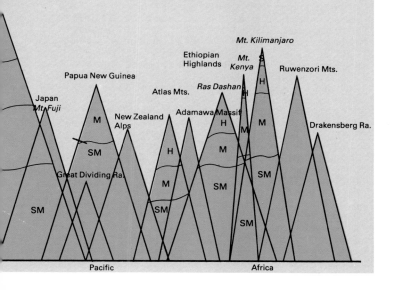

*Mt. Kilimanjaro*

Ethiopian
Highlands

*Mt.
Kenya*

Ruwenzori Mts.

Papua New Guinea

Atlas Mts.

*Ras Dashan*

S

Japan
*Mt. Fuji*

M

New Zealand
Alps

Adamawa Massif

H

Drakensberg Ra.

SM

H

H

M

M

M

Great Dividing Ra.

M

M

H

SM

SM

SM

SM

M

SM

SM

SM

Pacific

Africa

entire western side of North America and reaches its highest point in Mt. McKinley, Alaska, at 20,300 ft (6,187 m). To the west, the Sierra Nevada range in California has a highest peak of 14,495 ft (4,418 m). In Mexico, the Sierra Madre range includes the volcanoes of Popocatepetl (17,985 ft/5,482 m) and Ixtaccihuatl (17,342 ft/5,286 m). In the eastern United States, the relatively small range of the Appalachian Mountains is of very ancient origin; they reach a peak of only 6,686 ft (2,038 m), and are not conspicuous for their high mountain flora.

South America is dominated by the Cordillera of the Andes, extending almost 3,080 miles (8,000 km) from Venezuela to Patagonia. In some places it covers an area 370 miles (600 km) wide. The highest peaks in the Andes are Bolivia's Illampu (22,977 ft/7,000 m) and Illimani (22,592 ft/6,886 m), and Argentina's Aconcagua (22,831 ft/6,959 m).

The mountains of Europe, with the exception of the Alps, are of comparative insignificance in terms of height. The highest mountains in the north are the Grampians in Scotland (Ben Nevis – 4,406 ft/1,343 m) and the peaks of Scandinavia (8,104 ft/2,470 m). In central Europe, apart from the Alps (Mont Blanc – 15,781 ft/4,810 m) there are mountainous areas in France: the Massif Central and Cevennes (6,188 ft/1,886 m), the Jura (5,577 ft/1,700 m) and the Vosges (4,669 ft/1,423 m); and in eastern Europe: the Carpathians, (the Riesengebirge, the Tatra mountains and the Transylvanian Alps (8,743 ft/2,665 m)). The great Mediterranean peninsulas – the Iberian, Italian and Balkan – are all mountainous with a particularly interesting and very distinctive, indigenous alpine flora of relatively recent origin.

The most important mountains in the Iberian peninsula are the Pyrenees (Pico de Aneto – 11,168 ft/3,404 m), the Cantabrians (8,688 ft/2,648 m) and the numerous Spanish mountain ranges (Sierra Nevada – 11,411 ft/3,478 m). Most important in the Italian peninsula are the Apennines (Gran Sasso – 9,554 ft/2,912 m) and the Apuane Alps, and in the Balkan peninsula: the Dinaric Alps to the west (Durmitor – 8,274 ft/2,522 m), the Rhodope Mountains to the east (9,596 ft/2,925 m) and a series of isolated mountains in Greece, renowned both in history and mythology – Mt. Olympus (9,560 ft/2,914 m), Mt. Parnassus (8,061 ft/2,457 m) and Mt. Taíyetos (7,897 ft/2,407 m). The Mediterranean islands, too, have their mountains: Mt. Ida in Crete (8,058 ft/2,456 m), Mt. Etna in Sicily (10,902 ft/3,323 m) and the Monti del Gennargentu in Sardinia (6,345 ft/1,834 m).

To the east, Europe is bounded by two great mountain chains, rich in many interesting species of alpine plants; these are the Ural Mountains (6,214 ft/1,894 m), which extend from north to south for about 1,240 miles (2,000 km), and the Caucasus Mountains which reach their highest peak in Mt. Elbrus at 18,480 ft (5,633 m).

In Asia, some of the mountains reach heights of over 26,000

*The succession of altimetric zones of vegetation can be seen clearly on the slopes of Kilimanjaro, Africa's highest mountain.*

ft (8,000 m) and it is here that the highest mountains in the world are to be found, distributed as massifs, plateaux and upland plains, often exceeding 13,120–16,404 ft (4,000–5,000 m). In central Asia, three vast mountain chains spread out from the great high mountain plateau of the Pamirs: to the east and south-east the Karakorum (K2 – 28,251 ft/8,611 m), the Himalayas (Mt. Everest – 29,028 ft/8,847 m) and the mountains of Yunnan and Küen Lun; to the north-east Tien Shan (24,406 ft/7,439 m), the Altai Mountains (14,783 ft/4,506 m), and the mountains of Mongolia; and to the west the Hindu Kush range (25,262 ft/7,700 m), the mountain chains of Turkestan, the Elburz Mountains (Mt. Demavend, 18,933 ft/5,771 m) and the mountains of Transcaucasia and Anatolia (Mt. Ararat – 16,945 ft/5,165 m).

Also in Asia are the mountains of Lebanon (11,024 ft/3,360 m), origin of the famous cedars of Biblical fame. Of interest, too, are the mountains of Japan, which reach their highest peak in the extinct volcano of Mt. Fuji (12,395 ft/3,778 m). Notable too, are the mountains of western New Guinea (Mt. Jaya – 16,502 ft/5,030 m).

In Africa, the main mountains are situated in the north and centre of the continent. The great Atlas Mountains (13,665 ft/4,165 m) dominate the north-western sector, forming an imposing bulwark between the Mediterranean area and the Sahara Desert. To the east, besides the high Ethiopian upland

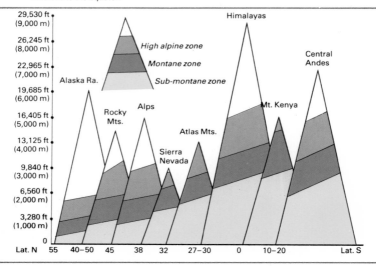

The progress of vegetal zones through the changes in latitude, from the Arctic and Antarctic to the Equator.

plains (Ras Dashan – 13,976 ft/4,260 m), are Mt. Kenya (17,057 ft/5,199 m) and the volcanic Mt. Kilimanjaro which reaches 19,340 ft (5,895 m), the highest peak in the continent. These are isolated massifs which look enormously impressive as they rise up from the extensive grasslands of the great savannahs. The central range culminates in the Ruwenzori mountains (16,795 ft/5,119 m) known in legend as the 'mountains of the moon', while in South Africa, the Drakensberg range reaches a maximum altitude of 11,621 ft (3,542 m).

The highest mountains in Australasia are Mt. Cook in New Zealand – 12,349 ft/3,794 m and the Great Dividing Range in Australia – 7,310 ft/2,228 m.

Mountains are the natural environment of alpine plants but not all thrive in the same conditions or at the same altitudes. While plants on Mt. Kilimanjaro grow at an altitude of 11,480 –19,020 ft (3,500–5,800 m), in the Himalayas they grow at 13,120–19,680 ft (4,000–6,000 m), in the Alps at 5,900–9,840 ft (1,800–3,000 m) and at 1,640–4,260 ft (500–1,300 m) in the mountains of Scotland.

The altitudinal level at which alpine plants live is known as the high alpine zone and is the highest of the three altimetric zones used in demarcating the altitudinal distribution of vegetation. The lower level, known as the sub-montane zone, includes the vegetation of the coast, plains and hills or, in other words, all forms of vegetation including plants that are not

*Distribution of altimetric zones in an alpine range.*

Snow
zone

High alpine
zone

Alpine
zone

Sub-alpine
zone

Upper montane
zone

Lower
montane
zone

Sub-montane zone

High alpine zone

Montane zone

Sub-montane zone

affected by altitude. In the middle latitudes, this zone extends from sea level to 1,640–3,280 ft (500–1,000 m); it extends to 660–980 ft (200–300 m) in central Europe, and to 4,920 ft (1,500 m) in North Africa.

The intermediate level is known as the montane zone and is usually well forested. In Europe, such wooded areas generally consist of beech, conifers and larches, while in North America they consist of maple, poplar and forests of spruce and pine. At this level, the effects of altitude (i.e. variations in temperature, rainfall, etc.) greatly influence the type of plants that grow there.

The upper limit of the montane zone is, as a rule, clearly defined by a natural demarcation line, the so-called timber-line or tree-line. Trees simply cannot grow above a certain level and their absence creates a boundary that is easily recognizable on any mountain. The montane zone extends upwards from the limit of the sub-montane zone to about 4,920–7,220 ft (1,500–2,000 m) in the middle latitudes; near the Equator it rises to about 9,840–11,480 ft (3,000–3,500 m), descending right down to sea level towards the Poles. The extent of the montane zone can easily be seen by studying the position of the timber-line on various mountains. The timber-line in equatorial mountain zones may be at an altitude of up to twice that of temperate mountain regions, and becomes gradually lower towards the Poles until it reaches sea level, as in northern Scandinavia, Alaska, and northern Canada. Apart from the altitudinal timber-line, there is also a latitudinal timber-line which indicates the polar limit of the forests. Strictly speaking, of course, there is neither a sub-montane nor a montane zone in these regions as high alpine plant life is to be found as far down as sea level.

The montane zone consists of several bands of distinct altimetric variations, recognizable by their different types of vegetation. Two zones in particular can be identified: a lower montane, consisting mainly of broad-leaved, deciduous forests in the northern hemisphere, and an upper montane of evergreen coniferous forests. Alpine plants can sometimes be found in the upper montane zone, especially in clearings, open spaces and on rocks.

Alpine plants are in their element in the high alpine zone which extends beyond the upper boundary of the forests to the perpetual snows or to the peaks of mountains that do not reach the snow-line. Here, too, several successive altimetric bands can be observed, which, on temperate mountains, consist of the following zones: sub-alpine, alpine, high alpine and snow zone.

The sub-alpine zone – also called sub-alpine scrubland or upland moor – is typified mainly by rather stunted, twisted shrubs with an occasional solitary tree or group of trees, such

as larches or pines, rising from the scrub. Dominating the scene, however, are clumps of shrubs, such as rhododendrons, dwarf pines, dwarf alders. The sub-alpine scrublands consist largely of dense thickets of shrubs interspersed with extensive areas of heathland covered with bilberry shrublets, broken here and there by open grassy areas. The upper limit of the sub-alpine zone coincides with the cessation of woody vegetation; solitary trees are not found above a certain altitude and shrubs disappear as well, giving way to open spaces occupied by herbaceous plants, all of which are low-growing although a few may be somewhat woody.

The alpine zone is typified by pastures: the continuous herbaceous vegetation is interrupted or relieved only by outcrops of rocks, natural rocky walls and mountain streams, marshlands or other watery types of terrain. Mountain plants thrive in these surroundings and the spectacle of masses of alpine flowers in bloom in these great, open spaces can be breathtaking.

Compact, herbaceous vegetation does not continue beyond the alpine zone; it is replaced by grassy patches here and there and sporadic areas of vegetation. This is the high alpine zone, home of the dwarf willow and ground-hugging, cushion-like plants. Here, however, are to be found many of the loveliest alpine flowers such as the soldanella, gentian, ranunculus (alpine buttercup), anemone and violet.

Torrents, streams, perpetual snows and glaciers all help to keep alpine plants supplied with water for most of the year (see page 30).

The highest zone of all – the snow zone – is undoubtedly the most beautiful and most fascinating. Primulas, saxifrages, rock jasmine and poppies are just some of the more typical representatives of alpine flora to be found in this altimetric belt. Sporadic vegetation thrives among the natural heaps of rubble and stones, in rocky walls, and along the top of ridges. This is not only the habitat of cryptogams – plants without true flowers and seeds, such as lichens, mosses and algae, but also of many interesting and wonderful alpine plants. These plants live among the perpetual snows, exposed both to bright sunlight and intense cold – conditions they have learned to come to terms with by means of ingenious adaptations.

The upper limit of the snow zone is delineated by the perpetual snows and glaciers. Conditions can vary from one zone to the next and can even differ within a distance of only a mile or two, where there may be differences of exposure, slope or ground. In the Alps, for instance, this upper limit normally varies from 8,200 to 9,840 ft (2,500–3,000 m) but may be higher in certain local climatic conditions. Some glorious alpine flowers can often be seen even above 9,840 ft (3,000 m) where small grassy or rocky areas or sheltered gravelly slopes that are not snow-covered offer a reasonable habitat; it is not unusual for plants to be found growing even above 11,480 ft (3,500 m), although only very few reach an altitude of 13,120 ft (4,000 m). The following, however, have been observed at record-breaking altitudes: above 13,780 ft (4,200 m), for example, only *Ranunculus glacialis* and *Achillea atrata* have been seen; at altitudes of over 13,120 ft (4,000 m) *Androsace alpina*, *Linaria alpina*, *Saxifraga moschata*, *S. bryoides*, *Gentiana brachyphylla* have been observed, while several other species, namely *Achillea moschata*, *Agrostis alpina*, *Androsace pubescens*, *Campanula cenisia*, *Trisetum spicatum*, *Eritrichium nanum*, have been found at over 12,470 ft (3,800 m).

**The world of the high mountains**

The natural habitats of alpine plants possess certain unique characteristics, arising from particular conditions of temperature, light and soil. A mountain therefore represents an ecosystem or, rather, a combination of ecosystems, to which alpine plants have adapted by means of their own biological structures and mechanisms. High altitude plants are hence referred to as hypsophylous or hypsophile plants i.e. vegetal organisms that have adapted to high-altitude conditions.

Among the most important factors in determining how hypsophylous plants adapt are climatic elements such as temperature, rain- and snowfall, solar radiation and winds. It must be emphasized, however, that these elements do not affect individual plants but interact with them in such a way as

*Ultra-violet solar radiation slows down the growth of alpine plants to produce forms of dwarfing or nanism, as can be seen in this Yellow Alpine Anemone (Pulsatilla).*

to create a complex of factors that act on the vegetation of the system as a whole rather than on a group of single elements. As the temperature decreases, precipitation changes from rain into snow, enabling the intense solar radiation to warm the ground, thereby causing variations in the temperature of the ground itself. Any examination of climatic influences on plants should therefore take this interdependence into consideration.

Air temperature decreases with the increase in altitude by about 2°F (0.5°C) for every 330 ft (100 m); this is known as the thermal gradient. In the high alpine zone the air temperature can fall to below 32°F (0°C) for many months of the year. Variations in air temperature during the year play an extremely important role in the biology of alpine plants. Such variations directly influence the opening of buds, the growth of leaves, flowering and fruiting. They also have very important indirect effects, such as causing the snow to melt and the ground to become warmer. In many high altitude areas the annual temperature range – the difference between the average temperatures of the coldest and hottest months – can be extremely high, up to 77–86°F (25–30°C), with temperatures averaging 50°F (10°C) in the summer and 5°F (−15°C) in the winter. The daily temperature range in the mountains is particularly wide: the maximum daytime temperature may be as high as 59°F (15°C), and at night as low as −4°F (−20°C).

*The wide varieties of soil-type and rocky subsoil (screes, debris and crags) exert a determining influence on the growth, differentiation and diffusion of alpine plants.*

More important to plant life, however, are the fluctuations in soil temperature, for plants depend entirely on the soil for their sustenance. Temperature changes tend to diminish the closer one gets to ground level, and at even very shallow depths in the soil itself the difference between maximum and minimum temperatures becomes almost insignificant. For example, at an altitude of 4,920 ft (1,500 m) air temperatures of 59° F (15° C) by day and 39° F (4° C) by night have been recorded over a 24-hour period in the summer, whereas at a depth of 4 ins (10 cm) below the surface, the temperature only varied between 50° F (10° C) and 55° F (13° C). The soil thus mitigates extremes of temperature, allowing the survival of many plants which would otherwise be unable to bear either very high or very low temperatures.

This phenomenon is apparent in places where the soil is fairly deep and the indigenous plants or trees have formed a thick ground-cover. Where there is little or no soil – on outcrops of rock, where the ground is stony, among rubble or on exposed cliff faces and crags – the effects of solar radiation are much more intense. The rocks, especially those that are dark in colour, i.e. ultrabasic rocks (rocks containing iron and magnesium, with little or no silica), reach a very high temperature by day and cool down considerably, albeit slowly, during the night. In such an environment few plants are able to survive the wide fluctuations in temperature.

*Lichens are the first colonizers of the bare mountain rocks, an inhospitable environment for flowering plants.*

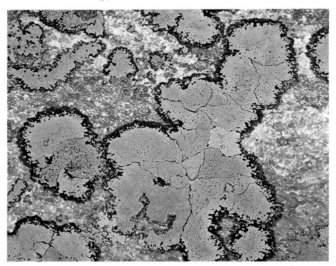

Alpine plants have developed a number of ingenious adaptations, enabling them to survive harmoniously and successfully in high mountain conditions. One of the more common adaptations is a protective covering of hairs; these hairs are usually very dense, forming a thick, felt-like coating on all the organs above ground, and serve to create a layer of air around the plant. This layer acts as a thermal 'cushion' in which the normal temperature is midway between that of the plant's interior, which is usually lower, and that of the atmosphere, which is generally higher. As the hairs usually consist of air-filled cellular structures, they give a whitish or silver-grey appearance to the leaves, branches, and often to the flowers; this pale colouring serves to repel solar radiation and thus diminish the effect of the sun's rays.

Many mountain plants protect themselves against low temperatures and constant thermal fluctuations by growing in thick tufts, closely packed mats or masses. Similarly, the density of the stems and leaves forms a compact vegetal layer within which the temperature is slightly higher than that of the ground and lower than that of the air.

Plants that live on exposed rocks or in crevices and fissures where there is little soil, are able to withstand the extreme temperatures thanks to their deep root systems, which are often very thick and woody.

High altitude plants also possess certain physiological char-

*Snow provides a reserve supply of water and protection from the intense cold, encouraging the rapid growth of many alpine plants which often flower while the thaw is still in progress.*

acteristics which enable them to withstand very low temperatures, even for prolonged periods. By means of photosynthesis, alpine plants often produce soluble sugars instead of starch, which is an insoluble sugar; these remain in the plant's cells and increase the concentration of its own internal solutions. Such soluble sugars make it harder for the cellular solutions to freeze, as they lower the freezing point by several degrees. Plants equipped with this mechanism can therefore survive even at night-time temperatures of +5° to −4°F (−15° to −20°C) at altitudes of over 13,120 ft (4,000 m).

According to some authorities, this high concentration of sugars also promotes the formation of pigments, ranging from dark blues to violets and reds, which would certainly explain the predominance of dark blue and red alpine flowers, and also account for the fact that the branches and leaves of high altitude plants frequently display reddish hues.

Light is another important factor affecting plants at high altitudes. Atmospheric density on mountains is lower than on the plains, which means that solar radiation reaches the level of the soil more easily and with higher intensity. Alpine plants are protected from this great intensity of light by the covering of hairs and the reddish colouring of their branches and leaves. Ultra-violet radiation is particularly strong at high altitudes, and has a stunting effect on plant growth; alpine species are therefore small in size and have a low-growing,

*Distribution of the main types of rock in the Alpine range.*

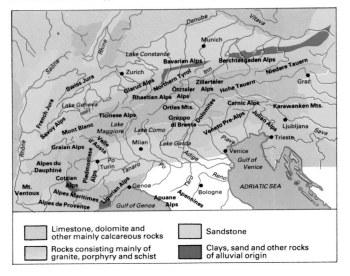

| | Limestone, dolomite and other mainly calcareous rocks | | Sandstone |
| | Rocks consisting mainly of granite, porphyry and schist | | Clays, sand and other rocks of alluvial origin |

often prostrate, habit, a phenomenon known as nanism or dwarfing.

An essential climatic element for all plants is water. Rainfall is always considerable on hills, and tends to increase with altitude until a height is reached at which it becomes snowfall. As a rule, therefore, an abundance of water is available to alpine plants, either in the form of rain or snow, annual precipitation usually amounting to 60–78 ins (1,500–2,000 mm). This does not mean, however, that alpine plants are adapted to living in wet conditions. In fact, the opposite is very often the case: high altitude plants frequently show adaptations to dry conditions (xerophilia) and many alpines can be termed true *xerophytes* (or *xerophiles*). The availability of water is a variable factor in the life of alpine plants. It is more important to determine the amount of water effectively absorbed by a plant than how much is actually deposited in the ground from the atmosphere.

Numerous factors are responsible for the variation in the amount of water absorbed by plants: for example, the type of soil, angle of slope, presence of snow, and wind action all influence a plant's capacity to absorb water.

The greatest influence is exerted by the actual type of precipitation, which may either be liquid in the form of rain, or solid in the form of snow. Once the snow zone has been reached – at about 9,510–10,500 ft (2,900–3,200 m) in the Alps

*Distribution of some calcicole and silicicolous plants in the Alps.*

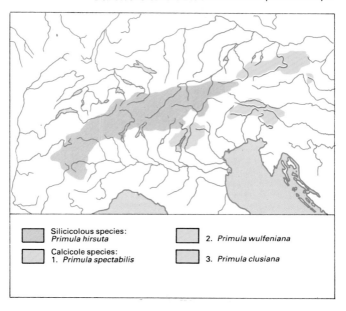

Silicicolous species:
*Primula hirsuta*

Calcicole species:
1. *Primula spectabilis*

2. *Primula wulfeniana*

3. *Primula clusiana*

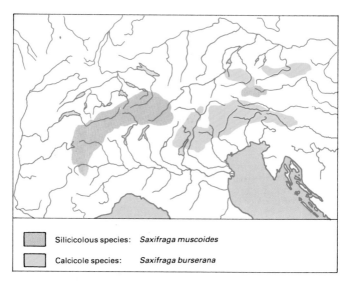

Silicicolous species:   *Saxifraga muscoides*

Calcicole species:   *Saxifraga burserana*

– precipitation is almost always in the form of snow and the vegetation has to make use of whatever water this provides. Naturally, the water supplied by snow differs considerably from rain, since it settles on the ground in solid form and is therefore not immediately available to a plant. As the thick blanket of snow gradually builds up, a vast amount of water is accumulated which is rapidly released to the plants when the thaw begins. It follows that only a very small amount of water is available to them in winter; because of the low temperature, however, the plants are resting throughout this season and therefore have no great need of moisture. When the snows melt, although an excessive amount of water suddenly becomes available, much of it is dispersed due to the angle of slope, the fact that the ground is impervious and so on. Very often the snow thaws too quickly for the plants to make use of more than a very small amount of water. Alternatively, their need for a certain amount of water may not come until later in the season, when the snow has disappeared. Mountain plants are therefore often xerophilous, since they are forced to adapt to extremely dry conditions.

Xerophilous plants are quite frequently found in high mountain areas, especially among species that have adapted to living on rocks or in stony places where the ground itself contributes to the speedy elimination of available water. Xerophilous adaptations are apparent in certain structural features which make alpine xerophytes easily recognizable. Such plants frequently grow in a carpet or mat formation, in order to retain water; they also tend to have well-developed root systems with very long, sturdy roots that grow down into the rock fissures in their search for moisture.

Succulent plants that store water in their stems and leaves are also common. Some of the more typical succulents adapted to high-altitude conditions are the evergreens, *Sempervivum* and *Jovibarba*, and the *Sedum* species of the family Crassulaceae; such adaptations can also be seen, however, in various species of saxifrage, androsace and primula, especially in their leaves.

The fact that the ground is covered by snow over a long period, besides affecting the availability of water, also has a direct influence on other aspects of plant development. For example, while plants are covered by a blanket of snow, no light can penetrate through to them. Since the temperature remains relatively benign under the snow during the winter, many plants are able to spring back into vegetative activity as soon as the snow melts or, as with the genus *Soldanella*, even before the snow has completely thawed. In one particular locality, where the air temperature was 1.4°F (−17°C), the temperature at soil level under a 20-in (50-cm) layer of snow was found to be 30°F (−1°C), a difference of at least 29°F

(16°C) between the temperature at ground level and the temperature of the air above the blanket of snow. Plants that are indigenous to this environment overcome the crushing weight of the snow by adopting a prostrate or creeping habit, a form displayed by many familiar alpines.

The long period when the ground is covered by snow thus has a strong influence on a number of vegetal associations. For instance, a detritus-loving plant such as *Androsace alpina* (Rock Jasmine), which grows in the siliceous rubble of the Alps, can cope with being snow-bound for periods of up to 11 months; equally, the bryophytes (mosses and liverworts) manage to survive with only one snow-free month a year. On the other hand, plants of the genus *Salix* (Willow), such as *Salix herbacea*, need at least two to three months to grow, while the grass-like plants of the genus *Carex* (Sedge), such as *Carex curvula*, cannot tolerate snow-bound conditions for more than seven to eight months.

The heavy mists that occur frequently at high altitudes can be a significant factor affecting the alpine habitat in several ways. To a limited extent, they are a source of water, in that drops of moisture form both on the ground and on the plants. Mists also tend to reduce the amount of light that reaches the plants, although it has been shown that they can in fact help to distribute light more evenly because it is refracted by their component water particles, thus enabling diffused light to reach areas that would otherwise be in the shade.

High winds are another common climatic feature of high mountains. Most frequently encountered at the summit, they often blow with great force for long periods, and thus constitute an almost continuous influence on plant growth; this is partly direct, visibly affecting the plants themselves, and partly indirect, affecting the montane surroundings in general. The indirect effect is usually detrimental to the vegetation, in that the wind tends to dry the ground and thus seriously damage a plant's ability to absorb water. Furthermore, by carrying small particles of rock away with it, the wind inevitably causes soil erosion. It also causes deep drifts of snow to build up in some areas, preventing the spread of certain plant associations. This continuous wind action leads some plants to resist uprooting, by forming very strong root systems and by restricting their growth above ground to a creeping habit or by clinging to the surface.

The most important direct effect on plants, however, is caused by the wind drying the air; this creates an increase in the plant's transpiration, i.e. the exhalation of water vapour from the surface of the leaves and other exposed parts of the plant, and a subsequent demand for more water from the ground. Alpine plants have developed certain adaptations to prevent an excessive water loss through transpiration,

*Draba aizoides is an alpine plant that grows mainly on calcareous subsoils.*

thus ensuring their survival even in the windiest sites. A further example of such adaptations is their tendency to grow in cushion-like or compact carpet formations, which effectively reduces water elimination; the small leaves also help to minimize water loss, and many species of the genera *Draba*, *Androsace* and *Saxifraga*, for example, have very tiny leaves indeed. A covering of hair and the thickening of leaf surfaces serve a similar purpose.

Another very important element which combines with the climatic factors of heat, light and water in creating the montane ecosystem is, of course, the earth itself, and in particular the subsoil in which the plants' root systems grow. The subsoil is formed by the weathering and decomposition of rocks just beneath the surface, and by the combined action of the climatic factors and the micro-organisms that inhabit this environment. Alpine plants are very sensitive to the type of ground in which they grow. Such factors as depth of soil, degree of moisture, chemical composition of the soil (the degree of acidity or silica content), the size and composition of the soil particles, give rise to numerous types of montane soil, each with its own distinctive vegetal characteristics and typical plant associations.

The nature of the rocks which constitute the subsoil has an extremely important effect on the vegetation. In mountain areas the surface soil is often very shallow because meteoric

activity and other factors which determine the formation of the ground militate against the creation of very deep or complex layers. Because the rocks have been broken down very little, they are therefore frequently on or close to the surface; the plants which are able to take root on them tend, therefore, to be dependent on a particular type of rock. For example, calcareous and dolomitic rocks create a particularly distinctive habitat, as they provide a subsoil in which calcium-rich alkaline solutions are present. These solutions influence water absorption, aeration of the soil, and the utilization of other chemical substances, which, in turn, produce a marked effect on the plants.

Plants that are adapted to growing in these types of ground conditions, with basic or alkaline soils, are called calcicole or basophile plants, and are widespread in mountain ranges with calcareous or dolomitic rocks. Some typical examples of common calcicole species in the Alps are *Dryas octopetala, Androsace helvetica, Linaria alpina, Potentilla caulescens* and *Thlaspi rotundifolium.* Siliceous rocks, or rocks that have a high silica content, also provide a habitat suitable for a characteristic type of flora (silicicolous species). These rocks usually have an acid soil which is often compact, badly aerated, calcium-free and moderately damp; only certain species are able to adapt to and flourish on such terrain. Plants which grow singly and prefer acid soils are known as calcifuge, ossiphile or

33

acidophile; they grow freely on crystalline rocks, detritus and among moraines formed from gneiss and schist. Among the commoner species in the Alps are *Artemisia laxa, Saxifraga exarata, Salix herbacea, Geum reptans* and *Oxyria digyna*. Although some of these plants only grow on a siliceous subsoil, they are nevertheless closely akin to certain other plants which only grow in calcareous soil. Such species are referred to as vicarious species, because each acts in a vicarious capacity for the other on the two types of subsoil. For instance, the calcicole alpine species *Draba aizoides, Rhododendron hirsutum* and *Gentiana clusii* are replaced in acid subsoils by the calcifuge species *Draba hoppeana, Rhododendron ferrugineum* and *Gentiana kochiana*.

In addition to influencing the distribution of individual alpine species, the subsoil also determines the types of plants that populate the high mountain ranges. For example, the dwarf willows *Salix retusa* and *S. reticulata*; the pastureland species *Sesleria coerulea* and *Carex sempervirens; Androsace helvetica* and *Draba tomentosa*, representing pioneer associations; stunted forest or dwarf shrubland species such as *Rhododendron hirsutum* and *Rhodothamnus chamaecistus* – these are all basophilous plants, that is, they have a marked preference for an alkaline soil. Conversely, the dwarf willow *Salix herbacea, Oxyria digyna*, a pioneer plant of acid moraines, and the association of mosses and lichens found in snow-covered dells (*Polytrichetum sexangularis*) are all forms of high altitude vegetation that will only grow in an acid subsoil.

The degree of acidity in the ground solutions is not, however, the only factor which influences the distribution of high altitude flora and vegetation. Equally important in determining whether certain species and types of vegetation can establish themselves on a particular terrain is the structure of the soil, that is the size and composition of its particles. Detritus on the slopes at the foot of the rock face, irregular heaps of boulders at the edge of glaciers, the screes and steep, pebbly gorges among the crags, the slopes covered with sporadic tufts of grass, and the snow-filled gullies at the boundary-line of the perpetual snows are all features of the alpine environment characterized by different types of soil structure: this is a vital element in determining water movement and the ability of plants which become established to arrest the slow progress of continuous landslips.

Lastly, of great importance to the distribution and biology of alpine plants is the morphology of the mountains themselves – a factor which depends neither on climatic characteristics nor on the soil, yet is closely linked to both. Two particularly significant morphological features are the steepness of a slope and its aspect. Steepness is very clearly of fundamental

Saxifraga bryoides *(below) and* Gentiana bavarica *subsp.* imbricata *(bottom) are examples of alpine plants that prefer to live on siliceous subsoils (silicicolous species).*

*Fog and mists are common meteorological phenomena in high mountains, helping to provide alpine plants with small supplies of water.*

importance, playing a vital part in determining local environmental conditions because of its close interaction with climate and soil. For example, a slope of as little as 5–10° will only allow surface water to trickle slowly; serious landslides are therefore unlikely and vegetation stands a good chance of becoming established. In contrast, where there is a steep slope of more than 40–50°, water runs too fast to really irrigate the ground, thus creating dry conditions. At the same time, the fast-running water carries down disintegrated rock fragments, preventing plants from growing on them or destroying the tenacious few that have managed to establish themselves. The angle of inclination also has a direct influence on the length of time the snow remains on the slope and determines variations in the incidence of sunlight.

The aspect is also an important factor, especially on mountains subject to a variety of climatic conditions on their slopes. For instance, in the mountain ranges of temperate zones, south-facing slopes experience different climatic conditions from those facing north; the former, with their much longer period of insolation, reach higher temperatures than the latter and the snow melts sooner, resulting in a higher snow-line. Conversely, on north-facing slopes zones of vegetation occur much lower. The aspect also affects the distribution of rain- and snowfall on the mountains. Precipitation in tropical as well as temperate ranges is frequently brought about by moist air currents which travel from one particular direction and make contact with the mountain from that one side. Because of the barrier created by the height of the mountain range itself, all the rain or snow falls on the same side as that affected by the moist air currents, with the result that one side of the mountain enjoys a wet climate while the opposite side is dry; this creates environmental conditions totally at variance with each other and produces different types of vegetation.

The above discussion aims to give an indication of the wide variety of environmental conditions with which alpine plants have to contend in the upper mountain reaches. The valleys and ravines, rocky precipices and glaciers all create such varied local conditions that each zone, even over a very limited distance, may have its own particular climate, often completely different from that of the immediately adjoining area. These strictly local microclimates have a considerable effect on the flora and vegetation, and often account for the presence of certain plants not found elsewhere in the immediate neighbourhood. The prevalence of these microclimatic situations is largely responsible for creating the highly varied landscape that is typical of high mountain scenery and contributes to its fascination.

## How alpine plants survive

Given these abnormal environmental conditions, the ecological situations in which mountain plants tend to live are often so extreme and inhospitable as to threaten their very survival.

The most obvious factor determining the biology of alpine plants is the brevity of their reproductive cycle. As already pointed out, snow may often remain on mountains for many months, during which vegetative activity virtually stops or is reduced to a minimum. The entire reproductive cycle, therefore, from the opening of the buds to the sprouting of the leaves, flowering, fruiting and dispersal of the seeds, must be completed within a few months. During this short period, the plants make every possible use of all the resources available while the warmer weather lasts. To guarantee their survival, mountain plants have developed a cycle that gives priority to the reproductive process, that is, flowering and the formation of fruit and seeds.

This emphasis asserts itself in many ways, the most obvious being the striking colours of the flowers themselves. The flowers of alpine plants are often quite spectacular, some large, like the anemones, alpine buttercups and gentians, others, like the orchids, primulas and artemisias, clustering together in brightly coloured groups, their colours ranging

*Precocious flowering is quite a common phenomenon in alpine plants, their flowers often developing even in the snow, as with this Soldanella.*

from dark blue to pink and yellow. Bright coloration is an efficient mechanism for attracting insects and other pollen-carrying creatures that enable fertilization and subsequent seed formation to take place. An alpine plant will often sacrifice all its strength in the formation of flowers, even at the expense of its vegetative system. This accounts for the number of mountain plant types to be found which, despite their reduced scale and small size, produce large, showy flowers – often prolifically – in contrast with the apparently very limited development of the rest of the plant. Typical examples are *Gentiana acaulis*, many of the campanulas and the cushion-shaped saxifrages.

The short period in which the biological cycle of alpine plants must be completed – sometimes as little as two to three months when the thaw sets in late – does not, however, prevent the full process from being accomplished. Since the temperature beneath the snow remains moderately warm, the essential reproductive phases are often well advanced so that when the snows start to melt the plant is already preparing to flower. In some species, the plants are ready to flower even before the snow has completely gone, presenting that wonderful sight of flowers bursting through the snow, often before their leaves have started to appear. Typical of these are the soldanellas, crocuses, snowdrops, and certain types of gentian.

*Pollinating insects are of essential biological importance during the short cycle of alpine plants.*

Another fairly frequent phenomenon is the appearance of viviparity in alpine plants: the formation of bulbils on the stem or among the flowers. When these small bulbs fall to the ground they reproduce the plant without involving the process of flowering and pollination. Examples of bulbil formation can be seen in *Polygonum viviparum, Poa alpina* and *Lilium bulbiferum.*

The vegetative phase in the growth of alpine plants, as already indicated, is of secondary importance to the reproductive phase. It is nevertheless essential for the plant to grow and to create reserves that can be drawn upon both for reproduction and for the following season's growth. Most mountain plants are perennials, that is, species that survive from one year to the next by means of their underground systems or the few stems or branches above ground that have lain dormant under the snow. These plants are able to preserve their buds at soil level or on a few very low branches, protected by dry leaves or by their perules. The buds are thus ready to burst into activity as soon as the new season arrives, and to form branches, leaves and flowers. Perennial plants are therefore much better suited to a mountain environment than annuals, very few of which are to be found. An annual grows from seed and has to go through all the reproductive stages, starting life as a seedling, developing a stem with leaves and flowers which will in turn produce seeds, in the space of a few months. To do

this, a seed requires a certain amount of moisture to germin-
ate, as well as a considerable amount of heat. It is inevitable
therefore that the biological cycle of annual plants takes considerably longer than that of perennials which recommence
growth as soon as the snow disappears.

Bearing in mind the effects of the environmental conditions
described, it is not difficult to understand why many mountain
plants are so distinctive in appearance, structure and habit –
genetic characteristics which persist even when the plant.is
grown away from its natural surroundings. The appearance
and habit of any alpine plant are therefore two of the most
important factors in identifying mountain flora.

Herbaceous annual species are very scarce in high mountains and it has been calculated that not more than five per cent
(and possibly as low as two to three per cent) of plants on most
mountains are annuals. Among the commoner annuals found
in the Alps are some species of the genera *Arenaria*, *Euphrasia*
and *Rhinanthus*.

Among the perennial species, plants with an erect habit are
in the minority. This biological type spends the winter with its
underground system dormant, its growth bud resting just
below the surface. With the arrival of the warmer season, in
due course, the bud produces leaves and flowers.

Acaulescence is a typical feature of alpine plants (this means
that they are stemless or nearly so). Plants characterized by
this habit have a crown of leaves (the rosette) at their base,
surrounding a slender stalk (the scape), which bears flowers
but no leaves. Acaulescent plants are very common among
mountain flora and examples can be found in a great many
types of primula, some gentians and campanulas and numerous composites, such as *Homogyne*, *Carlina* (stemless thistle), *Senecio* (groundsel), *Arnica* (mountain arnica), *Hieracium*
(hawkweed).

Plants with a cushion-forming habit are probably the most
frequently encountered biological type among the alpines,
together with similar types which have the appearance of a
densely-woven carpet. They are almost invariably perennials,
with a woody stem and a robust root system which may
extend 8–12 ins (20–50 cm) or more into the ground, and is
even capable of penetrating rock fissures, where it becomes
firmly anchored. This root system enables the plants to withstand wind action and helps them to locate nutritive solutions
deep in the tortuous cracks of the rocks. At the top of the root
system, just above the ground, the heavily lignified stem
splays out to form numerous short, creeping branches, each of
which is equipped with short, vertical branchlets covered with
tiny, closely-packed leaves and bright flowers.

The density of the branches and leaves acts as a protective
system against the meteorological agents described above.

*Habits of mountain species: an example of a plant with an erect habit* (Gentiana lutea).

*Habits of mountain species: below is an example of a tufted plant* (Thlaspi rotundifolium); *opposite is an acaulescent plant* (Primula auricula).

The cushion-formation is clearly a habit that has developed to give the best possible protection against the action of the wind and to enable the plant to withstand the strong thermal radiation caused by the heating of the rocks, the drying effects of the air, the thermal imbalances between air and soil, the loss of water through transpiration and the continuous pressure of the blanket of snow that may be many feet deep and last for months.

Of the numerous alpine species of a cushion-, clump- or mat-forming habit, those most commonly seen in the Alps include such species as *Minuartia recurva* and *Silene acaulis* among the Caryophyllaceae; several of the *Papaver* (poppies); several of the *Sedum* (Crassulaceae); many of the saxifrages (such as *Saxifraga oppositifolia, S. retusa, S. burseriana, S. caesia, S. diapensioides, S. bryoides*); several of the *Trifolium* (trefoils); *Loiseleuria procumbens* (*Azalea procumbens*) of the monotypical family Ericaceae; many species of the *Androsace* genus (*A. helvetica, A. vandellii, A. alpina* [*glacialis*], *A. wulfeniana*); several primulas and gentians and, finally, the carpet-forming *Galium* species.

A number of woody perennials that are indigenous to high mountains adopt a very shrub-like habit, even though the typical environmental conditions favour well-branched, broadly-spreading bushes of a rather stunted nature. Wind action and the layers of snow are also factors which discour-

age plants from growing to any great height, with the result that, from a distance, these shrubs look like great random patches of green, growing at different angles to the ground. Rhododendrons, for example, develop a shrubby habit; the two most widespread species in the high alpine zone, above the forest vegetation, are *Rhododendron hirsutum* and *R. ferrugineum* which only reach a height of 1–2 ft (30–60 cm), although in the Himalayas, where they are typical, they can grow to a height of 3–6 ft (1–2 m). On the other hand, although dwarf willows are botanically classified as shrubs, they adopt a completely prostrate habit; their small leaves lie parallel to the ground and bear short, erect inflorescences in brilliant shades of yellow or red.

There are also several plants that are exclusive to the tropical mountains of America and Africa which have an altogether different habit, as is seen in the typical 'giant' phenomenon exhibited by plants which are botanically regarded as perennials. Instead of branching out laterally into a broadly spreading shape, they grow upwards to a height of 20–30 ft (6–9 m) with a short, thick trunk which has a felt-like surface and is somewhat pliant due to the lack of tissue lignification. These plants have a short, simple stem from which spring numerous very large leaves only a foot or so from the ground; these are linear or lanceolate in shape, arranged in a spiral formation and closely clustered at the top to form a dramatic terminal

*Habits of mountain species: below, a mat-forming, cushion-shaped plant* (Silene acaulis); *bottom, a prostrate-spreading shrub* (Pinus montana *or Mountain Pine*).

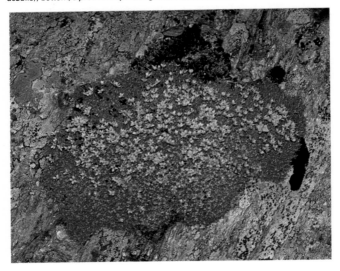

In the steppe-like grasslands of tropical mountains several types of herbaceous plant have a characteristic, almost tree-like, habit; typical of these 'giant' plants are the giant Lobelias and tree Senecios of Mt. Kenya, shown below.

rose of leaves. When the plant flowers, an inflorescence emerges from the centre of the leaves; this may be either long or broad but is, in either case, highly distinctive; it is covered by a great number of flowers to form either an axis, which may be oblong or cylindrical, at the very top of the plant, or a group of closely clustered, leafy rosettes.

Because of their distinctive habit and remarkable size, these giant plants are easily recognizable in the upland meadows of tropical mountains where they form one of the most outstanding features of the landscape. Such plants are widely found in the *páramos* or high altitude pastures of the Andes, from 9,840–14,760 ft (3,000–4,500 m), in tropical Africa on Mt. Kenya, the mountain range of Ruwenzori, on Mt. Kilimanjaro and in the mountains of Ethiopia, from 11,480–16,400 ft (3,500–5,000 m) – that is, in high mountain environments where the snow falls only sporadically and the luminosity and solar radiation are very intense. Some of the more characteristic species to be found growing in these conditions are the genus *Lobelia* (Campanulaceae), widespread throughout Africa, various species of the giant *Senecio* (Compositae) in the African mountains, the genus *Espeletia* (Compositae) in the Andes, and the *Puya raimondii* (Bromeliaceae) which is typical of the Peruvian Andes.

At the upper limit of the tree-line there are numerous forms of high altitude vegetation; pastures and screes, the banks of torrents and streams, snow-beds and woodland clearings are all populated with a wide variety of flowering plants.

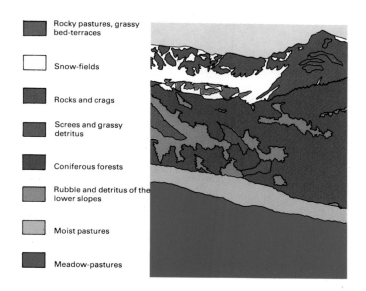

Rocky pastures, grassy bed-terraces

Snow-fields

Rocks and crags

Screes and grassy detritus

Coniferous forests

Rubble and detritus of the lower slopes

Moist pastures

Meadow-pastures

## High altitude vegetation

While mention has been made of the variety of ecological features, characteristic habitats and the peculiar growth habits of alpine plants, the types of vegetal association which are typical of high mountains remain to be discussed. To give a systematic description of the various forms of high mountain vegetation, we will deal with the altimetric zones in succession, from the montane to the high alpine.

The high altitude woodlands belong to the upper montane zone and are the last vestiges of the extensive forests to be found in the montane zone of nearly all continents. Here, alpine flowers can be seen blooming between conifers, in clearings and on rocks, in their search for the light that is otherwise denied them by the dense canopy of the trees. Anemones, aconites, violets and wild pinks peep out amid luxuriant carpets of grass and orchids. The great rocks and boulders which lie among the trees provide a strange landscape. This kind of environment creates a special type of ecosystem that encourages the growth of plants preferring a rocky subsoil but which thrive on moisture, the latter being provided mainly by the lush moss that covers the rocks and stones.

Beyond the timber-line, the trees become sparser, leaving only intermittent groups or isolated trees. This is the realm of

the high altitude scrublands, the sub-alpine zone, where vegetation is in the form of very large, dense clumps of shrubs, sometimes almost prostrate but more often 3–10 ft (1–3 m) high. In the Alps, the most characteristic species are the dwarf mountain pine (*Pinus mugo*), green elder (*Alnus viridis*) and rhododendrons, while the shrubby, high-altitude vegetation of the central African mountains consists of numerous members of the heath family (*Erica, Philippia*).

In Europe, the so-called alpine heathlands are the habitat, largely, of bilberries (*Vaccinium myrtillus, V. uliginosum*) which grow freely among the clumps of dwarf mountain pines and rhododendrons; they are typical suffruticose or shrub-like plants, about 8–16 ins (20–40 cm) in height, bearing edible fruit. The term 'heathlands', however, is inexact and often misleading as true heathlands are typical of the coastal and hilly areas of western Europe, consisting of low, shrubby plants, mainly of a dwarf heather, the wild ling *Calluna vulgaris*. Among the pines and bilberries flourish many brightly-hued herbaceous species such as violets, louseworts and milkworts.

Typical features of high mountain scenery are the pastures and meadows – vast areas of grassland, consisting mainly of perennial plants, but differing greatly in the type of soil, degree of dryness, chemical composition of the subsoil and their floral population. These regions of high altitude herbaceous

vegetation are sometimes referred to as pasture, meadow or field, without distinction; this is especially incorrect as regards the last term, which generally denotes an area where the herbaceous vegetation is regularly harvested, sometimes more than once a year, and fertilized. A field therefore contains herbaceous vegetation directly controlled by man whereas pasture land remains in its natural state or, at most, is subject only to the temporary effect of grazing animals.

Many types of alpine meadows are to be found in the mountains of Europe, from the very lush to areas where the grass is much thinner and shorter.

The commonest type of pastures, growing on a calcareous subsoil, consists of a ubiquitous evergreen vegetation: blue moor grass with bluish spikelets (*Sesleria coerulea*), and an evergreen sedge (*Carex sempervirens*), which forms a grassy carpet on the warmer slopes, usually facing south, where solar radiation lasts for several hours each day. In these conditions, the snow thaws quickly and the soil, partly because of the underlying calcareous rocks, becomes warm, which aids the drying-out of the surface subsoils. The pastures are therefore well drained and thickly carpeted. The plants which are typical of this kind of environment are often pilose and include gentians (*Gentiana angustifolia*, *G. verna*), louseworts (*Pedicularis rostrato-spicata*, *P. verticillata*), bird's-eye primrose (*Primula farinosa*), alpine aster (*Aster alpinus*), *Ranunculus seguieri, Vitaliana primuliflora,* silver crane's bill (*Geranium argenteum*), mountain oxytropis (*Oxytropis montana*) and hairy hawkweed (*Hieracium villosum*).

The type of pasture most frequently found on a siliceous subsoil, in contrast, consists of bent grass, which forms a thick herbaceous carpet on humus-rich, fairly moist soil, the dominant plant being recurved sedge (*Carex curvula*), distinguishable by its leaves which are often arched backwards. Plants growing in this type of terrain are nearly always acidophilous, some of the commonest and most widespread genera being the primulas (*Primula glutinosa, P. integrifolia, P. minima*), gentians (*Gentiana kochiana, G. alpina*), and pulsatillas (*Pulsatilla alpina, P. vernalis*) as well as *Saponaria pumila, Ranunculus pyrenaeus, Trifolium alpinum, Androsace carnea, Minuartia sedoides* and *Phyteuma hemisphaericum*. At lower levels, where the snow-fall is less, another type of pasture thrives on a siliceous subsoil, consisting of a dwarf grass-like plant, *Festuca halleri*, which has purplish-brown spikelets.

Among the vegetation found in the European alpine pastures are fescue grass (*Festuca varia*), typical of south-facing slopes with a dry, siliceous subsoil; sedge, *Carex ferruginea* which thrives on the loam-rich, moderately wet, marly or clayey soil where the snow remains for a long time; and alpine grass (*poa alpina*), found mainly in well-manured pastures.

Pastures of sedge are quite common in the Alps. They are mown or scythed several times a year and provide a hospitable environment for a number of multi-hued flowers such as nigritellas (*Nigritella nigra, N. rubra*), alpine astragalus (*Astragalus alpinus*), *Centaurea montana, Erigeron alpinus* and *Pedicularis rostrato-spicata*. The pastures of alpine grass are especially distinctive: frequently grazed by farm animals, they are well manured and, as a result, the herbaceous vegetation flourishes so luxuriantly that they are known as 'fat meadows', with a profusion of veronicas, forget-me-nots (*Myosotis alpestris*) and crocuses.

On land where animals graze regularly, and particularly where the surface of the soil is acid, the combined effect of the soil and the trampling of hooves results in the formation of dry pastures where the vegetation is often nothing more than a degenerate form of the plants normally associated with other types of pasture. These are the mat-grasslands, pastures typified by a small grass-like plant, mat-grass or nard (*Nardus stricta*), easily recognizable by its modest, one-sided, erect spike. Although mat-grass is often the only type of plant to be seen in these grasslands, a few other species are sometimes found, with flowers of varying brilliance or showiness; they include many of the gentians (*Gentiana lutea, G. pannonica, G. punctata, G. purpurea*), campanulas (*Campanula scheuchzeri*), orchids (*Leucorchis albida, Coeloglossum viride*) as well

Coniferous forests are found on the upper levels of the montane zone; at their upper limit they give way to the vegetation of the high alpine zone of pasture and rocks.

*The snow-beds (below), steep screes (bottom) and glacial moraines (opposite) are some of the most typical environments of mountain flowers where many of the loveliest alpine flowers are to be found.*

as the mountain arnica (*Arnica montana*), *Geum reptans* and *Hieracium aurantiacum*.

There are types of pasture which require particular conditions such as very shallow soil or soil that is deep and wet. Among the former are the typical high altitude pastures found among the windy, rocky ridges where the temperature may fall to −40°F (−40°C) in winter and rise to 122°F (50°C) in summer, due to the thin layer of snow that is always being blown away by the wind. Plants that grow in these conditions must be able to withstand extremes of temperature, strong winds and often excessive drought in summer. They are exemplified by the edelweiss (*Leontopodium alpinum*), glacier pinks (*Dianthus glacialis*), saussureas (*Saussurea alpina*) and, in less exposed positions, *Dryas octopetala, Salix retusa* and *Loiseleuria procumbens*.

In the cool, damp, flatter sites where a deep, humus-rich soil builds up, generally at lower altitudes and at the level of the timber-line, very lush, grassy pastures are often to be found. Among the plants that grow there are the monkshoods or aconites (*Aconitum napellus, A. vulparia*) as well as *Veratrum album, Adenostyles alpina, Cortusa matthioli, Allium victorialis* and *Saxifraga rotundifolia*.

Another type of grassy environment, quite different from those described above, is to be found in the depressions and snow-beds of the upper mountain reaches. Here the snow may remain for almost the whole year, only melting slowly and leaving the ground temporarily water-sodden, still at very low temperatures. The soil may remain uncovered for a period of not more than two to three months, but during this time the exposure to sunlight at such a high altitude can be so strong as to dry out the ground quickly, occasionally even producing arid conditions. The plants that grow here must be able not only to withstand a long period of snow cover but also to complete their natural cycle within an extremely short space of time. Under such conditions a very distinctive flora thrives, which differs according to whether the soil is calcareous or siliceous. Typical of the calcareous upper snow-beds are such plants as the dwarf willows (*Salix reticulata, S. retusa*), saxifrages (*Saxifraga androsacea, S. sedoides*) and soldanellas (*Soldanella alpina*), *Gnaphalium hoppeanum, Callianthemum coriandrifolium, Primula clusiana, Gentiana pumila*. In the siliceous upper snow-beds closely related species, often of the same genera, tend to grow, including *Salix herbacea, Soldanella pusilla, Gnaphalium supinum, Gentiana bavarica* and *Arenaria biflora*. Common to both types of soil is the moss *Polytrichum norvegicum* which often forms a thick, extensive carpet under the melting snow.

When the free flow of water is impeded by the nature of the subsoil or where there are springs or small streams, these damp conditions give rise to a distinctive hygrophilous alpine flora. Plants that grow in this environment must be able to tolerate the high humidity of the soil as well as withstand the peculiar characteristics of the subsoil. Marshes and bogs compact the soil and so reduce the availability of oxygen, to produce conditions of near asphyxia, and the development of a generally acid humus. In contrast, oxygen circulates actively in the water flowing in streams, forming a bicarbonate of calcium solution which is deposited on the rocks. The water has a mitigating effect on temperatures which remain at a favourable level, with only minimal changes: winter temperatures are mild and summer temperatures low. Among the plants which grow in high, moist sites are the butterworts (*Pinguicula alpina, P. vulgaris*), cottongrass (*Eriophorum scheuchzeri*), rushes (*Juncus jacquinii*), some of saxifrages (*Saxifrage aizoides, S. stellaris*), willowherb (*Epilobium alsinifolium*), as well as numerous sphagnum mosses and ordinary mosses.

It is, however, the rocky mountain habitats that give rise to the most characteristic and best known of European alpine flowers. Some of the most beautiful alpine species make their home in the screes, fissures, ridges and narrow ledges of practically insurmountable cliff faces.

Two types of environment predominate in these rocky domains: the first consists of stony slopes, some of which form

*Some of the most beautiful alpine plants, such as the Saxifrages and Campanulas, grow on rocky walls, often in quite precarious sites.*

*Many typical alpine species grow well in the wet mountain environments offered by marshlands (below) and peat-bogs or upland moors (opposite).*

screes, moraines and detritus, whilst others are made up of larger boulders which lie at the foot of cliffs, in ravines or on glacier edges where there is little or no soil. The second type of rocky environment consists of vertical crags and rock faces in whose fissures small amounts of topsoil build up; this provides a roothold for small, undemanding plants that are able to tolerate the excessive summer heat of the rocks and the low winter temperatures; these low temperatures are unalleviated by any protective covering of snow, since the cliff faces are too steep for it to settle. Again, it is the type of subsoil that determines the plant species and only those that react well to the particular rock type – calcareous or siliceous – will take root and thrive.

The rich and varied flora that is produced by these environments in the Alps and in many other ranges is a limitless source of interest and wonder for any walker, mountaineer or botanist.

Plants growing in calcareous detritus and natural rubble often show special adaptations to this particular type of subsoil; these may take the form of creeping or underground stolons – very long, and deep root systems that seek a firmer anchorage than is offered by the loose stones of the screes. The flowers that grow in this environment include some of the most beautiful of the alpine species, such as poppies, violets, campanulas and saxifrages. It would be impossible to include

a complete list here, but notable varieties are: *Papaver rhaeticum, Viola biflora, Campanula cochlearifolia, Saxifraga oppositifolia, Draba aizoides, Thlaspi rotundifolium* (a typical colonizer of detritus), *Linaria alpina, Achillea atrata, Hutchinsia alpina, Leucanthemopsis alpina* and *Doronicum grandiflorum.*

Conversely, plants which thrive on siliceous detritus are well suited to the often damp or wet, acid soil that forms on the rocks and, in particular, on the glacier edges of mountains of crystalline (granite, diorite, etc.) and schistose rock. Gentians (*Gentiana bavarica*), saxifrages (*Saxifraga bryoides, S. aspera*), artemisias (*Artemisia genepi* or *genipi*) as well as *Oxyria digyna, Ranunculus glacialis, Geum reptans, Androsace alpina, Achillea nana,* ferns and lichens all grow well on the detritus slopes, moraines and heaps of siliceous rubble.

The vertical rock face is the realm of the mat- and cushion-forming species. Here, the plants are small, white, hairy and sometimes fleshy, with large, brightly coloured flowers. They are perennials with sturdy rhizomes and strong roots which penetrate deep into the rock fissures. They are thus protected from the intense cold, wind and the strong rays of the sun. Among the alpine plants whose natural habitat is the calcareous crags are numerous saxifrages (*Saxifraga paniculata, S. burserana, S. crustata, S. cochlearis,* etc.), some campanulas (*Campanula morettiana, C. raineri, C. zoysii*), primulas

(*Primula auricula*), drabas (*Draba dubia, D. tomentosa*) and globularias (*Globularia cordifolia*) as well as androsaces (*Androsace helvetica*), valerians (*Valeriana saxatilis*) and potentillas (*Potentilla caulescens, P. clusiana*).

Although the flora of the siliceous rocks is less differentiated than that of the calcareous, several species are characteristic of this environment, such as *Androsace vandellii, Artemisia eriantha, A. laxa, A. glacialis*, and *Primula viscosa*.

The various habitats of the high alpine zones – pastures, upland marshes, peat-bogs, detritus, screes and cliff faces – occur and have similar characteristics on all mountains in the temperate regions. For example, the Rocky Mountains, the Pyrenees, the Caucasus and the Himalayas all exhibit the vegetation typical of the high alpine zone, although they may have different distinctive flora.

Tropical mountains, however, possess some characteristics which are peculiar to them alone. Here, the uppermost zone, which is nearly always at a height of over 11,480–13,120 ft (3,500–4,000 m), is characterized by vast stretches of grassland, closely resembling plateaux or tablelands, covered in low-growing vegetation occasionally broken by a few of the strange giant plants mentioned above. In the Andes, for example, the high altitude pastures, known as *páramos*, possess these characteristics to a greater or lesser degree, while the *puna*, a type of grass-like steppe that occurs at about 13,120 ft (4,000 m) is almost completely dry because of low precipitation combined with the damage caused by the heavy grazing of llamas and vicuñas. In Africa, the tablelands of Ethiopia, Kenya and the Ruwenzori mountain range of the Uganda-Zaïre border are rich in such alpine flowers as helichrysums (*Helichrysum* sp.), alchemillas (*Alchemilla* sp.), gentians, primulas and the giant lobelias and senecios.

Beyond the pastures, screes and rocks are the perpetual snows and glaciers. Here the vegetation ceases and gives way to the land of eternal ice where no mountain flower is able to grow. Only cryptogams can survive on the frozen peaks: lichens cover the more exposed rocks, and a few microscopic algae manage to withstand the extreme conditions of these upper reaches. The fascinating beauty of the alpine flowers has been left behind and climbers who have struggled this far know that their uphill journey will no longer afford the sight of the gaily-coloured flowers of plants lodged in crevices, spread out in carpets on steep slopes or perched on the narrow ledges of rock faces. In the intense, dazzling light of the mountain summits there are no flowers to transform the landscape with their magical colours – the red of the primulas, the blue of the campanulas, the yellow of the poppies; there is only the white of the glaciers and the scudding clouds, the grey of the rocks and the deep blue of the sky.

## Variety and rarity of alpine flora

Alpine flowers, with their wide variety of forms and colours, are undoubtedly among the most beautiful flora in the world. Mountain landscapes would not hold such fascination were it not for the brightly-hued plants that flourish there. They attract many people who are not expert climbers but who derive intense pleasure from spending time, however short, among the great, green expanses or the steep, rugged slopes of the mountains, finding refreshment there after the strains and stress of city life.

The wide variety of alpine flowers is part of a precious heritage, closely linked to all the features of a mountain environment – rocks, glaciers, streams and wildlife. Alpine flora began to develop immediately after the formation of the mountain ranges and was thus one of the earliest components of that complex ecosystem.

The majority of the mountain chains in Europe, Asia and America, as already explained, are of relatively recent geological origin – they were formed certainly not more than 60 million years ago. The flora of these mountains then developed through a series of processes which has produced the variety of different species in existence today. In the evolution of alpine plants, a very important role was played by the glaciations of the Quaternary era which caused most of the

59

*Some genera of plants are particularly prolific in alpine flora. Among the most common are gentians, saxifrages, campanulas, primulas. Representatives of two very widespread genera are shown – below (a primula) and opposite (a saxifrage).*

northern hemisphere, as far as approximately 50° north, to be covered by a thick ice-sheet. These glaciations also affected the mountain ranges of temperate zones, not only destroying many species in existence since the Tertiary era but also bringing about the differentiation of new species.

Mountains were thus among the most active centres for the formation of new plant species, a fact demonstrated by the large number of species contained in several genera, such as *Primula, Gentiana, Saxifraga, Androsace, Penstemon* and *Phlox.* Many species of these genera are exclusively mountain plants and strictly localized in their distribution; for instance, there are approximately 350 known species of the genus *Saxifraga,* of which at least 39 are localized in the Alps, while the genus *Phlox* comprises 60 known species, nearly all of which are North American, 20 being exclusive to the Rocky Mountains.

The geological history of mountains has therefore played an important role in the creation of this large variety of species, and in many cases, glaciations have confined these plants to restricted areas, giving rise to so-called endemic species which are very localized. The Alps, the Rocky Mountains and the Pyrenees are all rich in endemic species which, in some cases, are limited in distribution to a single mountain or even to a single peak. For example, *Dianthus alpinus, Papaver burseri, Draba dolomitica* and *Saxifraga valdensis* are all local-

ized within restricted areas of the Alps, as are *Saxifraga presolanensis*, limited to the Presolana Pass (northern Italy), *Draba ladina* to the mountains of Engadine (Switzerland), *Callianthemum kerneranum* to Monte Baldo (northern Italy) and *Saxifraga florulenta* to the central part of the Alpes-Maritimes.

Following the highly active period of differentiation of species in the Quaternary era, a number of genera developed species which were purely mountain types and it is these that are to be found most frequently in the pastures, on the screes and on rocks. For instance, most people recognize primulas, saxifrages, gentians, campanulas and androsaces as typical mountain species which constitute a large percentage of high altitude flora. This wide variety of forms is further differentiated by a remarkable range of colours.

**Endangered and protected species**

In conclusion we must stress the need to protect alpine flora. There are two basic reasons for safeguarding alpine plants, one aesthetic, the other purely scientific. If we are to continue enjoying the beauty of mountain flowers, it is essential for everyone to recognize the importance of protecting them. Random and thoughtless picking must be avoided at all costs,

and no plants should ever be dug up in the hope that they can be transplanted successfully to a suburban rock garden. The pleasure they will give can only be short-lived, and the plants will almost certainly die. A few photographs, or one or two specimens, carefully picked without uprooting the whole plant, must suffice. The scientific reason why alpine flora should not be tampered with concerns the localized distribution of many alpine species. Endemic species which only exist in a particular group of mountains – or only on a single peak – are extremely vulnerable and their destruction could easily mean their total extinction. The harm thus caused would represent an irreplaceable genetic loss.

For many years, attempts have been made to avoid such risks by conserving rare species in alpine botanical gardens and reproducing them 'in captivity'. Alpine gardens of this nature were originated during the latter part of the nineteenth century with the aim of bringing together examples of mountain plants from every continent. Nowadays, however, such gardens are devoted almost entirely to the conservation of endangered alpine species and many governments have introduced legislation to protect their rarest wild plants. Among the species protected in the Alps, for instance, are the red-flowered primulas, lilies (such as the Martagon or Turk's-cap lily), aquilegias, edelweiss and many species of dianthus, saxifrage and orchid. In the British Isles 61 species are strictly

protected under the Wildlife and Countryside Act of 1981, including rare alpines such as *Gentiana nivalis* and *Saxifraga cernua.*

In addition, an international agreement, the Convention on International Trade in Endangered Species (CITES) requires that the importation and exportation of certain plants, including all orchids, be licensed. EEC countries implement these stipulations particularly strictly for terrestrial orchids taken from the wild.

An alpine garden is, however, at best an artificial environment and although the soil and climate are carefully chosen to suit them, the plants are deprived of their natural surroundings and cut off from their own particular ecosystem. By far the best way of safeguarding alpine plants is to keep them in their natural setting; hence conservation of their natural environment is vital. Numerous natural parks and reserves, where both the plants and their surroundings are protected, have already been established in mountain areas all over the world. But the efforts of scientists to conserve high altitude flora will be in vain unless every visitor to the mountains understands the need for such work. Decisions taken at a political level to give legislative and financial support to such schemes must be reinforced by an awareness of the need to conserve not only alpine flora, but the environment of our planet as a whole. To fail to do so is to put at risk our very survival.

**ALPINE FLOWERS**

## 1 ACAENA MICROPHYLLA Hook f.

**Family** *Rosaceae*
**Description** A tufted, herbaceous plant, prostrate-spreading, with short, ascending branches. Leaves pinnate-compound, stipulate, ¾–1¼ ins (2–3 cm) long and stalked with 7–13 sub-rounded, sessile (or subsessile) leaflets, about ⅛ in (3–4 mm) long, dentate or serrate. Flower stalks short, pilose, with very small bracts. Flowers joined in dense terminal heads, about 1 in (2.5 cm) diameter, distinguished by long red or reddish-brown spines protruding from the head for about ½ in (1 cm). Sepals 4, oval, greenish-yellow. Corolla absent. Stamens 2; inferior ovary forming a dome that bears the spines.
**Size** 1¼–2 ins (3–5 cm).
**Flowering period** October–February (in southern hemisphere).
**Ecology and distribution** Pastures and grasslands, hilly and montane grasslands and by streams, from 1,310 to 3,935 ft (400–1,200 m). Endemic to New Zealand; although found among the hills and mountains of both the North and South Islands, it is not a common plant.
**Notes** The genus *Acaena* includes 150 species, all indigenous to the southern hemisphere; 15 of these are exclusive to New Zealand.

---

## 2 ACANTHOLIMON ULICINUM (Willd.) Boiss.
*A. androsaceum* (Jaub. et Spach) Boiss.

**Family** *Plumbaginaceae*
**Description** A low-growing, tufted, more or less stemless, shrub-like plant forming dense, leafy, much-branched cushions. Leaves linear or lanceolate-linear, triangular in section, grey-green or glaucous, slightly rough margin, mostly basal, close-growing, ¼–¾ in (5–20 mm) long and less than ⅟₁₆ in (0.7–1 mm) wide. Numerous short flowering stems, slightly larger than the leaves, each bearing one or two spikes. Flowers pink, joined into an apical spike formed by 3–7 spikelets; bracts and bracteoles oblong-lanceolate, acuminate. Calyx pink, funnel-shaped-tubular, approx. ½–¾ in (12–14 mm) long, with limb formed of 5–10 lobes, expanded-conical. Corolla tubular, funnel-shaped-campanulate.
**Size** 1¼–2 ins (3–5 cm)
**Flowering period** June–August.
**Ecology and distribution** Rocks, natural rubble, precipices and steep ridges of craggy terrain, especially on basic or serpentine subsoils, from 1,415 to 3,935 ft (1,200–3,000 m). Found in Crete, Lebanon, the southern part of the Balkan peninsula and the mountains of Anatolia.

## 3 ACHILLEA CLAVENNAE L.
Yarrow, Milfoil

**Family** *Compositae*
**Description** A tufted, more or less stemless, herbaceous plant with a creeping rhizome from which emerge the ascending epigeal stems. Leaves partly basal, elliptical or oblong-spatulate in outline, incised, slightly lobed with a few well-spaced segments, sometimes dentate, greenish-grey due to the numerous silvery hairs; stem leaves shorter, lanceolate-spatulate. Inflorescence of 5–10 heads gathered at the end of the stem to form a corymb on a long peduncle. Each head is ½–¾ in (1–2 cm) wide with a hemispherical involucre consisting of numerous over-lapping bracts. Disc flowers pale yellow or off-white; 5–8 ray-florets white, with spreading sub-rounded ligules.
**Size** 4–10(–12) ins (10–25(–30) cm).
**Flowering period** July–September.
**Ecology and distribution** Rocks, detritus of the lower slopes and naturally formed rubble on a calcareous sub-soil, from 4,920 to 8,200 ft (1,500–2,500 m). Endemic to the calcareous central and eastern Alps, from Lake Lugano to the Carniola Pass, the Dinaric Alps and the mountains of the western Balkan peninsula (Albania, Macedonia, Greece).

---

## 4 ACHILLEA MOSCHATA Wulf.
Musk Milfoil

**Family** *Compositae*
**Description** A herbaceous perennial, stemless or nearly so, strongly aromatic, with one or more slightly pilose ascending stems. Leaves mainly basal, pale green, pinna-tisect, oblong in outline, divided only once into short linear lobes which are acute or acuminate, sometimes dentate and perpendicular at the axis which is broad, almost winged. Inflorescence of 3–25 heads close together in terminal corymb, approx. ½–¾ in (10–14 mm) wide. Involucre, hemispherical, short, with numerous lanceolate bracts, brown at the edge. Disc florets, yellow or pale yellow, bisexual; 6–8 ray-florets, white, all female, with patent, broadly obovate or sub-rounded, almost strap-shaped, ligules.
**Size** 2–8 ins (5–20 cm).
**Flowering period** July–September.
**Ecology and distribution** Stony places, the pebbly ground flanking streams, moraines, dry pastures and crags on a siliceous subsoil, from 4,595 to 11,155(–12,465) ft ((1,400–3,400(–3,800) m). Exclusive to the Alps, where it is fairly common from Savoy to the eastern Alps, and to the southern Apennines.
**Notes** An aromatic and medicinal plant with a diuretic and tonic effect, it has recently been recognized as a subspecies of *A. erba-rotta* All. A protected plant.

## 5 ACONITUM NAPELLUS L.
Monkshood

**Family** *Ranunculaceae*
**Description** A showy perennial with a tuberous rhizome and erect, sturdy stem. Leaves alternate, palmately divided almost to the base into linear lobes, about 1/16–5/16 in (1–8 mm) long, often dentate-incised. Flowers purplish-blue, joined in a dense terminal spike. Calyx petal-like, coloured, formed from an upper sepal into a helmet-shape, approx. 1/3–3/4 in (7–14 mm) long, with two sub-rounded lateral sepals and two lower lanceolate sepals. Petals transformed into cylindrical nectaries, incurved and uncinate at the apex.
**Size** 20–60 ins (50–150 cm)
**Flowering period** July–September.
**Ecology and distribution** High pastures, moist meadows and other grassy places where animals have grazed, especially near the alpine summer pastures, from (1,640–)2,625 to 6,560(–9,515) ft ((500–)800–2,000(–2,900) m). Very common in all the central-southern European mountains, the British Isles, and Scandinavia. In central Europe it also descends into the plains. A few variants even reach the Urals and Caucasus.
**Notes** The species described above has now been divided into several different species which can be distinguished by certain characteristics and helmet-like calyx. A protected species.

## 6 ACONITUM VULPARIA Reichb.
Wolf's Bane
*A. lycoctonum* auct. pro parte

**Family** *Ranunculaceae*
**Description** A sturdy, herbaceous perennial with erect stem. Leaves alternate, palmately divided more than half-way into 3–5 main segments, deeply lobed-dentate, three-lobed at the apex. Flowers yellow or pale yellow, pedunculate, terminal raceme forming a lax inflorescence. Calyx petal-like, coloured, formed of 5 unequal sepals, the upper forming a cylindrical-conical helmet 3/4–1 in (15–25 mm) long and 1/8–1/3 in (3–8 mm) wide, two ovate-lanceolate laterals and two lanceolate or linear inferiors. Petals transformed into cylindrical nectaries by being folded into a semi-spiral formation.
**Size** 20–60 ins (50–150 cm).
**Flowering period** June–August.
**Ecology and distribution** Woods, pastures, grassy or stony places, on any subsoil, from (985–)1,640 to 7,875 ft ((300–)500–2,400 m). Commonly found in the Alps, Apennines, Carpathians and widespread in the hilly areas of central-northern Europe.
**Notes** Closely related to this species is *A. lamarckii*, widespread in the central-southern mountains of Europe and distinguishable by its more branched leaves and more compact, many-flowered inflorescence. Both are protected plants.

## 7 ADONIS PYRENAICA DC.
Pyrenean Pheasant's-eye

**Family** *Ranunculaceae*
**Description** A herbaceous perennial with simple stem or slightly branched at the base. Basal leaves on long petioles, bipinnate or tripinnate in linear segments; stem leaves sessile. Flower golden-yellow, borne singly at the apex of each stem, approx. 1½–2½ ins (4–6 cm) diameter. Sepals 5, about half the length of the petals, hairless. Petals 12–18, elliptical or oblong-spatulate. Fruit consisting of numerous achenes, 6 mm (¼ in) long, semi-hairless, equipped with a short, recurved beak.
**Size** 4–12(–16) ins (10–30(–40) cm).
**Flowering period** June–July.
**Ecology and distribution** Stony places, detritus of the lower slopes, natural rubble and rocks mainly of a calcareous nature, from (4,265–)4,920 to 7,545(–7,875) ft ((1,300–)1,500–2,300(–2,400) m). While infrequent in the Pyrenees, it is also found in one particular locality in the Alpes Maritimes, Mt. Pelat, where it is nevertheless very rare.

---

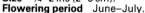

## 8 AETHIONEMA OPPOSITIFOLIUM (Pers.)
Hedge

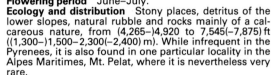

**Family** *Cruciferae*
**Description** A small tufted perennial, forming dense leafy cushions, with short branches. Leaves slightly fleshy, orbicular or obovate, opposite or nearly so, sessile, densely clustered, delicately papillose, margins sometimes rough. Flowers pink, in short constricted terminal racemose-capitate inflorescences. Petals 4, ¼–⅓ in (6–8 mm) long and ⅛–⅙ in (3–4 mm) wide, obovate, finely veined. Stamens 6, with yellow anthers.
**Size** ¾–2 ins (2–5 cm).
**Flowering period** June–July.
**Ecology and distribution** Rocks, steep rocky terrain, natural rubble and detritus, from 6,560 to 9,840 ft (2,000–3,000 m). Sporadic in the mountains of Asia Minor (Syria, Lebanon, Anatolia), the southern Caucasus and Transcaucasia.

## 9 AETHIONEMA THOMASIANUM J. Gay

**Family** *Cruciferae*
**Description** Grows in small, lax tufts. Stems greenish-grey, rather thick. Leaves ovate or elliptical, sessile, fleshy, pale green or greyish, numerous and alternate on the stem. Flowers pale pink or parma violet with red throats, sometimes veined in dark red, clustered into a compact terminal inflorescence in a hemispherical corymb. Petals 4, oblong, approx. ⅙–¼ in (4–5 mm) long. Fruiting corymbs very dense; siliquae small, flat and winged.
**Size** 2–8 ins (5–20 cm).
**Flowering period** (May–)June–July.
**Ecology and distribution** Stony places, natural rubble and detritus, with a mica-schist content, from 6,335 to 7,875 ft (1,900–2,400 m). A very rare species, endemic to the Cogne valley in the Graian Alps.
**Notes** A strictly protected species because of its rarity and very localized distribution.

---

## 10 AJUGA PYRAMIDALIS L.
Pyramid Bugle

**Family** *Labiatae*
**Description** An erect, herbaceous perennial with a pyramidal habit. Stem simple and pilose. Leaves opposite, arranged in two rows, oval, obtuse, with a short petiole, or sessile, pilose, spreading and semi-incurved towards the outside. Flowers sky-blue or pale purplish-blue, arranged in whorls in the axils of the large, leafy bracts which are longer than the flowers, reddish-green at the base shading up to brownish-red, deep purple or a bluish-shade, fading towards the top. Calyx ½ in (1 cm) long, with a short tube and acuminate teeth. Corolla two-lipped with a cylindrical tube, the limb having a very short upper lip and the lower being divided into three lobes of which the two laterals are oblong, obtuse, while the central, retuse lobe, widens outwards.
**Size** 4–12 ins (10–30 cm).
**Flowering period** (May–)June–August.
**Ecology and distribution** Pastures, open grassy or stony places, clearings in woods and spinneys, on any subsoil although with a preference for acid ground, from (2,295–)4,265 to 7,220(–9,185) ft ((700–)1,300–2,200(–2,800)) m. Quite common in all the European mountains (the Pyrenees, Alps, Apennines, Carpathians, and Balkan Mountains), including the British Isles and Scandinavia.

## 11  ALLIUM INSUBRICUM  Boiss. et Reut.

**Family** *Liliaceae*
**Description**  A more or less stemless, bulbous, herbaceous plant. Erect stem, incurved at the top. Leaves basal, numerous, linear, grass-like, up to ¼ in (5 mm) wide, blue-grey. Terminal inflorescence consists of a downward-facing, densely packed umbel, surrounded by a large, thin, membranous, whitish bract formed by the split spathe. Flowers pink or mauvish-pink, 3–5 to each inflorescence, sub-campanulate or converging approx. ¾ in (1.8–2 cm) long, with 6 oblong tepals.
**Size**  8–12 ins (20–30 cm).
**Flowering period**  July–August.
**Ecology and distribution**  Rocks, pastures and natural rubble, on a calcareous or dolomitic subsoil from (2,950–)4,920 to 6,890 ft ((900–)1,500–2,100 m). Occasionally found in the calcareous Pre-Alps including the southern Alps between Lake Como and Lake d'Iseo.
**Notes**  Endemic to the Lombardic Pre-Alps. A protected species.

---

## 12  ALLIUM VICTORIALIS  L.
Alpine Leek

**Family** *Liliaceae*
**Description**  A more or less stemless plant with an oblong, fibre-covered bulb; it has 2–3 large basal leaves, oblong-elliptical, gradually tapering, ¾–2½ ins (2–6 cm) wide, folded longitudinally. Its yellow flowers are grouped into a dense terminal inflorescence at the apex of the flower stalk. The more or less spherical umbel of the inflorescence is surrounded by a membranous, yellowish-white involucre; numerous flowers on short peduncles. Six yellowish or greenish tepals, erect-spreading, approx. ¼ in (5–6 mm) long; the stamens project beyond the tepals.
**Size**  12–24(–30) ins (30–60(–75) cm).
**Flowering period**  (June–)July–August.
**Ecology and distribution**  Grassy places, stony pastures, rocks, high moorlands of dwarf broom, mountain pine, on various types of subsoil, mainly calcareous, from (4,595–)4,920 to 8,530 ft ((1,400–)1,500–2,600 m). Although rather rare, this plant is fairly prolific in localized areas of the mountains of southern Europe (the Pyrenees, Alps and Carpathians) as well as in the Caucasus and central Urals. Closely related species, sometimes referred to by the same name, are distributed in the Altai Mountains and the mountains of north-western America.
**Notes**  A protected species in some countries.

## 13 ANAPHALIS MARGARITACEA (L.) Benth. et Hook.

**Family** *Compositae*
**Description** An erect, herbaceous plant, with a simple or branched stem, with a silvery-white woolly covering. Numerous alternate leaves, linear or linear-lanceolate, 2–6 ins (5–15 cm) long, white-tomentose on the lower surface. White flowers arranged in heads in lax, leafless corymbs. Each head surrounded by an involucre formed of numerous series of pure white bracts with a group of small yellow flowers in the middle.
**Size** 12–32 ins (30–80 cm).
**Flowering period** June–August(–September).
**Ecology and distribution** Montane forests, shady places and woodland clearings, from 2,950 to 5,905 ft (900–1,800 m). Found in the mountains of North America, from Alaska and north-western Canada to California and New Mexico as well as north-eastern Asia.
**Notes** It is grown in Europe as an ornamental plant.

## 14 ANDROSACE ALPINA (L.) Lam.
Rock Jasmine

**Family** *Primulaceae*
**Description** A low, well-branched, herbaceous plant forming fairly compact, extensive mats growing close to the ground and consisting of a large number of rosettes. Leaves joined together in a closely packed rosette to each branch, forming a compact cushion; leaves ⅙–⅓ in (4–8 mm) long and ¹/₁₆ in (1.5 mm) wide, linear-spatulate, fleshy, pointed or blunt, covered with short star-shaped hairs. Flowers solitary (one to each rosette), pink or white shaded with pink, yellow throats, sub-sessile or with a short peduncle, emerging from the dense leafy cushion. Corolla about ¼ in (5 mm) wide with a short tube and 5 expanded, slightly concave, obovate, rounded lobes.
**Size** ¾–2½ ins (2–6 cm) – the flowering branches.
**Flowering period** July–August.
**Ecology and distribution** Rocky detritus, stabilized rubble, debris and stony places, generally on siliceous rocks, from 6,235 to 10,825(–13,780) ft (1,900 to 3,300(–4,200) m). Endemic to the Alps; fairly frequent.
**Notes** All the European species of *Androsace* are protected, especially those with the most limited distribution area such as entries 14, 15, 17 and 18.

## 15 ANDROSACE CARNEA L.
Rock Jasmine

**Family** *Primulaceae*
**Description** A small, more or less stemless plant forming tufts fairly close together, sometimes in a lax mat. Creeping branches with closely-packed basal rosettes of linear or awl-like leaves, ½–⅝ in (1–1.5 cm) long and approx. 1/16 in (1–2 mm) wide, entire, sometimes pilose. Erect flower stalks, either hairless or thickly pilose according to the variety, with an umbel of 1–6 flowers borne on short peduncles at the apex. Flowers pink, occasionally white, with yellowish throats; obconic calyx with 5 short lobes. Corolla ¼–⅓ in (5–8 mm) with a short tube and a limb formed of 5 oblong or oblanceolate lobes, apically rounded.
**Size** 1¼–4(–6) ins (3–10(–15) cm – the flowering stems.
**Flowering period** June–August.
**Ecology and distribution** Pastures, stony places, natural detritus and rubble, on various types of subsoil but with a preference for acid ground, from (4,595–)6,560 to 9,840 ft ((1,400–)2,000–3,000 m). Fairly frequent in the Pyrenees and Cevennes as well as the western and central Alps.
**Notes** A protected plant.

---

## 16 ANDROSACE CHAMAEJASME Wulf.
Rock Jasmine

**Family** *Primulaceae*
**Description** A small, more or less stemless, pilose, stolon-bearing plant with creeping branches with numerous leafy rosettes fairly close together. Dense, radiate or flat rosettes consisting of spatulate or lanceolate-spatulate, obtuse leaves, ¼–½ in (0.5–1 cm) long and approx. ⅛ in (2–3 mm) wide, with long silky white hairs forming a ciliate margin. Erect flower stalks distinctly pubescent with an umbel of 2–8 closely-packed flowers at the apex, the flowers emerging from the axil of a corona of lanceolate bracts the same length as the peduncles. White flowers with yellow throats, shading to pink towards the end of flowering period; corolla ¼–½ in (6–10 mm) wide, a very short tube and 5 lobes broadly obovate or almost sub-rounded and apically obtuse.
**Size** 1¼–3¼(–5) ins (3–8(–12) cm) – flowering stems.
**Flowering period** June–August.
**Ecology and distribution** Stony places, rocks and rocky pastures, especially on a calcareous subsoil, from (3,280–)5,575 to 8,860(–9,840) ft ((1,000–)1,700–2,700 (–3,000) m). Found in the Pyrenees (where it is very rare), the Alps (especially in the west), Carpathians, Urals, Caucasus, Himalayas, the Arctic Euro-Asiatic ranges, from northern Russia to Siberia, the Rocky Mountains and Arctic regions of North America.

## 17 ANDROSACE HAUSMANNII Leybold
Rock Jasmine

**Family** *Primulaceae*
**Description** A small tufted plant, branching from the base, forming lax more or less spherical or hemispherical cushions. Leaves ¼–½ in (5–10 mm) long and approx. ⅛ in (1–3 mm) wide, oblong-lanceolate or oblanceolate, and covered with star-shaped silvery hairs, in compact basal rosettes. Flowers white or occasionally pink, with yellowish throats, growing singly in the centre of each rosette of leaves, sessile or sub-sessile. Calyx shortly campanulate. Corolla ¼ in (4–5 mm) wide with a very short tube and a limb with 5 broadly obovate or sub-rounded lobes, apically obtuse or slightly emarginate.

**Size** ¾–2 ins (2–5 cm).
**Flowering period** July–August.
**Ecology and distribution** Crags, natural rubble and detritus, rock fissures, on a calcareous or dolomitic subsoil, from (4,920–)6,235 to 10,170 ft ((1,500–)1,900–3,100 m). Endemic to the eastern calcareous Alps, from the Gruppo di Brenta to the Salzburg Alps.
**Notes** A protected plant.

---

## 18 ANDROSACE HELVETICA (L.) All.
Rock Jasmine

**Family** *Primulaceae*
**Description** A small, hardy plant forming compact cushions consisting of numerous small, erect branches covered with short columnar, leafy rosettes. Leaves small, very densely packed, ⅛ in (3 mm) long and 1/16 in (1 mm) wide, linear-spatulate, grey-green, covered with simple hairs. Flowers white, with yellow throats, growing singly at the apex of each leafy rosette, sub-sessile, just emerging from the leafy cushions. Calyx has 5 acuminate, bristly sepals. Corolla approx. ¼ in (4–6 mm) wide with a very short tube and rotate limb with 5 spreading or almost rolled back, obovate, obtuse lobes.

**Size** ¾–1½ ins (2–4 cm).
**Flowering period** May–July(–August).
**Ecology and distribution** Crags, rocky ridges, crevices in rocks and detritus, on a calcareous subsoil, from 5,905 to 9,840(–11,485) ft ((1,800–3,000(–3,500) m). Endemic to the Alps. Also reported in the Pyrenees but confirmatory evidence for this is lacking.
**Notes** A protected plant.

## 19  ANDROSACE LACTEA L.
Rock Jasmine

**Family** *Primulaceae*
**Description**  A tufted, herbaceous plant forming loose mats, very branched at the base, equipped with underground stolons from which the flowering branches emerge. It is distinguished by its long, slender flower stalks. Leaves lanceolate-linear or linear, in dense rosettes along the stolons, ½–⅝ in (1–1.5 cm) long. Erect or ascending, delicate flower stalks with an umbel of 1–6 flowers at the top surrounded by a small corona of bracts. Floral peduncles 1–2 ins (2.5–5 cm) long. Flowers white with yellow throats. Corolla ⅓–½ in (8–12 mm) wide with a very short tube and a limb formed of 5 obovate, clearly emarginate, spreading lobes.

**Size**  ¾–4(–6½) ins  (2–10(–16) cm)  – the flowering stems.

**Flowering period**  (June–)July–August.
**Ecology and distribution**  Stony places, natural detritus and rocks, on a calcareous subsoil, from 3,280 to 7,875 ft (1,000–2,400 m). Widespread in the mountains of central Europe, from the Jura and Alps to the Carpathians and Dinaric Alps. Most commonly found towards the east of the Alpine range, especially in the northern calcareous sector; in the southern sector it has only been found in the foothills near Vicenza.

---

## 20  ANDROSACE SARMENTOSA Wall.

**Family** *Primulaceae*
**Description**  A stemless, herbaceous plant, thickly covered with long white hairs. It has numerous stolons, 4–6 ins (10–15 cm) long, which spring from the base among the leaves, dark red, with a leafy rosette at the apex. Basal leaves in rosette form, densely packed, lanceolate-spatulate, obtuse, outer ones incurved, each narrowing down to a short petiole. Erect flower stalk with an apical inflorescence in the form of a dense umbel surrounded by an involucre of ovate or oblong, lanceolate bracts close to the flowers. Flowers pink or red with a tubular calyx with 5 obtuse, oblong lobes. Corolla ⅓–⅝ in (8–16 mm) wide with a short cylindrical tube, open yellow throat and a flattened, circular limb formed of 5 broadly obovate, entire lobes.

**Size**  4–6 ins (10–15 cm).
**Flowering period**  April–July.
**Ecology and distribution**  Rocks, open stony places and craggy slopes, from 9,840 to 13,125 ft (3,000–4,000 m). Endemic to the eastern Himalayas (central Nepal, Sikkim, Kashmir).

## 21 **ANDROSACE VILLOSA** L.
Rock Jasmine

**Family** *Primulaceae*
**Description** A small, stemless white-silky plant, well-branched at the base, stolon-bearing, forming dense clumps of closely-packed leafy rosettes. Leaves basal in more or less spherical rosettes, ¼ in (5 mm) long, lanceolate or obovate-spatulate, sessile, acuminate-aristate, villose. Erect flower stem equipped with a dense terminal umbel of 2–5 fragrant, white flowers, with short peduncles, emerging from a corona of linear bracts. Flattened, circular corolla, ¼–½ in (6–10 mm) wide, very short tube, narrow yellow or reddish throat and an expanded limb formed of 5 obovate, apically rounded, lobes.
**Size** 1¼–2(–4) ins (3–5(–10) cm).
**Flowering period** June–August.
**Ecology and distribution** Stony places, rocks, dry pastures, on a calcareous or dolomitic subsoil, from 4,920 to 8,200(–9,840) ft (1,500–2,500(–3,000) m). Fairly widespread in the Pyrenees, Alps, Apennines and other mountains of southern Europe. Very closely related species are also found in the Caucasus and in the mountains of central Asia.

---

## 22 **ANTENNARIA CARPATICA** (Wahl.) Bluff et Fing.
Carpathian Cat's-foot

**Family** *Compositae*
**Description** A small, perennial, dioecious plant, more or less stemless, without stolons. Leaves lanceolate, nearly all basal, attenuate, apically acute, pilose or white-tomentose. Stem leaves alternate, lanceolate or linear, shorter than the basal ones. Inflorescence of 2–6 heads, densely packed at the top of the stem to form a compact terminal corymb. Head ¼–⅓ in (6–8 mm) long with a hemispherical involucre, campanulate or sub-cylindrical, formed of numerous brown or blackish, acuminate, linear bracts. Flowers all tubular, pure white or yellowish-white; stamens protruding from the reddish corolla and fused to form a tube through which the style passes, to emerge with its yellow stigma, above the stamens.
**Size** 2–8 ins (5–20 cm).
**Flowering period** June–August.
**Ecology and distribution** Pastures, stony and open grassy places and rocky ridges, mainly on an acid subsoil, from 4,920 to 10,170 ft (1,500–3,100 m). Widespread in the Pyrenees, Alps and Carpathians, where it is endemic.
**Notes** A polyploid species from certain tetraploid forms distributed in Scandinavia, the Urals and Euro-Asiatic Arctic regions (*A. villifera*).

## 23 ANTENNARIA DIOICA (L.) Gaertn.
Cat's-foot

**Family** *Compositae*
**Description** A small, tufted, more or less stemless, dioecious plant with a sturdy oblique rhizome and creeping, rooting stolons from which arise numerous erect stems. Leaves mostly basal, obovate-lanceolate or oblanceolate, attenuate, apically obtuse or acute, ½–1½ ins (1–4 cm), white-woolly; leaves of sterile buds in dense rosettes at the end of the stolons. Stem leaves, lanceolate, villose, pressed closely to each stem. Inflorescence of 2–8 heads, close together in dense terminal umbel. Head sub-cylindrical or campanulate, approx. ½ in (10–12 mm) wide in the female plants and approx. ¼ in (5–6 mm) in the male. Numerous involucral red or pink bracts in the female heads and white or yellowish in the male. Flowers are pink or white and all tubular.
**Size** 2–8 ins (5–20 cm).
**Flowering period** May–July(–August).
**Ecology and distribution** Pastures, woodland clearings, high moorlands and dry stony places, from (1,640–)4,920 to 9,840 ft ((500–)1,500–3,000 m). Common in all European mountains, especially in the British Isles, Scandinavia and the Caucasus as well as the Arctic regions of Europe, Asia and North America. In the far north of Europe, this plant descends into the lowlands.

---

## 24 AQUILEGIA ALPINA L.
Alpine Columbine

**Family** *Ranunculaceae*
**Description** A herbaceous plant, its erect stem has long, sparse hairs on the lower part and is densely villose on the upper. Large basal leaves, bi- or triternate, with segments divided into two or three. Stem leaves alternate, slightly divided or linear. Flowers sky-blue or bright blue, 2–3¼ ins (5–8 cm) in diameter, solitary or in groups of 2–3 at the apex of the stem, directed downwards. Sepals 5, same colour as petals, ovate or oblong, 1¼–1¾ ins (30–45 mm) long and ⅝–1 in (14–22 mm) wide. Petals 5, with limb approx. ⅝–¾ in (14–17 mm) long and ⅓–½ in (8–11 mm) wide, extending backwards to form a straight or curved spur, ¾–1 in (18–25 mm) long.
**Size** (6–)8–32 ins ((15–)20–80 cm).
**Flowering period** July–August.
**Ecology and distribution** Dry pastures, stony and grassy places, woods and rocks, from (3,280–)4,920 to 8,200(–8,530) ft ((1,000–)1,500–2,500(–2,600) m). Widespread, but not frequent, in the Alps, especially towards the west, and in the northern Apennines.
**Notes** Endemic to the Alps and Apennines. Its survival threatened, it is now a protected plant.

## 25  AQUILEGIA COERULEA  James

**Family** *Ranunculaceae*
**Description**  An erect, herbaceous plant, only slightly branched, with mainly basal leaves, large, on long petioles, ternate-compound, with 2–3 ternate leaflets and rounded lobes. Flowers large, 1–3⅛ ins (2.5–8 cm) wide, solitary at the apex of the branches. Sepals 5, elliptical or oblong, acuminate, petal-like, violet-blue in colour and sometimes with white. Petals 5, white or yellowish-white, deeply concave, obovate, fairly truncate or crenate at the apex, each flower extending backwards at the base to form a straight or slightly curved, coloured, slender spur, 1¼–2½ ins (2.8–6 cm) long. Stamens numerous, yellow, enclosed within the corolla.
**Size**  (8–)10–28 ins ((20–)25–70 cm).
**Flowering period**  June–August.
**Ecology and distribution**  Cool shady woods, grassy places and rocks, from 5,905 to 10,825 ft (1,800–3,300 m). Endemic to the Rocky Mountains from Montana to New Mexico and Arizona.
**Notes**  The flowers are used as the emblem of the state of Colorado.

## 26  AQUILEGIA EINSELEANA  Schultz
Einsel's Columbine

**Family** *Ranunculaceae*
**Description**  An erect, sub-acaulescent herbaceous plant with a simple or slightly branched stem, more or less hairless below and sparsely glandular-pubescent above. Leaves mostly basal, biternate, with segments divided into two or three, often barely incised, fan-shaped. Stem leaves entire, linear. Flowers violet or violet-purple, solitary or in groups of 2–3 at the apex of the stem, 1–1½ ins (2.5–4 cm) wide, folded back laterally or downwards. Sepals 5, coloured, oval, ⅝–¾ in (15–19 mm) long and approx. ⅓ in (7–8 mm) wide. Petals 5, with limb ⅓–½ in (8–10 mm) long and ¼–⅓ in (6–9 mm) wide, extending backwards to form a straight spur, approx. ¼–½ in (7–10 mm) long.
**Size**  4–18 ins (10–45 cm).
**Flowering period**  June–July.
**Ecology and distribution**  Open stony places, natural rubble and rocky outcrops in woods, on a calcareous or dolomitic subsoil, from (820–)2,625 to 5,905(–9,185) ft ((250–)800–1,800(–2,800) m). Widespread, but quite rare, in the calcareous southern Alps, from Lombardy to the Julian Alps, in the Dolomites and the calcareous Salzburg Alps.
**Notes**  Endemic to the Alps. A protected plant.

## 27 AQUILEGIA FLABELLATA Sieb. et Zucc.

**Family** *Ranunculaceae*
**Description** An erect, more or less stemless, herbaceous plant, tufted, with a rhizome covered by the bases of the old leaves. Leaves mostly basal, numerous, on long petioles and almost sheathed, palmate, ternate-compound, with orbicular-fan-shaped leaflets, 1¼–2 ins (3–5 cm) wide, with three-lobed or incised segments, apically crenate-rotund. Stem leaves short, ternate, sessile and sheathed. Flowers pure white, 2–3 to each flowering stem, pointing downwards. Sepals erect and widely spreading, oblong or elliptical, narrowing towards the base, approx. ¾ in (15–18 mm) long and ½–¾ in (12–14 mm) wide. Petals erect with oblong limbs, rounded or slightly emarginate, approx. ½–¾ in (12–15 mm) long, equipped at the base with a short spur sharply incurved at the end.
**Size** 5–10 ins (12–25 cm).
**Flowering period** May–June.
**Ecology and distribution** Scrubland and damp woods, at about 2,625 to 4,920 ft (800–1,500 m). A frequent species in the mountains of Japan.

## 28 AQUILEGIA FORMOSA Fisch.

**Family** *Ranunculaceae*
**Description** A herbaceous perennial, with few branches or branched only at the base, with slender, delicate stems. Leaves large, the lower on long petioles, ternate-compound, with ternate or incised segments, rounded, oblong or sub-spatulate. Flowers red and yellow, solitary at the apex of the branches, large, 1½–2 ins (4–5 cm) wide, curved downwards at the base. Sepals 5, dark red, oblong, acuminate, with a greenish tip. Petals 5, cylindrical-conical, upper part yellow, extending backwards at the base to form a long, straight, bright red conical spur with a small hook at the end. Stamens numerous, yellow, closely packed, much longer than the petals.
**Size** 10–32 ins (25–80 cm).
**Flowering period** June–August.
**Ecology and distribution** Montane woods, damp fields and by mountain streams, from 2,950 to 5,905 ft (900–1,800 m). Common in the mountains of the western United States: the Rocky Mountains and Sierra Nevada.

## 29 AQUILEGIA PYRENAICA DC.
Pyrenean Columbine

**Family** *Ranunculaceae*
**Description** A herbaceous plant with an erect, uniflorous stem. Leaves mostly basal, large, biternate, with segments divided into two or three, fan-shaped, hairless or nearly so. Stem leaves are smaller, slightly incised or almost linear. Flowers large, deep violet-blue, directed downwards. Sepals 5, same colour as petals, ¾–1¼ ins (2–3 cm) long and ½–⅝ in (10–16 mm) wide, broadly ovate or oblong. Petals 5, oblong limb, ½–¾ in (12–15 mm) long and ⅓–½ in (8–10 mm) wide extending backwards to form a slender conical, straight or slightly incurved spur at the end, ½–⅝ in (10–16 mm) long. Stamens as long as the petals.
**Size** 4–12 ins (10–30 cm).
**Flowering period** July–August.
**Ecology and distribution** Rocky or stony places, from 5,905 to 8,200 ft (1,800–2,500 m). Endemic to the Spanish and French Pyrenees and to northern Spain (Santander).
**Notes** It is quite rare; a protected plant.

---

## 30 ARABIS ALPINA L.
Alpine Rock-cress

**Family** *Cruciferae*
**Description** An erect, herbaceous perennial with leaves in basal rosettes and stems branched at the base. Lower leaves obovate or oblong, narrowing to a short petiole, irregularly dentate; stem leaves sessile, oval or lanceolate, amplexicaul, apically acute and irregularly dentate. Flowers, white, grouped into dense apical, or sometimes lateral, inflorescences. Sepals 4, yellowish, slightly bag-like at the base, half the length of the corolla. Petals 4, ¼–½ in (6–10 mm) long with an oblique limb. Siliquae ¼–½ in (6–10 mm) long, approx. ¹⁄₁₆ in (1.5–2 mm) wide, spreading.
**Size** (2½–)4–16 ins ((6–)10–40 cm).
**Flowering period** (April–)May–August(–September).
**Ecology and distribution** Rocks, screes, wet crags and shady grassy areas, mainly on calcareous rock, from (2,625–)3,280 to 9,840(–10,500) ft ((800–)1,000–3,000 (–3,200) m). Very common in all European mountains: the Pyrenees, Alps, Apennines, Carpathians, including the British Isles and Scandinavia; also common in Asia: the Caucasus and Himalayas, and North America.

## 31 ARCTOSTAPHYLOS UVA-URSI (L.) Spreng.
Bearberry

**Family** *Ericaceae*
**Description** A low-growing, evergreen, prostrate shrub, with creeping branches, the end branchlets ascending and densely leafy. Leaves leathery, alternate, obovate, spatulate or elliptical, wedge-shaped at the base ¾ in (2 cm) long. Flowers white tinged with pink, clustered into a short, racemose, drooping inflorescence of 3–12 flowers on short peduncles ⅛–⅙ in (3–4 mm) long. Corolla urn-shaped, ⅙–¼ in (4–6 mm) long, with 5 pink apical teeth turning outwards; superior ovary. A sub-rounded fruit of ¼–⅓ in (6–8 mm) in diameter, turning red when ripe.
**Size** 2–8(–20) ins (5–20(–50) cm) – ascending branches.
**Flowering period** (March–)April–July(–September).
**Ecology and distribution** Exposed stony places, upland moors, dry pastures and detritus, on any type of subsoil although with a preference for calcareous rock, from (1,640–)3,280 to 8,200(–8,860) ft ((500–)1,000–2,500 (–2,700) m). Very common in the mountains of Europe: the Pyrenees, Alps and Apennines, in the British Isles and Scandinavia, and in Asia and North America.
**Notes** Similar to the Bearberry is *Arctostaphylos alpina*, the Black Bearberry, which is distinguished by its soft, short-lived, serrate leaves and greenish-white flowers.

## 32 ARENARIA CILIATA L.
Hairy Sandwort

**Family** *Caryophyllaceae*
**Description** A herbaceous, prostrate-spreading plant, strongly branched at the base with ascending branches. Leaves opposite, elliptical, spatulate or oblanceolate, with veins protruding on the lower surface, ciliate on the margin of the lower part of the blade. Flowers white, in groups of 2–7 in short apical cymes, ¼–½ in (5–10 mm) wide. Sepals ovate-lanceolate, acute. Petals 5, elliptical, oblong or ovate, longer than the sepals. Stamens 10, with white anthers; spherical ovary with 3 styles.
**Size** 2–10 ins (5–25 cm) – when flowering.
**Flowering period** July–August(–September).
**Ecology and distribution** Pastures, stony places, rubble and detritus, on a fairly calcareous subsoil, from (4,595–) 5,905 to 10,500 ft ((1,400–)1,800–3,200 m). Very common in the mountains of central Spain, the Pyrenees, Alps, northern Apennines, Carpathians, northern Arctic and sub-Arctic regions of Europe, Asia and North America.
**Notes** This species is very variable in the shape and size of its flowers and leaves.

## 33  ARENARIA PURPURASCENS  Ramond ex DC.
Pink Sandwort

**Family**  *Caryophyllaceae*
**Description**  A prostrate-spreading perennial, with short erect or ascending stems with scale-like leaves near the base. Leaves elliptical-lanceolate or lanceolate, ¼–½ in (5–10 mm) long, acute, clearly 1-nerved, ciliate at the base. Flowers red or light purplish-red, sometimes white, ½–¾ in (7–14 mm), in groups of 2–4 in dense apical cymes. Peduncles tomentose, same length as the sepals, approx. ¼ in (4.5–6.5 mm). Petals 5, oblong, spreading, almost twice as long as the sepals. Stamens pink.
**Size**  1½–4 ins (4–10 cm).
**Flowering period**  July–August.
**Ecology and distribution**  Damp rocks, detritus and rocky fissures, from 5,905 to 9,185 ft (1,800–2,800 m). Common in the Pyrenees and northern Spain (the Cantabrian Mountains).
**Notes**  Endemic to the Iberian Mountains.

---

## 34  ARMERIA ALPINA  (DC.) Willd.
Mountain or Alpine Thrift
*A. montana* (Mill.)

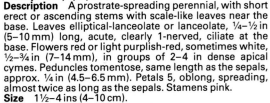

**Family**  *Plumbaginaceae*
**Description**  A stemless, herbaceous perennial, with a thick, oblique rhizome. Leaves all basal, grass-like, erect or nearly so, 1¼–3¼ ins (3–8 cm) long and 1⁄16–1⁄8 in (1–4 mm) wide, with 1–3 nerves, slightly ciliate at the base. Flower stalk, leafless, terminating in a dense, more or less spherical head, ¾–1 in (2–2.5 cm), with a corona of scarious or brownish bracts at its base. Flowers pink or pinkish-lilac, very close together. Calyx funnel-shaped, with awns shorter than tube. Corolla tubular, with a short tube and 5 lanceolate lobes, truncate or retuse, widely spreading in full bloom.
**Size**  4–10(–12) ins  (10–25(–30) cm) – the flowering stem.
**Flowering period**  July–September(–October).
**Ecology and distribution**  Pastures, damp fields and detritus of the lower slopes, screes, on any type of subsoil, from (4,595–)6,560 to 9,840(–10,170) ft ((1,400–)2,000–3,000(–3,100) m). Quite common in the Pyrenees, Alps, Apennines, eastern Carpathians and sporadically in the Balkan Mountains.
**Notes**  A protected plant.

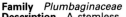

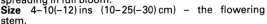

## 35 ARNICA MONTANA L.

Arnica, Mountain Arnica
*A. alpina*

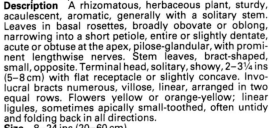

**Family** *Compositae*
**Description** A rhizomatous, herbaceous plant, sturdy, acaulescent, aromatic, generally with a solitary stem. Leaves in basal rosettes, broadly obovate or oblong, narrowing into a short petiole, entire or slightly dentate, acute or obtuse at the apex, pilose-glandular, with prominent lengthwise nerves. Stem leaves, bract-shaped, small, opposite. Terminal head, solitary, showy, 2–3¼ ins (5–8 cm) with flat receptacle or slightly concave. Involucral bracts numerous, villose, linear, arranged in two equal rows. Flowers yellow or orange-yellow; linear ligules, sometimes apically small-toothed, often untidy and folding back in all directions.
**Size** 8–24 ins (20–60 cm).
**Flowering period** (May–)June–August.
**Ecology and distribution** Pastures, sparse woods, unmanured fields, on acid soil, from 3,280 to 9,185 ft (1,000–2,800 m). Found in the Iberian Mountains, the Pyrenees, Alps, northern Apennines, Carpathians and other central European mountains and also in the hills of central-northern Europe as far north as southern Scandinavia.
**Notes** A medicinal plant; an alkaloid with a neurotonic effect as a stimulant and digestive is extracted from its rhizome and leaves. A protected plant.

## 36 ARTEMISIA ATRATA Lam.

Dark Alpine Wormwood

**Family** *Compositae*
**Description** A more or less stemless, tufted, herbaceous plant, greyish-green, hairless. Leaves mostly basal, on long petioles, bipinnatisect, in linear segments perpendicular to the axis, acute or acuminate. Stem leaves alternate, very reduced. Terminal inflorescence consists of a long raceme of pendent heads with short peduncles. Head in the shape of a fairly broad paintbrush ⅓ in (8 mm) wide, covered by an involucre of greyish-green bracts with a brown margin. Flowers only slightly longer than the involucre, yellow, pale yellow or greenish yellow.
**Size** 4–16 ins (10–40 cm).
**Flowering period** July–August.
**Ecology and distribution** Stony places, dry meadows and pastures, from 5,905 to 7,875 ft (1,800–2,400 m). A very rare species, sporadically distributed from the Cottian to the Julian Alps; endemic.

## 37  ARTEMISIA ERIANTHA  Ten.
*A. petrosa* Fritsch

**Family**  *Compositae*
**Description**  A more or less stemless, tufted perennial, silky-tomentose, greyish in colour. Stems ascending with numerous stalked basal leaves, cuneate-spatulate, biternate, with linear-lanceolate lobes; stem leaves sessile, shorter, digitate. Inflorescence oblong, dense, consisting of a leafy raceme of heads borne on short peduncles. Head sub-cylindrical-hemispherical, approx. ¼ in (5–7 mm) wide, covered with lanceolate involucral bracts, pilose-tomentose, consisting of 25–50 small yellow or pale yellow flowers with a densely pilose corona on the outside.
**Size**  2–4(–10) ins (5–10(–25) cm).
**Flowering period**  July–September.
**Ecology and distribution**  Stony places and craggy slopes, on a siliceous subsoil, especially in the western sector of its distribution area, from 6,560 to 10,170 ft (2,000–3,100 m). Uncommon, but occasionally found in the Pyrenees, western Alps, central Apennines, Carpathians and mountains of the Balkan peninsula.
**Notes**  A similar species to *A. genipi* (see entry 38).

---

## 38  ARTEMISIA GENIPI  Weber
Genipi
*A. spicata* Wulfen

**Family**  *Compositae*
**Description**  A small, tufted perennial, semi-rosulate, with one or more greenish-grey ascending stems, pilose-silky. Lower leaves in rosette form, roughly cuneate-spatulate, palmatifid, divided into 3 linear segments often also divided; stem leaves smaller, sub-sessile, less incised, continuing right up to the inflorescence, consisting of a leafy spike of short heads, shorter than the leaves. Inflorescence dense, erect at first then drooping. Head small, sub-cylindrical, ⅛–⅓ in (3–8 mm) in diameter, consisting of 10–15 flowers, covered with an involucre of greyish-green, woolly bracts ending in a blackish point. Flowers yellow, only slightly longer than the bracts.
**Size**  2–4(–12) ins (5–10(–30) cm).
**Flowering period**  July–September.
**Ecology and distribution**  Rocks, rubble, detritus of the lower slopes and moraines, on a siliceous subsoil, from (6,890–)7,220 to 10,170(–12,465) ft ((2,100–)2,400–3,100 (–3,800) m). Quite common in the Alps, where it is endemic.
**Notes**  A very similar species to *A. eriantha* (see entry 37), from which it is distinguished by its heads which have fewer flowers and whose corolla is generally hairless. A protected plant.

## 39 ARTEMISIA GLACIALIS L.
Glacier Wormwood

**Family** *Compositae*
**Description** A herbaceous, tufted, more or less stemless, silvery-grey perennial, with numerous ascending stems emerging from each tuft, branched above. Leaves mostly basal, silky-woolly, greyish, stalked, spatulate-laciniate, divided into 5 segments, each segment divided into linear lobes. Stem leaves, alternate, reduced; 3–9 heads clustered into a short raceme on each branch. Head approx. ¼ in (5–6 mm) diameter, covered with white-woolly involucral bracts, sub-cylindrical, broadening at the apex. Flowers golden-yellow, very slightly longer than the involucre.
**Size** 2–6 ins (5–15 cm).
**Flowering period** July–August(–September).
**Ecology and distribution** Rocks, detritus of the lower slopes, rubble, moraines and stony places in general, on a mainly siliceous subsoil, from (4,920–)5,905 to 10,500 ft ((1,500–)1,800–3,200 m). Endemic to the western and central-western Alps, but relatively rare.
**Notes** A protected species because of its rarity.

## 40 ASTER ALPINUS L.
Alpine Aster

**Family** *Compositae*
**Description** A herbaceous perennial, tufted, more or less stemless with one or more ascending, epigeal stems. Leaves mostly basal, lanceolate-spatulate, narrowing into the petiole, acute or obtuse at the apex, entire, almost channelled; stem leaves alternate, lanceolate, short. Inflorescence in the form of a terminal, solitary head 1⅜–1¾ ins (3.5–4.5 cm) diameter. Flat receptacle with involucre consisting of numerous green linear, overlapping bracts. Disc-florets yellow or orange-yellow, tubular, about 20–40 ray-florets, violet, pale mauve or purple, with lanceolate or almost linear ligules, nearly equal to – or slightly longer than – the diameter of the disc.
**Size** 2–8(–16) ins (5–20(–40) cm).
**Flowering period** July–August(–September).
**Ecology and distribution** Pastures, grassy or stony places, dry fields and craggy sites on various types of subsoil although preferring a calcareous content, from (2,950–)4,595 to 10,170(–10,500) ft ((900–)1,400–3,100 (–3,200) m). Frequent in all central-southern European mountains: the Pyrenees, Alps, Apennines, Carpathians and the Balkan Mountains, the Caucasus, in the mountains of Iran and central Asia; at lower altitudes in Russia and north-western Asia to Siberia.
**Notes** A protected species.

## 41 ASTER PYRENAEUS Desf. ex DC.
Pyrenean Aster

**Family** *Compositae*
**Description** A herbaceous, erect or ascending perennial, stem simple or branched towards the top, pilose. Leaves alternate, broadly lanceolate, sessile and auriculate at the base, amplexicaul, with a slightly dentate margin, bristly, acute. Flowers in terminal heads, solitary at the apex of each branch, 1½–2 ins (4–5 cm) in diameter. Flat receptacle; involucre formed of numerous lanceolate, villose bracts. Disc-florets yellow, tubular; ray-florets, 20–40 in number, violet or purple, with a linear or nearly spatulate-linear ligule, slightly longer than the diameter of the disc.
**Size** 16–24(–36) ins (40–60(–90) cm).
**Flowering period** July–September.
**Ecology and distribution** Pastures, damp fields and grassy or stony places, from 3,280 to 6,560 ft (1,000–2,000 m). Endemic to the French Pyrenees, especially in the west and centre, although quite rare.

## 42 ASTRAGALUS ALPINUS L.
Alpine Milkvetch
*Phaca minima* All.; *P. astragalina* DC.

**Family** *Papilionaceae*
**Description** A tufted, spreading perennial, subacaulescent, with stems branched at the base, slender, ascending, pubescent. Leaves imparipinnate, 1½–4 ins (4–10 cm) long, with 7–12 pairs of elliptical leaflets, ovate or oblong, fairly pubescent; stipules oval, ⅛–¼ in (3–5 mm) long. Flowers variegated in white and violet or blue, arranged on a lax terminal raceme of 5–15 flowers, slightly drooping. Calyx short, almost swollen. Corolla pea-like with 5 petals and standard ½–¾ in (10–14 mm) long, nearly equal to the keel, tinged with violet at the apex and white-winged.
**Size** 3–8 ins (8–20 cm).
**Flowering period** July–August.
**Ecology and distribution** Infertile fields and pastures, grassy and stony places, dry ground and rocks, on any type of subsoil, from (3,280–)5,905 to 9,840(–10,170) ft ((1,000–)1,800–3,000(–3,100) m). Very widespread in all the mountains of central-southern Europe (the Pyrenees, Alps and Carpathians), in central Asia (the Himalayas and Altai Mountains), in the Caucasus and Arctic regions of Europe and Asia.

## 43 ASTRAGALUS SEMPERVIRENS Lam.
Mountain Tragacanth
*A. aristatus* L'Hérit.

**Family** *Papilionaceae*
**Description** A tufted, herbaceous perennial, prostrate-spreading, branched at the base, forming dense mats, pilose. Stems woody, rigid, covered by old leaves and persistent petioles transformed into spines. Leaves paripinnate, ¾–2¾ ins (2–7 cm) long, greyish-green, pilose, terminating in a short acuminate point; leaflets in 4–10 pairs, oblong or oblanceolate. Flowers pale mauvish-pink or white tinged with pink, clustered into a dense terminal inflorescence shorter than the leaves, formed of 4–8 flowers. Calyx pilose, cylindrical-conical, with 5 long teeth. Corolla pea-like, with a standard ½–¾ in (1–2 cm) long, recurved or flat, slightly longer than the other petals.
**Size** 2–16 ins (5–40 cm).
**Flowering period** (June–)July–August
**Ecology and distribution** Stony places, rocky slopes and detritus, on fairly calcareous ground, from 3,280 to 8,860 ft (1,000–2,700 m). Found in the mountains of the Iberian peninsula (Sierra Nevada and the Pyrenees), the Alps (especially the western range) the central Apennines and the mountains of Greece.
**Notes** In addition to this more frequent species, 2 sub-species, *muticus* and *nevadensis*, are known in the Iberian peninsula and another, *cephalonicus*, in the Balkan peninsula.

---

## 44 ASTRANTIA MAJOR L.
Great Masterwort, Mountain Sanicle

**Family** *Umbelliferae*
**Description** An erect, showy, herbaceous plant, sparsely leaved, branched. Basal leaves 3¼–6 ins (8–15 cm) wide, on long petioles, palmatisect with 3–7 oblong lobes, densely serrate. Stem leaves sessile, sheathed. Inflorescence consisting of a simple terminal umbel, ½–¾ in (1–2 cm) wide, surrounded by an involucre formed of numerous oblong acuminate 3–5 veined bracts, ½–¾ in (1–2 cm) long, greenish or purple above, whitish below. Flowers small, approx. ¹⁄₁₆ in (1 mm) long, dense, much shorter than the involucre, greenish white with a reddish tinge.
**Size** 12–32(–40) ins (30–80(–100) cm).
**Flowering period** June–August(–September).
**Ecology and distribution** Woods, clearings, montane fields and pastures, with a preference for calcareous ground, from (1,970–)3,280 to 6,560(–7,550) ft ((600–)1,000–2,000(–2,300) m). Frequent in the mountains of central and southern Europe (the Pyrenees, Alps, Apennines, Carpathians), and eastwards as far as the Caucasus.
**Notes** A protected species.

## 45 ASTRANTIA MINOR L.
Lesser Masterwort

**Family** *Umbelliferae*
**Description** A slender, erect, herbaceous plant, often branched at the base. Basal leaves, large, on long petioles, palmatisect, with 7(9) deeply serrate-lanceolate segments. Stem leaves and bracts sparse, divided into 3 narrow segments. Inflorescence a simple terminal umbel, approx. ½ in (1–1.2 cm) wide, surrounded by an involucre of 10–12 lanceolate-acuminate bracts, whitish, sometimes tinged with red. Flowers small, white or yellowish-white, 10–20 in number, almost the same size as the involucre or slightly shorter.
**Size** 6–16 ins (15–40 cm).
**Flowering period** (June–)July–August.
**Ecology and distribution** Stony pastures, clearings in the woods, rocks and rock faces, mainly on acid soil, from (3,280–)4,265 to 8,860 ft ((1,000–)1,300–2,700 m). Quite common in the Pyrenees, western and central Alps and the Apennines.

## 46 BICUCULLA EXIMIA (Ker) Millsp.
*Dicentra eximia* (Ker) Torr.

**Family** *Fumariaceae*
**Description** An acaulescent, herbaceous plant with a scaly, glaucescent rhizome. Basal leaves on long petioles, ternate-pinnatifid, with pinnatifid lobes formed of oblong or ovate, toothed segments. Stem slender, sub-equal to the leaves, with a compound apical raceme incurved at the base. Flowers pink, red or purplish, clustered in short cymes at the end of the raceme branches, with slender linear bracts, ⅝–1 in (1.5–2.5 cm) long and ¼–½ in (6–10 mm) wide at the base. Calyx consisting of 2 short ovate sepals. Corolla, 4 petals of which 2 are large, concave, swollen at the base, and 2 are linear-spatulate, crested on the back.
**Size** 8–24 ins (20–60 cm).
**Flowering period** May–September.
**Ecology and distribution** Open rocky places, woods and grassy areas, from 1,640 to 6,560 ft (500–2,000 m). Found in the mountainous areas of the eastern states of North America (Allegheny Mountains) from Pennsylvania to Tennessee and Georgia.

## 47 BISCUTELLA LAEVIGATA L.
Buckler Mustard

**Family** *Cruciferae*
**Description** A more or less stemless, tufted perennial with basal leaves from which spring numerous epigeal stems. Basal leaves oblong-spatulate or lanceolate-spatulate, lengthily attenuate, entire or small-toothed, 3¼–6 ins (8–15 cm) long. Stem leaves infrequent and alternate, sessile, narrower and shorter than the basals. Flowers yellow or pale yellow in lax racemose inflorescences and often branched, even from the base. Sepals half the length of the petals. Petals 4, ⅛–⅓ in (4–8 mm) long, obovate. Siliqua flat, divided into two sub-rounded valves between which is the style.

**Size** (4–)6–20(–28) ins ((10–)15–50(–70) cm).
**Flowering period** (April–)May–August(–September).

**Ecology and distribution** Crags, rubble, dry pastures and open grassy places, mainly on calcareous ground, from (1,640–)3,280 to 8,530(–9,190) ft ((500–)1,000–2,600(–2,800) m). Common in the Pyrenees, Alps, Apennines and nearly all the mountains of Europe.

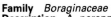

## 48 BUGLOSSOIDES GASTONII (Benth.)
I. M. Johnston
*Lithospermum gastonii* Benth.

**Family** *Boraginaceae*
**Description** A perennial with a short rhizome from which emerge several erect, non-branched, pilose epigeal stems. Leaves lanceolate or ovate-lanceolate, acute or acuminate, semi-amplexicaul, becoming denser towards the top of the stem, 1¼–2½ ins (3–6.5 cm) long and ½–1 in (1–2.5 cm) wide, with appressed hairs. Flowers violet-coloured at first turning to blue, in short terminal cymes, sometimes almost lost among the upper leaves. Calyx tubular with lanceolate-linear lobes. Corolla funnel-shaped, approx. ½–¾ in (12–14 mm) long, with a limb flaring out into 5 lobes with a central furrow marked by a white line. Stamens attached to inside of corolla tube.
**Size** 4–12 ins (10–30 cm).
**Flowering period** July–August.

**Ecology and distribution** Shady side of rock faces, outcrops of rock in montane woods, grassy crags and rubble, from (2,625–)3,280 to 6,560 ft ((800–)1,000–2,000 m). Endemic to the western Pyrenees in France; quite rare.

## 49  BUPLEURUM ANGULOSUM L.
Hare's-ear

**Family** *Umbelliferae*
**Description** A herbaceous perennial with an erect, sparsely-leaved stem and numerous dead leaves covering its base. Lower leaves very long, linear or narrowly lanceolate with a shorter petiole than the blade; upper leaves 3–5, broader, cordate-amplexicaul at the base. Flowers greenish or greenish-yellow, clustered into apical inflorescences in the form of a compound umbel. Main umbel consisting of 3–6 rays surrounded at the base by 3–4 ovate-lanceolate bracts. Secondary umbels 3–6, each one like a single flower, surrounded by a corona of 4–6 greenish-yellow bracteoles, broadly ovate or subrounded, spoon-shaped; flowers small, numerous.
**Size** 4–16(–20) ins (10–40(–50) cm).
**Flowering period** July–August.
**Ecology and distribution** Rocks and stony places, on a calcareous subsoil, from 4,920 to 7,550 ft (1,500–2,300 m). Endemic to the Pyrenees and mountains of north-eastern Spain.

---

## 50  CALCEOLARIA BIFLORA Lam.

**Family** *Scrophulariaceae*
**Description** An acaulescent, herbaceous plant, with 3–10 flower stems, with a dense rosette of broadly rhombic or lanceolate-ovate leaves, 4–6 ins (10–15 cm) long, the peripherals lying close to the ground and the central ones erect, strongly veined, upper surface dark green, slightly pubescent, lower surface lighter in colour, margin crenate-serrate towards the apex. Flower stalk pubescent, with a lax umbellate panicle, formed of 2–4 yellow flowers on long peduncles. Calyx 4-parted, in ovate-acute segments, glandular-pubescent on the outside. Corolla two-lipped with a very small upper lip, ovate, divided into two, and a lower lip rather like an inflated bag, almost hemispherical, with red spots on the inside.
**Size** 8–12 ins (20–30 cm) – the flowering stems.
**Flowering period** January–March.
**Ecology and distribution** High altitude steppes and pastures, at about 8,200 to 9,840 ft (2,500–3,000 m). Widespread in the great mountain system of the Andes, from northern Chile almost as far south as Patagonia.

## 51  CALLIANTHEMUM CORIANDRIFOLIUM

Reichenb.

*C. rutaefolium* (L.) Reichenb.; *Ranunculus rutaefolius* L.; *R. berardi* Vill.

**Family**  *Ranunculaceae*

**Description**  A tufted, herbaceous perennial, with one or more stems emerging from the base. Leaves mostly basal, on long petioles, imparipinnate, deeply incised into 4–6 lateral lobes and one terminal, lobes all pinnatifid in oblong, rounded segments. Stem leaves alternate, short, sessile. Flowers white with orange centre, sometimes pink, solitary, terminal at apex of stems. Calyx short, herbaceous. Corolla open, ¾–1⅜ ins (2–3.5 cm) in diameter, consisting of 5–12 obovate or elliptical petals, slightly retuse at the apex, with a yellow claw. Stamens numerous, yellow, spreading; carpels numerous, small, greenish.

**Size**  2–10 ins (5–25 cm).

**Flowering period**  (June–)July–August.

**Ecology and distribution**  Pastures, dry grassy places, stony and detrital sites, often near melting snow, on any type of subsoil, from 5,900 to 9,515(–9,840) ft (1,800–2,900(–3,000) m). A rare plant, sometimes seen in the mountains of central-southern Europe (the Pyrenees, Alps, Carpathians and the mountains of the western Balkan peninsula).

**Notes**  Similar species have been reported in the mountains of central Asia.

---

## 52  CALLIANTHEMUM KERNERANUM (or KERNERIANUM)  Freyn ex Kerner

**Family**  *Ranunculaceae*

**Description**  A small, sub-acaulescent, tufted plant, with spreading epigeal stems and basal leaves. Leaves on long petioles, pinnatifid blade, deeply incise-dentate lobes in oblong segments acute or acuminate, often incurved and almost overlapping each other. Stem leaves very short, incised, sessile. Flowers white, terminal, with a short green calyx of 5 sepals; corolla open, almost broadly campanulate, 1–1¼ ins (2.5–3 cm) diameter, consisting of 10–12 oblong or nearly linear petals, white, often veined in pink or red, rounded at the apex. Stamens numerous, yellow; carpels small.

**Size**  ¾–2¾ ins (2–7 cm).

**Flowering period**  June–July.

**Ecology and distribution**  Grassy or stony pastures and detritus, near to melting snow, on a calcareous subsoil, from 5,250 to 7,220 ft (1,600–2,200 m). Endemic to Monte Baldo in northern Italy and the southern slopes of the central-eastern Alps where it is quite frequent.

## 53 CALTHA LEPTOSEPALA DC.
Slender-sepalled Marsh Marigold

**Family** *Ranunculaceae*
**Description** A low-growing, more or less stemless densely tufted plant, very branched at the base. Leaves mostly basal, ovate, dark green, shiny, cordate at the base, stalked. Flowers showy, 1¼–2½ ins (3–6 cm) in diameter, arranged in lax few-flowered cymes. Corolla white, open, often goblet-shaped, consisting of 8–12 oblong or obovate petals, concave, rounded at the apex. Stamens numerous, yellow.
**Size** 4–8(–12) ins (10–20(–30) cm).
**Flowering period** June–July(–August).
**Ecology and distribution** By mountain streams, in wet fields and marshlands, from 6,560 to 9,840 ft (2,000–3,000 m). Found in the Rocky Mountains and mountain ranges of north-western America, from south-western Canada (British Columbia) to the western United States (Arizona and New Mexico).

---

## 54 CAMPANULA BARBATA L.
Bearded Bellflower

**Family** *Campanulaceae*
**Description** A more or less stemless, tufted, herbaceous plant, with a basal rosette of leaves and one or two flowering, leafless, hirsute stems. Basal leaves lanceolate or spatulate, entire, obtuse, sometimes with a wavy margin; stem leaves very sparse, linear, short. Flowers pale blue, occasionally white, on short peduncles, pendent, united in an apical raceme, often nearly unilateral, of 3–9 flowers. Calyx, short lobes one-third the length of the corolla, interspersed with small reflexed appendages. Corolla ⅝–1¼ ins (1.5–3 cm) long, cylindrical-campanulate, with 5 spreading ovate-triangular lobes and with a showy fringe of long hairs on the margin.
**Size** 4–12 ins (10–30 cm).
**Flowering period** June–August.
**Ecology and distribution** Pastures, stony places and sparse woods, on a mainly acid subsoil, from (2,625–)3,280 to 8,530(–9,515) ft ((800–)1,000–2,600(–2,900) m). Rather frequent and widespread in the Alps and Carpathians as well as the mountains of southern Norway.

## 55 CAMPANULA CENISIA L.
Mont Cenis Bellflower

**Family** *Campanulaceae*
**Description** A dwarf, herbaceous plant with prostrate-ascending stems and numerous stolons bearing sterile leafy rosettes. Leaves of the basal rosettes obovate or elliptical, obtuse, hairless, sessile, ciliate, sometimes fleshy, very closely packed; stem leaves oblong or obovate. Flowers large, mauvish-blue, solitary at the apex of the short flowering stems. Calyx hirsute. Corolla broadly campanulate, ½–⅝ in (1–1.5 cm) in diameter, with a short tube, cut almost to the base into 5 lanceolate-acuminate lobes, fully recurved when in full bloom. Anthers orange-yellow.
**Size** ¾–2(–4) ins (2–5(–10) cm) – when in flower.
**Flowering period** June–August(–September).
**Ecology and distribution** Rocks, detritus of the lower slopes, moraines, rubble and gravelly streams, on any type of subsoil although often found on calcareous rocks, from 6,235 to 10,170(–12,470) ft (1,900–3,100(–3,800) m). Endemic to the Alpine range, it is distributed from the Cottian to the Rhaetian Alps.

---

## 56 CAMPANULA COCHLEARIFOLIA Lam.
Fairy's Thimble
*C. pusilla* Haenke; *C. bellardii* All.; *C. pumila* Curt.

**Family** *Campanulaceae*
**Description** A tufted, herbaceous plant with a slender, branched rhizome, forming numerous ascending epigeal stems. Basal leaves stalked in lax, sub-rounded rosettes, truncate or cordate at the base, strongly toothed. Stem leaves lanceolate, slightly serrate. Flowers sky-blue or mauvish-blue, solitary or in small apical groups on the flowering stems, tending to be pendent especially when in bud. Calyx very short with spreading lobes. Corolla approx. ½–¾ in (12–20 mm) long, hemispherical at the base then campanulate, with 5 short, broad lobes.
**Size** 2–4(–8) ins (5–10(–20) cm).
**Flowering period** June-August(–September).
**Ecology and distribution** Rocky places, rubble, detritus of the lower slopes and gravelly streams on a fairly calcareous subsoil, from 3,280 to 9,840(–11,155) ft (1,000–3,000(–3,400) m). Very frequent in the Pyrenees, Vosges, Jura, Alps, Carpathians and mountains of the Balkan peninsula.

## 57 CAMPANULA EXCISA Schleich. ex Murith
Perforate Bellflower

**Family** *Campanulaceae*
**Description** A tufted, delicate, hairless, herbaceous perennial, with a slender rhizome, branched with sterile shoots and numerous flowering stems. Basal leaves cordate or sub-rounded which disappear at flowering-time; stem leaves linear or linear-lanceolate. Flowers light blue or mauvish-blue, solitary, pendent. Calyx short, with narrowly linear lobes, fully recurved. Corolla ¾–1⅜ ins (2–3.5 cm) long, with a cylindrical-campanulate tube with 5 undulate, ovate lobes, one-third the length of the corolla, which narrow sharply at their base.
**Size** 2–5(–6) ins (5–12(–15) cm).
**Flowering period** July–September.
**Ecology and distribution** Stony and rocky places and detritus of the lower slopes, on a gneissic or granitic subsoil, from (4,595–)5,250 to 7,545 ft ((1,400–)1,600–2,300 m). Endemic to the western and central Alps, from the Graian to the Lepontine Alps where it is quite frequent.

## 58 CAMPANULA PULLA L.
Solitary Harebell

**Family** *Campanulaceae*
**Description** A tufted, herbaceous plant with a slender rhizome, branched, from which emerge numerous graceful, epigeal stems, ascending or erect. Basal leaves oval or sub-rounded, absent at flowering-time; lower leaves oval, on short petioles, slightly crenate, upper leaves lanceolate. Flowers deep purple, solitary, pendent, broadly campanulate. Calyx short with linear lobes. Corolla approx. ¾–1 in (17–24 mm) long with a flared tube with 10 veins and short lobes.
**Size** 2¾–6 ins (7–15 cm).
**Flowering period** July–August.
**Ecology and distribution** Stony and grassy places, alpine pastures, rubble and rocks, on a calcareous subsoil, from 4,920 to 7,220 ft (1,500–2,200 m). Endemic to the north-eastern Austrian Alps.
**Notes** A protected species.

## 59 CAMPANULA RAINERI Perpenti
Rainer's Bellflower

**Family** *Campanulaceae*
**Description** A dwarf perennial, prostrate-ascending, with a woody rhizome that penetrates into the rock fissures, and short epigeal stems. Leaves close together, obovate or spatulate, narrowing into a short petiole, slightly serrate. Flowers light mauvish-blue, large, solitary at the apex of each epigeal stem. Corolla 1–1¼ ins (2.5–3 cm) long and 1¼–1½ ins (3–4 cm) wide, broadly campanulate, flared, with 5 very short, slightly channelled, slightly recurved lobes, ending with a short point.
**Size** 2–4 ins (5–10 cm).
**Flowering period** August–September.
**Ecology and distribution** Rocks, stony and craggy places, fissures in rock faces, rubble, on a calcareous subsoil, from (2,625–)4,265 to 7,220 ft ((800–)1,300–2,200 m). Endemic to the southern Alps (Lombardic Pre-Alps, from Lake Como to Lake Garda), where it is quite frequent.
**Notes** A protected species because of its limited distribution.

---

## 60 CAMPANULA SCHEUCHZERI Vill.

**Family** *Campanulaceae*
**Description** A tufted herbaceous plant with a branched rhizome, with numerous slender, delicate epigeal stems. Basal leaves round or cordate, on long petioles, crenate, nearly always absent at flowering-time. Stem leaves, linear, acute, ciliate at the base. Flowers mauvish-blue or violet, solitary or in groups of 2–3, erect or slightly bent. Calyx short with spreading linear lobes. Corolla campanulate, flared, ¾–1⅛ ins (18–28 mm), with 5 semicircular, recurved lobes.
**Size** 4–14(–20) ins (10–35(–50) cm).
**Flowering period** July–August(–September).
**Ecology and distribution** Pastures, stony places, rubble and grassy areas, on any type of subsoil, from (2,625–)4,595 to 10,170(–11,155) ft ((800–)1,400–3,100(–3,400) m). Very common in all the southern European mountains (the Pyrenees, Alps, Jura, Vosges, Apennines and Carpathians) and in the mountains of the Balkan peninsula.

## 61 CAMPANULA THYRSOIDES (or THYRSOIDEA) L.
Yellow Bellflower

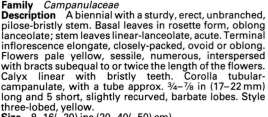

**Family** *Campanulaceae*
**Description** A biennial with a sturdy, erect, unbranched, pilose-bristly stem. Basal leaves in rosette form, oblong lanceolate; stem leaves linear-lanceolate, acute. Terminal inflorescence elongate, closely-packed, ovoid or oblong. Flowers pale yellow, sessile, numerous, interspersed with bracts subequal to or twice the length of the flowers. Calyx linear with bristly teeth. Corolla tubular-campanulate, with a tube approx. ¾–⅞ in (17–22 mm) long and 5 short, slightly recurved, barbate lobes. Style three-lobed, yellow.
**Size** 8–16(–20) ins (20–40(–50) cm).
**Flowering period** (June–)July–August(–September).
**Ecology and distribution** Alpine pastures, fields, rocky detritus, high alpine moorlands and outskirts of woods, on a calcareous subsoil, from (2,625–)4,920 to 8,530 (–9,020) ft ((800–)1,500–2,600(–2,750) m). Although found locally in scattered areas of the Alps, it is a rare plant; also found in the Jura and mountains of the Balkan peninsula.
**Notes** This is the only European mountain Campanula with yellow flowers, all the other species having flowers ranging from blue to violet and, rarely, white. A strictly protected species.

## 62 CAMPANULA TOMMASINIANA Koch

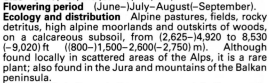

**Family** *Campanulaceae*
**Description** A tufted, herbaceous perennial with a short rhizome and numerous hairless, delicate, epigeal stems. Basal leaves small, ovate or sub-rounded, no longer present at flowering-time. Lower stem leaves elliptical or ovate, upper leaves lanceolate and narrowing to a long point, denticulate-serrate, sessile. Flowers violet-blue, set into the axils of the upper leaves and leaf-like bracts, pendent, with short peduncles. Calyx short with linear teeth. Corolla with a narrow cylindrical tube, slightly flared at the end into 5 short, lanceolate lobes, one-third to one-quarter the length of the corolla itself.
**Size** 8–12 ins (20–30 cm).
**Flowering period** July–August.
**Ecology and distribution** On the rocks of montane woods, preferably calcareous, from 1,970 to 4,920 ft (600–1,500 m). Endemic to the mountains of north-western Yugoslavia.
**Notes** This species is similar to *C. waldsteiniana*, widespread in the Dinaric Alps of north-western Yugoslavia. The latter is distinguished from *C. tommasiniana* by its much wider open corolla – rotate-campanulate – with lobes about half the length of the corolla.

## 63  CAMPANULA ZOYSII (or ZOISII) Wulf.
Crimped Bellflower

**Family** *Campanulaceae*
**Description** A delicate, tufted perennial, very branched at the base. Lower leaves ovate or sub-rounded, on short petioles, obtuse. Upper leaves lanceolate or linear. Flowers sky-blue, pale blue or violet, solitary at the apex of the epigeal stems. Calyx short with linear, spreading lobes. Corolla ½–¾ in (10–20 mm) long, very distinctively shaped being cylindrical-swollen in the lower part, then narrowing sharply before enlarging into 5 projections, each shaped like a short spur; it is constricted at the apex into a white throat with 5 small recurved teeth.
**Size** 2–4 ins (5–10 cm).
**Flowering period** June–August.
**Ecology and distribution** Crags and detritus of the lower slopes, on a calcareous subsoil, from 5,905 to 7,545 ft (1,800–2,300 m). Endemic to the eastern Alps from Vicenza in Italy to the Julian and Karawanken Alps in Austria; quite rare.
**Notes** A protected species.

---

## 64  CARLINA ACANTHIFOLIA All.
Acanthus-leaved Carline Thistle

**Family** *Compositae*
**Description** An acaulescent perennial with a showy rosette of leaves flat on the ground. Leaves spiny, pinnate-lobed or pinnate-parted with slightly spreading lobes, dentate-spinose, 8–14 ins (20–35 cm) long and 2¾–3½ ins (7–9 cm) wide, arachnoid on the underside and greenish on the upper. Flowers united in a dense inflorescence; this flower-head is solitary, sessile and positioned in the centre of the leaf rosette, 5–5½ ins (12–14 cm) wide, including the bracts, with numerous mauve then yellowish flowers. Bracts inside the involucre are narrow, linear, 1⅜–2¼ ins (35–55 mm) long, and yellowish, straw-coloured or bright yellow.
**Size** 4–8 ins (10–20 cm).
**Flowering period** July–September.
**Ecology and distribution** Grassy woods, dry pastures and stony slopes, preferably on a calcareous subsoil, from (1,970–)2,625 to 5,905 ft ((600–)800–1,800 m). Sporadic, but not frequent, in the Pyrenees, Alps, Cevennes, Carpathians, Apennines and mountains of the Balkan peninsula.
**Notes** A protected species in some areas.

## 65 CARLINA ACAULIS L.
Stemless Carline Thistle

**Family** *Compositae*
**Description** An acaulescent, herbaceous perennial with a thick vertical rhizome and a basal rosette of leaves flat on the ground. Leaves spiny, pinnate-parted or pinnatifid with acuminate, oblong, sub-opposite lobes, dentate-spinose on the margin 8–12 ins (20–30 cm) long and 2–2¾ ins (5–7 cm) wide, slightly pilose. Flowers united in a dense inflorescence to form a showy head; this is solitary, sessile, positioned in the centre of the leaf rosette, 2½–5 ins (6–12 cm) diameter including the bracts. Bracts inside the involucre are similar to a corona of strap-shaped flowers, silvery-white above, green or violet below, 1¼–1¾ ins (30–45 mm) long; numerous reddish-violet flowers clustered close together.
**Size** 4–6(–8) ins (10–15(–20) cm).
**Flowering period** July–September.
**Ecology and distribution** Dry pastures, stony and dry grassy places, on any type of subsoil but particularly frequent on calcareous soil, from (3,935–)4,920 to 9,185 ft (1,200–)1,500–2,800 m. Frequent in all the mountains of Europe (especially the south): the Pyrenees, Alps, Apennines and mountains of the Balkan peninsula.
**Notes** Declared a protected species in some areas.

---

## 66 CENTAUREA MONTANA L.
Mountain Cornflower

**Family** *Compositae*
**Description** An erect, herbaceous plant with a stiff stem, densely leafy, arachnoid-tomentose, with ovate, ovate-lanceolate or oblong-lanceolate leaves, tomentose on the lower surface, decurrent for some length on the stem giving a winged appearance. Flowers, ranging in colour from purplish-red to violet and blue, in solitary terminal heads. Head 2¼–3¼ ins (6–8 cm) wide, globose, with oblong or elliptical, fringed, involucral bracts, ¾–1 in (2–2.5 cm) long, dark brown to black. Central flowers tubular, red or violet, with protruding styles; peripheral flowers sub-campanulate, double the length of those in the centre, laciniate with 5 or more blue or violet-blue linear segments.
**Size** 4–32 ins (10–80 cm).
**Flowering period** May–July(–September).
**Ecology and distribution** Dry pastures, exposed craggy places and dry fields, mainly on a calcareous subsoil, from 3,280 to 6,890 ft (1,000–2,100 m). Very frequent in all the central European mountains (the Pyrenees, Ardennes, Alps, Apennines, Carpathians and Dinaric Alps).
**Notes** A similar species to *C. triumfetti* (see entry 68), from which it differs in its larger, more decurrent leaves and darker brown bracts. A protected species.

## 67 CENTAUREA NERVOSA Willd.
Plume Knapweed

**Family** *Compositae*
**Description** A sturdy perennial, with an erect, greyish-green stem. Leaves alternate, lanceolate or narrowly lanceolate, on short petioles or sub-sessile, small-toothed, growing closer together towards the top of the stem. Flowers purplish-red or violet-red, usually in a solitary head at the apex of each stem. Head globose, 2–3¼ ins (5–8 cm) wide, covered with an involucre of lanceolate bracts ¾–1 in (2–2.5 cm) long, apically fringed, with a long, recurved, feathery appendage at the top giving the bracts an almost pilose-arachnoid appearance, especially when the flower is in bud. Flowers in centre of head are short, slightly longer than the bracts; peripheral flowers are larger, fringed into numerous slender, linear segments.
**Size** 4–16 ins (10–40 cm).
**Flowering period** July–August.
**Ecology and distribution** Pastures, open grassy places, dwarf pine and rhododendron moorlands, on any type of subsoil, from (2,625–)3,610 to 8,530 ft (800–)1,100–2,600 m). Quite frequent in the Alps, northern Apennines, eastern Carpathians and the mountains of the Balkan peninsula.
**Notes** Nowadays, it is sometimes regarded as a sub-species of *Centaurea uniflora*, a rather variable species.

## 68 CENTAUREA TRIUMFETTI All.
*C. variegata*

**Family** *Compositae*
**Description** A herbaceous perennial with an erect sturdy, pilose-arachnoid stem. Leaves greyish-green, arachnoid-tomentose, alternate, lanceolate or linear-lanceolate, briefly decurrent on the stem. Flowers pink or violet-red, united into a solitary dense apical head more or less spherical; involucre formed from oblong or lanceolate bracts, fringed along the upper half like a comb, dark or light brown or whitish. Central flowers red with showy anthers, linear, deep violet; peripheral flowers twice the length of the central ones, laciniate in pink or violet-coloured linear segments.
**Size** 4–28 ins (10–70 cm).
**Flowering period** May–July.
**Ecology and distribution** Fields, high altitude pastures, grassy and open stony places, mainly on a calcareous subsoil, from (2,625–)3,280 to 6,560(–7,875) ft ((800–)1,000–2,000(–2,400) m). Frequent in the European mountains (the Pyrenees, Alps, Apennines, Carpathians, mountains of the Balkan peninsula) and in the mountains of Asia Minor; it also descends into the lowlands of central and eastern Europe as far as the Ukraine and Crimea.
**Notes** This species is very similar to *C. montana* (see entry 66).

## 69 CERASTIUM LATIFOLIUM L.
Broad-leaved Mouse-ear Chickweed

**Family** *Caryophyllaceae*
**Description** A herbaceous plant with loose, leafy tufts and erect or ascending flowering stems, pilose-glandular or pubescent. Leaves opposite, grey-blue, ovate, acute, stiff, ½–1¼ ins (12–30 mm) long and ¼–½ in (5–10 mm) wide. Flowers white, solitary or in groups of 2–3, ⅝–¾ in (1.5–2 cm) wide, open, campanulate. Calyx short, with 5 sepals. Corolla of 5 petals, twice as long as the sepals, obovate, emarginate or deeply incised to about half-way.
**Size** 2–8 ins (5–20 cm).
**Flowering period** (June–)July–August.

**Ecology and distribution** Detritus, moraines, stony places, rubble, on a calcareous or dolomitic subsoil, from 5,250 to 10,500(–11,485) ft (1,000–3,200(–3,500) m). Quite frequent in the Alps, especially in the western and central zones; also found in the northern Apennines.

---

## 70 CERASTIUM TOMENTOSUM L.
Snow-in-summer, Dusty Miller

**Family** *Caryophyllaceae*
**Description** A tufted, herbaceous plant, white-tomentose with often delicate stems, very branched, spreading-ascending, intersecting with each other, erect terminal branches many flowered. Leaves opposite, lanceolate or linear, greenish-white or whitish, with a thick, close-growing tomentum, ½–1¼ ins (1–3 cm) long. Flowers white in loose terminal inflorescences of 2–15 flowers to each axis. Corolla flared, ¾–1 in (2–2.5 cm) in diameter; petals 5, obovate, with an attenuate claw and deeply emarginate limb.
**Size** 6–12(–18) ins (15–30(–45) cm).
**Flowering period** (May–)June–July.
**Ecology and distribution** Grassy and open stony places, rocky woodland clearings and pastures, preferably on a subsoil of basic rock, from 3,280 to 6,560(–7,545) ft (1,000–2,000(–2,300) m). Common in the central and southern Apennines and in Sicily. Previous records of this species from Greece, the Balkan peninsula and the Caucasus are in doubt, as it has been confused with other species such as *C. candidissimum* and *C. bierbersteinii*.
**Notes** Endemic to southern Italy and Sicily. Widely used as a garden plant for its showy, prolific white flowers and all-the-year-round silvery foliage.

## 71 CERASTIUM UNIFLORUM Clairv. (also Thom)

Glacier Mouse-ear Chickweed
*C. glaciale* Gaud.

**Family** *Caryophyllaceae*
**Description** A tufted, herbaceous perennial, woody at the base, forming lax leafy mats. Leaves opposite, very close together, oblong or obovate, ½–¾ in (10–18 mm) long and ⅛–¼ in (3–5 mm) wide, bright green. Flowers white, solitary at the apex of the flowering stems or united into groups of 2–3, ½–⅝ in (1–1.5 cm) wide, campanulate-flared. Sepals approx. ¼ in (5–7 mm) long; petals 5, obovate, deeply emarginate or bifid to almost half-way, traversed by greyish veins towards the claw, about twice the length of the sepals.
**Size** 1–4 ins (3–10 cm).
**Flowering period** July–August(–September).
**Ecology and distribution** Rocks, detritus of the lower slopes, moraines and rubble, on siliceous rocks such as gneiss and granite, from 6,235 to 10,500(–11,155) ft (1,900–3,200(–3,400) m). Frequent in the Alps, also found in the western Carpathians and northern Dinaric Alps.

---

## 72 CIRSIUM ERIOPHORUM (L.) Scop.

Woolly Thistle

**Family** *Compositae*
**Description** A very sturdy, herbaceous perennial with a thick rhizome and a simple or branched, erect stem covered with white-tomentose down. Leaves alternate, white-tomentose, pinnatifid, sessile or almost amplexicaul, divided into spaced-out, linear lobes, spiny at the apex. Head terminal, usually solitary, very large, 1½–2¾ ins (4–7 cm) wide, globose and expanded; involucre formed of numerous ovate-acuminate bracts, spiny at the apex, covered by a white tomentum. Flowers purple, violet-red or deep pink, all tubular emerging from the involucre rather like a broad paintbrush.
**Size** 24–60 ins (60–150 cm).
**Flowering period** July–September.
**Ecology and distribution** Uncultivated places, clearings in woods, by mountain paths, among shrubs and on ground used for grazing, on a calcareous subsoil, from (985–)3,940 to 6,560(–6,890) ft ((300–)1,200–2,000 (–2,100) m). Frequent in all European mountains (the Pyrenees, Alps, Apennines, Carpathians, Balkan Mountains and Scottish Highlands); also found at low altitudes, especially in central and eastern Europe.

## 73 CIRSIUM SPINOSISSIMUM (L.) Scop.
Spiniest Thistle

**Family** *Compositae*
**Description** A showy, erect perennial, very spiny, with a solitary, sturdy stem. Leaves alternate, oblong, erect-spreading, green, deeply divided into broad, spiny, spreading lobes; upper leaves closer together towards the apex of the stem below the head, amplexicaul, shorter than the others, often arcuate towards the top, yellowish-green or golden-yellow. Heads terminal, sessile, united into closely-packed agglomerates surrounded by the upper leaves. Head ¾–1 in (2–2.5 cm), consisting of an ovoid or globose involucre of spiny linear bracts. Flowers yellowish or golden-yellow, tubular, emerging like a thick paintbrush from the involucre.
**Size** 8–20(–48) ins (20–50(–120) cm).
**Flowering period** July–September.
**Ecology and distribution** Pastures, grassy places near alpine summer pastures, stony clearings, rubble and detritus of the lower slopes, generally on wet or damp ground, from (2,950–)4,920 to 8,860(–10,170) ft ((900–)1,500–2,700(–3,100) m). Very frequent in the Alps where it is endemic.

---

## 74 CORTUSA MATTHIOLI L.
Alpine Bells
*Androsace primuloides* Moench; *Primula matthioli* Richt.

**Family** *Primulaceae*
**Description** An acaulescent, herbaceous perennial with a branched rhizome from which emerges a rosette of dark green, rather conspicuous, cordate-orbicular or sub-rounded leaves, 3¼–5 ins (8–12 cm) wide, palmate-lobate with irregularly dentate lobes, pilose, on long petioles. Flower stem erect, pilose, with a terminal umbel of 3–15 pendulous flowers borne on unequal peduncles. Flowers purplish-pink, ½ in (1 cm). Calyx campanulate. Corolla 2–3 times as long as the calyx, conical-campanulate, divided almost half-way down into 5 ovate-lanceolate, obtuse or acute, lobes.
**Size** 4–12(–16) ins (10–30(–40) cm).
**Flowering period** May–July(–August).
**Ecology and distribution** Moist woods, thickets and wet rocks, on any type of subsoil, with a preference for limestone. Found in the Alps, Carpathians, Transylvanian Alps and mountains of the south-eastern Balkan peninsula.
**Notes** A protected species in some areas. Similar species are found in Russia, the Urals and the mountains of central Asia (*Cortusa altaica*).

## 75 CREPIS AUREA (L.) Cass.
Golden Hawksbeard

**Family** *Compositae*
**Description** A herbaceous, acaulescent perennial with a thick underground rhizome. Leaves, all basal, densely-packed, spathulate-runcinate or oblanceolate and wavy-dentate, hairless, shiny. Flowering stem with black glandular hairs on the upper part and a single terminal head. Head ¾–1¼ ins (2–3 cm) wide, with an ovoid or sub-cylindrical involucre formed of numerous linear bracts thickly covered with spreading, glandular black hairs. Flowers orange-yellow or reddish-orange, all strap-shaped, outer spreading, with linear ligules, toothed at the apex.
**Size** 2–8(–12) ins (5–20(–30) cm).
**Flowering period** June–September.
**Ecology and distribution** Pastures, grassy or stony places and rocky slopes, on any type of subsoil although with a preference for acid soils, from (2,950–)4,920 to 9,515 ft (900–)1,500–2,900 m). Frequent in the Alps, Apuane Alps, Apennines and the mountains of the western and southern Balkan peninsula.

---

## 76 CROCUS PURPUREUS Weston
Purple Crocus
*C. vernus* (L.) Wulf; *C. albiflorus* Kit.

**Family** *Iridaceae*
**Description** A small perennial growing from a corm. Leaves 2–4, erect, narrowly linear, emerging from the ground just as the flowering period starts, dark green with white veins, a little shorter than the open flower. Flower usually solitary, emerging from 1 or 2 basal, papery sheaths which remain wrapped around the flower stalks. Perianth white, violet or striped, formed of 6 oblong or elliptical tepals, pilose inside the base, the 3 inside being narrower than the 3 outside. Stamens 3, with yellow anthers.
**Size** ½–5 ins (6–12 cm) – the flowering plant.
**Flowering period** (February–)March–June; the flowering begins immediately after the snows have melted.
**Ecology and distribution** Wet meadows, damp pastures and grassy places, on any type of subsoil; it also grows in the sub-montane region but is more frequent in the montane zone and in the high alpine zone where it may be found at a height of 8,858 ft (2,700 m). Very common in the mountains of central-northern Europe (Iberian, Corsican and Balkan Mountains, the Pyrenees, Jura, Alps, northern Apennines and Carpathians).

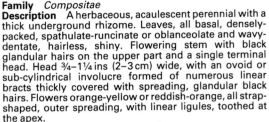

## 77 CYANANTHUS MICROPHYLLUS
Edgeworth

**Family** *Campanulaceae*
**Description** A small perennial with a creeping rhizome from which spring numerous epigeal stems which are prostrate at first then ascending, reddish, delicate, slightly pubescent. Leaves alternate, distant, lanceolate or ovate, cordate at the base, revolute on the margin, sessile or nearly so, approx. ¼–½ in (6–10 mm) long and ⅛–¼ in (3–5 mm) wide. Flowers violet-blue, solitary at the apex of the branches, sub-sessile or with a short peduncle. Calyx campanulate or nearly urn-shaped, green, covered with reddish-brown bristly hairs. Corolla campanulate, with a cylindrical tube approx. ⅝ in (1.5–1.7 cm) long; throat open, with numerous white thread-like fringes; limb nearly circular, formed of 5 narrowly obovate or elliptical acute lobes.
**Size** 6–12 ins (15–30 cm).
**Flowering period** June–August.
**Ecology and distribution** Open rocky areas, rubble and rocky pastures, from 10,825 to 12,800 ft (3,300–3,900 m). Endemic to the central Himalayas (Nepal and Kumaun).

## 78 CYPRIPEDIUM CALCEOLUS L.
Lady's Slipper Orchid

**Family** *Orchidaceae*
**Description** A sturdy, herbaceous plant with a horizontal rhizome. Stem epigeal, erect, cylindrical, slightly pilose, equipped with 3–5 alternate leaves, elliptical or broadly oval, 4–6¾ ins (10–17 cm) long and 1⅜–2¾ ins (3.5–7 cm) wide, with deeply sunken veins. Flowers 1–2, occasionally 3, unilateral, large, 2–2½ ins (5–6 cm) wide, positioned in the axil of leaf-like bracts and supported by an arching peduncle. Perianth formed of 6 tepals, 5 of which are elliptic-lanceolate, reddish or chestnut-brown, two of which have grown together into a single element; the sixth, known as the labellum or lip, is large, 1¼ ins (3 cm), yellow, inflated like a bulging pocket or slipper.
**Size** 6–24(–28) ins (15–60(–70) cm).
**Flowering period** May–July.
**Ecology and distribution** Clearings in woods, thickets of dwarf pine and grassy places, often on a calcareous subsoil, from (2,300–)3,280 to 6,560 ft ((700–)1,000–2,000 m). Quite rare but found sporadically in nearly all European mountains (the Pyrenees, Alps, central Apennines, Carpathians, in the British Isles, Scandinavia and the Balkan peninsula), in the Caucasus and north-eastern Asia, from Siberia to China and Sakhalin.
**Notes** Now rare because of indiscriminate picking. A strictly protected species.

## 79  DAPHNE STRIATA  Tratt.

**Family**  *Thymelaeaceae*
**Description**  A low-growing, woody, evergreen shrub, much branched, prostrate-spreading, with subterranean stems emerging from the ground at considerable distances from main plant. Leaves alternate, grouped at the top of branches just below the inflorescence, linear, linear-lanceolate or linear-spatulate, ¾–1¼ ins (2–3 cm) long, often incurved towards the base. Flowers pink or carmine-red, fragrant, sessile, united in dense terminal inflorescences of 8–12 flowers. Calyx very short with 4 coloured sepals. Corolla with a very long tube and flat and rounded limb with 4 oval or elliptical lobes. Fruit reddish.
**Size**  4–20 ins (10–50 cm).
**Flowering period**  May–July(–August).
**Ecology and distribution**  Dry pastures, stony places and rubble, mainly on a calcareous subsoil, from (3,280 –)5,250 to 8,200(–9,515) ft ((1,000–)1,600–2,500(–2,900) m). Quite frequent in the Alps, especially the central Alps; more rare in the French Alps.
**Notes**  Endemic to the Alps; a protected plant.

---

## 80  DELPHINIUM ELATUM  L.
Alpine Larkspur

**Family**  *Ranunculaceae*
**Description**  An erect, herbaceous perennial, stems pubescent (at least on the lower part). Leaves alternate, pinnatifid or pinnatisect, with 5 lanceolate lobes, serrate or incised, the upper ones trifid with lanceolate or linear lobes, entire. Flowers sky-blue or violet-blue, united in a long terminal racemose inflorescence, with long peduncles, positioned in the axils of two linear bracts. Calyx irregular, formed of 5 petal-like sepals, broadly elliptical or ovate, approx. ¾–⅞ in (14–21 mm) long, acute, with short hairs on the outside, 1½–3 times longer than wide, the upper sepal with a long cylindrical spur, incurved at the end. Petals 4, reduced to nectar-bearing scales.
**Size**  1 ft 4 ins–6 ft 6 ins (40–200 cm).
**Flowering period**  June–August.
**Ecology and distribution**  Pastures, grassy or stony places and alpine meadows, on any type of subsoil although with a preference for limestone, from 3,940 to 6,560(–7,875) ft (1,200–2,000(–2,400) m). Widespread in the Pyrenees, Alps, Carpathians and Arctic regions of northern Europe, Russia and Siberia.
**Notes**  A protected plant in some areas.

## 81 DIANTHUS GLACIALIS Haenke
Glacier Pink

**Family** *Caryophyllaceae*
**Description** A herbaceous plant with a short rhizome and leaves clustering into a tuft. Stems, one or two epigeal. Leaves opposite, linear, slightly wider in the upper half, fleshy-spiky, obtuse, often longer than the flowering stems. Flowers pink, solitary, approx. ½–¾ in (12–15 mm) in diameter. Calyx subtended by 2–4 ovate-acuminate bracteoles, the same length as the calyx, ½–1 in (12–16 mm) long. Corolla pink with whitish mouth, surrounded by small scales. Petals 5 with an obovate, expanded limb and dentate margin.
**Size** 2–4 ins (5–10 cm).
**Flowering period** July–August.
**Ecology and distribution** Stony places, pastures, grassy rocks and moraines, on granite, mica-schist or acid subsoils, from (6,230–)7,875 to 9,515 ft ((1,900–)2,400–2,900 m). Found in the eastern and central Alps (from the canton of Graubünden in Switzerland to the Hohe Tauern in Austria) and in the Carpathians; an endemic species.
**Notes** A protected species almost everywhere.

## 82 DIANTHUS MICROLEPIS Boiss.

**Family** *Caryophyllaceae*
**Description** A small, more or less stemless, tufted perennial, forming dense lax leafy cushions. Flowering stems, leafless or with 1–2 small opposite scale-like leaves. Basal leaves, narrowly linear, ½–¾ in (10–20 mm) long, densely packed. Flowers deep pink, usually solitary on the apex of the stems, occasionally in dense cymes of 2–3 flowers. Calyx subtended by 2 small bracts, tubular, flaring upwards, approx. ½ in (9–10.5 mm). Corolla of 5 petals with a short tube and a 5-lobed rhombic-subrounded limb, veined in red, apically small-toothed, approx. ¼ in (6–7 mm) long.
**Size** ½–4 ins (1–10 cm).
**Flowering period** June–September.
**Ecology and distribution** High altitude pastures and open grassy places, from 4,595 to 8,860 ft (1,400–2,700 m). Endemic to the mountains of south-western Bulgaria.

## 83 DODECATHEON PAUCIFLORUM (Dur.)
Greene
Shooting Stars
*D. pulchellum*

**Family** *Primulaceae*
**Description** An acaulescent perennial, with a rosette of oblong or oblanceolate, closely-packed leaves at the base. Flowering stem simple, with an umbel of pedunculate flowers at the top which bend downwards when blooming, equipped with a corona of small linear bracts. Flowers pink or purplish-pink. Calyx cylindrical-conical, with 5 lanceolate lobes. Corolla, tube short, yellow mouth and a 5-lobed, lanceolate or oblong, pink limb, ⅝–1¼ ins (1.5–3 cm) long, which completely folds back when in flower. Stamens and anthers acuminate, converging, protruding from the corolla.
**Size** 6–20 ins (15–50 cm).
**Flowering period** (April–)May–July.
**Ecology and distribution** Damp grassy places and marshy pastures, from (1,970–)3,280 to 11,810 ft ((600–) 1,000–3,600 m). Quite common, as are numerous other species of *Dodecatheon*, in the mountains of western North America, from British Columbia and Saskatchewan to California and Arizona.

---

## 84 DORONICUM GRANDIFLORUM Lam.
Large Flowered Leopard's Bane
*D. jacquini* Tausch; *D. scorpioides* W. et L.; *Aronicum scorpioides* Koch

**Family** *Compositae*
**Description** A densely tufted, herbaceous perennial with numerous erect flowering stems and an oblique or horizontal, thick rhizome. Leaves mostly basal, broadly ovate or sub-rounded, stalked, truncate or cordate at the base, regularly dentate, with a pilose margin; stem leaves alternate, sessile, cordate and clasping the stem. Heads 1½–2½(–3¼) ins (4–6(–8) cm) wide, solitary at the apex of the flowering stems which thicken immediately below the head; numerous involucral bracts in 2–3 rows. Discflorets, dark yellow, tubular; ray-florets numerous, yellow or golden-yellow, with linear ligules, up to ¾ in (2 cm) long.
**Size** 4–20 ins (10–50 cm).
**Flowering period** July–August(–September).
**Ecology and distribution** Stony places, detritus, moraines, rubble and debris, on a mainly calcareous subsoil, from (4,265–)5,575 to 8,530(–11,155) ft ((1,300–)1,700–2,600(–3,400) m). Frequent, often growing in dense colonies of numerous individual plants, in the Pyrenees and Alps as well as the mountains of Corsica and the southern Dinaric Alps.

## 85 DOUGLASIA LAEVIGATA A. Gray

**Family** *Primulaceae*
**Description** A small, acaulescent, herbaceous plant with one or more dense basal rosettes. Leaves close together, oblong or linear-lanceolate, acute, leathery, light green, ½–¾ in (12–20 mm) long, arranged to give a rayed effect in the rosette. Flower stem solitary, with a terminal umbel of flowers emerging from a corona of 4–6 oval-obtuse bracts, approx. ¼ in (6–8 mm) long. Umbels consisting of 2–5 pink flowers on long peduncles, with a campanulate tubular calyx. Corolla, with cylindrical tube twice the length of the calyx; flat and rounded limb, ¼–½ in (7–10 mm) wide, with 5 obtuse, elliptical-obovate lobes. Mouth edged in darker pink; stamens positioned below mouth.
**Size** 2¾–4 ins (7–10 cm).
**Flowering period** June–August.
**Ecology and distribution** Rocks, rocky or stony slopes and open ground, around 9,840 to 11,480 ft (3,000–3,500 m). Found in the Rocky Mountains, from British Columbia to Oregon.

## 86 DRABA AIZOIDES L.
Yellow Whitlow-grass

**Family** *Cruciferae*
**Description** An acaulescent, tufted plant with a tap-root which branches out into numerous dense rosettes of leaves. Stems short, leafless; basal leaves, linear, stiff, up to ¾ in (2 cm) long, with numerous stiff bristles on the margin and apex. Flowers golden-yellow, in dense terminal inflorescences, hemispherical or flat, containing 4–18 flowers. Corolla ⅓ in (8–9 mm). Petals 4, obovate or oblong, ¼–⅓ in (5–8 mm) long; stamens and styles protruding. Flat, elliptical silicles, approx. ¼–½ in (6–12 mm) long and approx. ⅛ in (2.5–4 mm) wide.
**Size** 2–4(–6) ins (5–10(–15) cm) – the flowering plant.
**Flowering period** (April–)May–July(–August).
**Ecology and distribution** Rocks, stony places, dry grassy pastures and fissures in crags, preferably on limestone, from (2,625–)4,595 to 10,500(–11,810) ft ((800–)1,400–3,200(–3,600) m). Widespread in the Pyrenees, Alps, Apennines and the mountains of Sicily, central-eastern Europe and the Balkan peninsula.

## 87 DRABA DUBIA Suter
*D. frigida* Sauter

**Family** *Cruciferae*
**Description** A herbaceous perennial in tufts of 2–5 individual plants with an erect, sub-acaulescent stem, covered with star-shaped hairs. Basal leaves in rosette form, obovate or almost spatulate, hirsute; stem leaves, alternate, 2–3, sometimes absent, obovate or elliptical, sessile. Flowers white, united at the apex of the stem into short racemose inflorescences, clustered together as flowering period starts. Sepals 4; petals 4, obovate, ⅛–¼ in (3–5 mm) long. Silicula oblong-elliptical, ¼–⅝ in (6–14 mm) long, with star-shaped hairs.
**Size** 2–6 ins (5–15 cm).
**Flowering period** (April–)May–August.
**Ecology and distribution** Screes, rocks and detritus of lower slopes, on any type of subsoil, from 3,935 to 10,500(–11,810) ft (1,300–3,200(–3,600) m). Quite common in the mountains of the Iberian peninsula (Sierra Nevada, Pyrenees) as well as in the Alps and Carpathians.
**Notes** Often confused with *Draba tomentosa* Wulf., which is rare, more densely covered with star-shaped hairs all over, has slightly larger flowers and prefers limestone soils.

---

## 88 DRACOCEPHALUM BULLATUM Forrest ex
Diels
Dragon-head

**Family** *Labiatae*
**Description** An erect, herbaceous perennial, with a violet-red pubescent stem, and numerous sub-rounded basal leaves, on long petioles, cordate-auriculate or sub-rounded at base, 1½–2½ ins (4–6.5 cm) long and wide, conspicuously crenate, with very prominent veins. Stem leaves, 3–4 pairs, on short petioles or sessile, sub-rounded, smaller than the basals. Inflorescence spicate, consisting of flowers in closely-packed whorls, 1½–2⅜ ins (4–6 cm) long. Bracts, obovate or sub-rounded, with acuminate teeth. Calyx approx. ¾ in (2 cm) long, with 5 teeth, 4 triangular acuminate and one rounded, with clearly visible nerves. Corolla tubular, two-lipped, violet-blue, with dark markings on the lower lip. Tube approx. ⅞ in (2.3 cm) long, obconical; limb formed of 4 sub-rounded lobes, approx. ⅙ in (4–4.5 mm) long, and a lower spotted lip folding downwards.
**Size** 4–12 ins (10–30 cm).
**Flowering period** July–August.
**Ecology and distribution** Rocky slopes, crags, screes, rubble, stony ground and alpine scrub, on a calcareous subsoil, from 9,840 to 13,125(–13,780) ft (3,000–4,000 (–4,200) m). Endemic to the mountains in the Li-chiang region of Yunnan province in southern China.

## 89 DRYAS DRUMMONDII Richards.

**Family** *Rosaceae*
**Description** A herbaceous perennial, woody at the base, acaulescent, with a creeping rhizome and sub-prostrate branches. Basal leaves on fairly long petioles, elliptical or obovate, rounded at the apex, attenuate or restricted at the base, crenate, white-tomentose on the lower surface. Flower stem longer than leaves, woolly-tomentose. Flowers yellow, solitary, bending downwards as they begin to open. Calyx, tube short, 8–9 ovate lobes, acute, pubescent-hirsute with blackish hairs. Corolla ⅞–1 in (22 –25 mm) wide, consisting of 8–10 oblong or obovate petals.
**Size** 3¼–6(–8) ins (8–15(–20) cm).
**Flowering period** June–August.
**Ecology and distribution** Stony places, walls and rocks from 3,940 to 9,840 ft (1,200–3,000 m). Common in the Rocky Mountains, from Canada to Montana and Oregon; also found in the Arctic regions of North America, from Alaska to Quebec and Labrador.

## 90 DRYAS OCTOPETALA L.
Mountain Avens

**Family** *Rosaceae*
**Description** A small, semi-woody, evergreen plant, sub-acaulescent, with much branched creeping stems forming huge leafy mats. Leaves close together on prostrate branches, oblong or ovate, ¼–¾ in (0.5–2 cm) long, dark green on the upper surface and white-tomentose on the lower, crenate-serrate. Flowers white, solitary at the apex of long axillary flower stalks. Calyx of numerous pilose sepals. Corolla 1–1½ ins (2.5–4 cm) in diameter, consisting of 7–10 (usually 8) sub-rounded or ovate-elliptical, obtuse petals. Fruit formed from numerous long achenes with persistent styles, featherlike ¾–1¼ ins (2–3 cm) long.
**Size** 1¼–6 ins (3–15 cm) – the flowering plant.
**Flowering period** May–July(–August).
**Ecology and distribution** Rocks, dry rubble and stony pastures, preferably on a calcareous subsoil, from 3,280 to 9,190 ft (1,000–2,800 m). Very common in the mountains of central and northern Europe but rarer in those to the south; widespread in the Caucasus and the circum-boreal belt of Eurasia and North America.
**Notes** A protected plant in the Alps and mountains of southern Europe.

## 91 DRYPIS SPINOSA L.

**Family** *Caryophyllaceae*
**Description** A bushy, herbaceous perennial, with erect very branched stems growing close together, quadrangular in cross-section. Leaves whorled, linear-subulate spiny, channelled, the upper ones pinnatifid-spiny. Flowers white or pink, united into a corymb of dense inflorescences with spiny bracts. Calyx tubular, with 5 spiny teeth. Corolla with 5 small petals divided into two, with small scales on the mouth. Stamens 5, with bluish anthers.
**Size** 3¼–12 ins (8–30 cm).
**Flowering period** June–August.
**Ecology and distribution** Open stony places, screes and rubble, preferably on a calcareous subsoil, from 2,625–9,840 ft (800–3,000 m). Quite frequent in the mountains of south-eastern Europe (eastern Alps, central Apennines, and the mountains of the western Balkan peninsula, from Yugoslavia to Greece).
**Notes** Two subspecies of the *Drypis* genus are particularly outstanding: *D. spinosa* is widespread in the high alpine and upper montane zone, and *D. jacquiniana* Murb. et Wettst., which is a coastal and hill subspecies 0 to 2,640 ft (0 to 800 m). The subspecies *spinosa* (above) is a protected plant.

---

## 92 EDRAIANTHUS PUMILIO (Portenschl.) A. DC.

**Family** *Campanulaceae*
**Description** A more or less stemless, tufted, dwarf perennial, with a thick, woody rhizome which branches into numerous ascending epigeal stems. Basal leaves are close together, linear, sessile, ⅓–¾ in (8–20 mm) long and approx. 1/16 in (1 mm) wide, often with revolute margins, densely hirsute and greyish on the upper surface, with a ciliate margin. Stem leaves, alternate. Flowers violet-blue or violet-coloured, rarely white, solitary or, at most, in groups of 2–3 at the apex of the stem. Corolla campanulate, ⅝–¾ in (14–18 mm) long, with oblong lobes, hairless.
**Size** ½–1¼(–2) ins (1–3(–5) cm).
**Flowering period** July–August.
**Ecology and distribution** Rocks, fissures in crags and stony places, on a calcareous subsoil, from 4,920 to 8,200 ft (1,500–2,500 m). Endemic to the western Balkan peninsula, it grows exclusively in Yugoslavia (the Biokova Mountains of Croatia).
**Notes** Numerous other species related to *Edraianthus* grow on other mountains in the Balkan peninsula and the Apennines; these include *E. graminifolius*, *E. parnassicus*, *E. dalmaticus*, *E. serbicus*, *E. serpyllifolius*.

## 93 EPILOBIUM FLEISCHERI Hochst.
Alpine Willowherb; Alpine Fireweed

**Family** *Onagraceae*
**Description** A herbaceous perennial with a thick prostrate rhizome from which emerge numerous erect or ascending epigeal stems. Leaves, alternate, hairless, narrowly lanceolate, thick, stiff, small-toothed. Flowers pink or violet-red, arranged in a lax terminal leafy inflorescence. Bracts leaf-like, decreasing in size towards the top. Floral peduncle, long, cylindrical, broadening towards the top. Calyx consisting of 4 acute, lanceolate sepals, darker violet-red than the corolla, arranged in a cross. Corolla pink, about 1 in (2.5 cm) wide, formed of 4 obovate or elliptical petals which alternate with the sepals, veined in red. Stamens 8, pink. Fruit, elongate capsule containing numerous seeds equipped with a feathery tuft of hairs, to be seen most clearly at the moment before dispersal.
**Size** 8–16 ins (20–40 cm).
**Flowering period** July–September.
**Ecology and distribution** Detrital sites, moraines, rubble, gravelly shores and banks of streams, preferably on an acid subsoil, from (2,295–)3,280 to 8,200(–8,860) ft ((700–)1,000–2,500(–2,700) m). Endemic to the Alps where it is fairly common.

---

## 94 ERICA HERBACEA L.
Spring Heath
*E. carnea* L.

**Family** *Ericaceae*
**Description** A low-growing, dense, bushy shrub with slender, ascending branches. Leaves small, linear, acuminate, needle-like, ¼ in (7 mm) long, united into whorls of 3–4. Flowers bright or flesh-pink, on short peduncles, spreading or leaning downwards, united into closely-packed terminal leafy inflorescences. Corolla tubular-urn-shaped ¼ in (6–8 mm) long, narrowing towards the top with dark red or blackish anthers protruding from it.
**Size** 6–12(–24) ins (15–30(–60) cm.
**Flowering period** (February–)March–June; the flowering period begins as the snows melt.
**Ecology and distribution** Woods, clearings, rubble and stony places, on a calcareous or dolomitic subsoil, from (985–)3,280 to 7,875(–8,860) ft ((300–)1,000–2,400(–2,700) m). Common in all the mountains of south-eastern Europe (the Alps, Apennines and Balkan Mountains).

## 95 ERIGERON ALPINUS L.
Alpine Fleabane

**Family** *Compositae*
**Description** A herbaceous perennial, pilose-hirsute, tufted, erect or ascending, with a stem that is simple or slightly branched at the top. Leaves, pilose, obovate-lanceolate or spatulate, narrow, sub-sessile, mostly basal but some on flowering stems, alternate. Head solitary, at the apex of each branch, 1–5 per plant, ¾–1¼ ins (2–3 cm) wide. Involucre formed of numerous linear, pilose-hirsute, bracts. Disc-florets yellow or reddish-yellow; ray-florets pink or pale violet, numerous, with long linear ligules about half the diameter of the disc. Between the marginal florets of the disc and those of the ray there is a distinctive row of sterile thread-like tubular florets.
**Size** 1¼–8(–16) ins (3–20(–40) cm).
**Flowering period** July–September.
**Ecology and distribution** Pastures, meadows, stony or rocky places, on any type of subsoil, from 4,920 to 8,200(–9,840) ft (1,500–2,500(–3,000) m). Frequent in the Pyrenees, Auvergne, Jura, Alps, central Apennines, eastern Carpathians, Caucasus, the mountains of Corsica, the Balkan peninsula and central Asia (Turkestan).

## 96 ERIGERON UNIFLORUS L.
One-flowered Fleabane

**Family** *Compositae*
**Description** A small, pilose perennial, tufted, more or less stemless with a solitary erect or ascending stem. Leaves nearly all basal, obovate-lanceolate, obtuse, ciliate, channelled; stem leaves sparse or absent. Head terminal solitary, ½–⅝ in (1–1.5 cm) wide, with an involucre of numerous linear bracts, pilose-woolly, arranged in two rows. Disc-florets yellow or pale yellow; ray-florets numerous, violet-pink, pale pink or white, with narrowly linear ligules a little shorter than the diameter of the disc. There are no sterile tubular florets, as in *E. alpinus*.
**Size** ¾–3¼(–5) ins (2–8(–12) cm).
**Flowering period** July–August(–September).
**Ecology and distribution** Stony places, moraines, rubble, detritus of the lower slopes and dry pastures, on any type of subsoil although with a preference for siliceous rocks, from (3,935–)6,235 to 9,840(–12,140) ft ((1,200–)1,900–3,000(–3,700) m). A widespread species, although not very common, in the Pyrenees, Auvergne, Alps, Apuane Alps, central Apennines, Carpathians, Caucasus and the mountains of Corsica and Scandinavia; also found in the central Himalayas and the Euro-Asiatic and North American Arctic regions.

## 97 ERINUS ALPINUS L.
Alpine Erinus, Fairy Foxglove

**Family** *Scrophulariaceae*
**Description** A small, more or less stemless, tufted plant, with an erect stem at the base of which is a rosette of spatulate leaves, crenate-serrate, ¼–¾ in (5–20 mm) long, narrowing into a short petiole. Stem leaves alternate, narrowly spatulate or oblanceolate. Flowers pink or violet-pink, in short racemes or terminal umbels. Calyx tubular with 5 acuminate teeth. Corolla slightly asymmetrical, with a slender narrow tube and two-lipped limb; the upper lip is divided into two, with two oblong-linear lobes, and the lower lip with 3 obovate lobes. All the lobes spread outwards, retuse or grooved to the centre by a darker-coloured vein. Stamens 4, enclosed within the corolla tube.

**Size** 2–6 ins (5–15 cm).
**Flowering period** May–August(–September).
**Ecology and distribution** Rocks, detritus and stony pastures, on a calcareous subsoil, from (3,280–)3,935 to 7,875 ft ((1,000–)1,200–2,400 m). Sporadically, in the mountains of Spain, the Pyrenees, western and central Alps and central Apennines as well as in Sardinia, the Balearic Islands and North Africa.
**Notes** A protected plant.

## 98 ERIOPHORUM SCHEUCHZERI Hoppe
Cottongrass

**Family** *Cyperaceae*
**Description** A more or less stemless, tufted, herbaceous plant with a grass-like appearance. Stem erect, green, circular in cross-section, with widely-spaced tubular bracts. Leaves numerous, mostly basal, linear, approx. ⅛ in (2–4 mm) wide which have mostly dried out by flowering-time and fold downwards – only a few remain green and erect. Flowers united in a single terminal inflorescence in spikelet-form, more or less spherical or oblong, which becomes a showy white plume after flowering, formed by the woolly-setaceous bristles of the perianth, ⅝–1 in (1.5–2.5 cm) long.

**Size** 4–8 ins (10–20 cm) when in flower; 8–20 ins (20–50 cm) after flowering.
**Flowering period** (May–)June–September(–October).
**Ecology and distribution** Wet places, by ponds, peat-bogs and marshlands, on any type of subsoil but with a preference for acid soils, from (4,920–)5,250 to 9,185 (–9,515) ft ((1,500–)1,600–2,800(–2,900) m). Common in the high mountains of Europe (the Pyrenees, Alps, northern Apennines, Carpathians and in Scandinavia) as well as in Asia and North America.
**Notes** A protected species in several countries.

## 99 ERIOPHYLLUM LANATUM (Pursh) Forbes
Oregon Sunshine

**Family** *Compositae*
**Description** A tufted, spreading or erect plant, with a woolly base, very branched with long, slender branches, thickly covered with white or greenish-white hairs. Leaves, linear or lanceolate, crenate-incised or entire (in var. *integrifolium*), short, opposite or in short fascicles. Flowers yellow, united in discoid head, ⅝–1 in (1.5–2.5 cm) wide. A small disc with numerous tubular florets crowded together; a large ray with ligulate florets, oblong limb, rounded or apically emarginate, bright yellow in the part nearest the centre and pale yellow in the distal part.
**Size** 4–20(–28) ins (10–50(–70) cm).
**Flowering period** June–July.
**Ecology and distribution** Open grassy pastures and dry stony places, from (1,640–)3,280 to 8,200 ft ((500–)1,000–2,500 m). Widespread in the northern and central parts of the Rocky Mountains, from British Columbia to Wyoming, and in California.
**Notes** This is the only species of the genus *Eriophyllum* that is widespread in the Rocky Mountains; the commonest variety, however, is *integrifolium* which has entire leaves.

---

## 100 ERODIUM MANESCAVI Cosson
Storksbill

**Family** *Geraniaceae*
**Description** An acaulescent perennial with a thick rhizome from which spring several leafless epigeal stems. Leaves exclusively basal, large, up to 12 ins (30 cm) long, lanceolate, pilose, pinnatisect, with ovate leaflets, deeply incised or pinnatifid, in dentate segments. Flowers carmine-red or violet-pink, ¾–1½ ins (2–4 cm) in diameter, 5–20 united in lax umbels. Each umbel emerges from a corona of sub-rounded bracts fused together in the form of a cup. Petals 5, oblong, obovate or elliptical, ⅝–¾ in (15–20 mm) long, deeply veined in a darker colour.
**Size** 8–16(–20) ins (20–40(–50) cm).
**Flowering period** July–August.
**Ecology and distribution** Montane meadows and high altitude pastures, from 2,625 to 7,545 ft (800–2,300 m). Endemic to the western and central Pyrenees.
**Notes** The fruits of this plant act as hygrometers as they are equipped with a long beak which, when ripe, twists itself into a spiral which becomes tighter or looser depending on the humidity of the atmosphere.

## 101 ERODIUM PETRAEUM (Gouan) Willd.
Rock Storksbill

**Family** *Geraniaceae*
**Description** An acaulescent, tufted, fragrant herbaceous plant, with ovate-oblong leaves, ½–2¾ ins (1–7 cm), pinnate-compound with pinnatisect leaflets in linear-lanceolate segments. Flowers pink or violet in lax terminal umbels, formed of 1–5 flowers, ⅝–¾ in (1.5–2 cm) in diameter. Petals 5, broadly obovate or subrounded, the two upper ones being conspicuously marked with deep-violet veins.
**Size** 1¼–2½(–6) ins (3–6(–15) cm).
**Flowering period** June–August.

**Ecology and distribution** Craggy and rocky places; the subspecies *glandulosum* grows on a granite or schistose subsoil, from (985–)1,970 to 10,500 ft ((300–) 600–3,200 m). Endemic to the Pyrenees, where it is nevertheless quite rare.
**Notes** This species is naturally rather variable, especially in size, pilosity, size and colour of flowers. Five subspecies have been identified, distributed in France and Spain; the subspecies illustrated is *glandulosum* (Cav.) Bonn. (syn. *Erodium macradenum* L'Hér.), exclusive to the Pyrenees.

---

## 102 ERYNGIUM ALPINUM L.
Alpine Eryngo, Queen of the Alps

**Family** *Umbelliferae*
**Description** An erect, herbaceous, glaucous-green plant, tending towards deep blue in the upper part. Basal leaves soft, entire, on long petioles, 6–10 ins (15–25 cm) long and 2–6 ins (5–15 cm) wide, with an ovate or cordate blade, irregularly dentate. Stem leaves sparse or absent, lanceolate, pinnately-parted or deeply dentate, spiny. Apical inflorescences averaging 2–5 on each plant, surrounded by an involucre of 10–20, lanceolate-pinnatifid, very long, sky-, dark- or silvery-blue showy bracts. Inflorescence in the form of a dense head, oblong or ovoid, 1¼–2 ins (3–5 cm) long, greenish-blue or violet-azure.
**Size** 12–28(–40) ins (30–70(–100) cm).
**Flowering period** (June–)July–September.

**Ecology and distribution** Grassy places, meadows and pastures, on any type of subsoil although with a preference for limestone, from (3,280–)3,940 to 8,200 ft ((1,000–)1,200–2,500 m). Found in the Jura, the Alps and the mountains of the northern Balkan peninsula.
**Notes** Infrequent, it has disappeared from certain areas altogether as a result of over-picking. A protected species.

## 103 ERYSIMUM HELVETICUM (Jacq.) DC.
Swiss Treacle-mustard
*E. dubium*

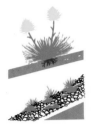

**Family** *Cruciferae*
**Description** A tufted perennial with a woody base and one or two flowering stems. Stems angular, pilose, short. Basal leaves in dense rosettes, silvery-green, linear, linear-lanceolate or oblanceolate, acuminate, narrowing for a considerable length at the base. Flowers bright yellow in contracted terminal panicles. Peduncles approx. ⅛ in (2–4 mm) long. Sepals bag-like, ⅓–⅝ in (9–15 mm) long. Corolla open, ⅝–¾ in (15–20 mm) in diameter. Petals 4, ⅝–1 in (15–25 mm) long, with a long claw and an expanded, obovate limb, ¼–½ in (5–10 mm) long. Siliqua greenish-grey, 1½–3¼ ins (4–8 cm) long and approx. ¹⁄₁₆ in (1–1.5 mm) wide.
**Size** 4–16(–24) ins (10–40(–60) cm).
**Flowering period** June–August.
**Ecology and distribution** Rocky places, crags, rubble, detritus and on the gravelly bottoms of streams, on any type of subsoil (schist, limestone, dolomite, etc.), from (985–)1,970 to 8,860(–10,170) ft ((300–)600–2,700(–3,100) m). Found in the Pyrenees, Alps, Apennines and mountains of the Balkan peninsula.

---

## 104 EUPHRASIA MINIMA Jacq. ex DC.
Alpine Eyebright

**Family** *Scrophulariaceae*
**Description** A small, erect annual, slightly branched or branchless, with opposite leaves, oval or sub-rounded, sub-sessile, dentate-serrate, pilose, ¹⁄₁₆–½ in (2–11 mm). Bracts short, sub-equal to the leaves. Flowers sessile, united into a short dense terminal spike and subtended by the bracts. Calyx tubular-campanulate, two-lipped, with acuminate lobes. Corolla two-lipped, in various colours, approx. ¼ in (5–6 mm) long. Tube cylindrical; limb with upper lip entire or bilobed, purple or whitish, and lower lip three-lobed, yellowish or orange-yellow, with linear, emarginate, patent lobes incurved downwards.
**Size** ¾–4(–10) ins (2–10(–25) cm).
**Flowering period** July–September.
**Ecology and distribution** Pastures, alpine meadows, stony and open grassy places, preferably on acid sub-soils, from 3,280 to 10,500(–11,480) ft (1,000–3,200 (–3,500) m). A very frequent species in all the mountains of central and southern Europe (the Pyrenees, Auvergne, Vosges, Alps, Apennines and Carpathians as well as in Corsica and the Balkan peninsula).

## 105 EUPHRASIA SALISBURGENSIS Funck
Salzburg Eyebright

**Family** *Scrophulariaceae*
**Description** A small, erect annual, colour varying from green to reddish-brown, with a much branched stem and ascending branches. Leaves opposite, lanceolate, wedge-shaped, acute, ⅛–⅝ in (3–15 mm), each with 3–5 pairs of obtuse teeth, often rust-red in colour. Bracts similar to the leaves, larger, with acuminate teeth. Flowers sessile, approx. ¼ in (6–8 mm) long, growing in dense terminal spikes from the axils of the bracts. Calyx short, with 5 teeth. Corolla two-lipped with cylindrical tube. Upper lip of corolla short, violet, usually bilobed; lower lip spreading, three-lobed, white with a yellow mark at the base, emarginate lobes.
**Size** 2–8(–10) ins (5–20(–25) cm).
**Flowering period** July–September(–October).
**Ecology and distribution** Pastures, grassy places, rubble, and open woods, on a calcareous subsoil, from (1,310–)2,625 to 8,530(–10,825) ft ((400–)800–2,600 (–3,300) m). Very common and widespread in all the European mountains (the Pyrenees, Jura, Vosges, Alps, Apennines, Carpathians, the Balkan Mountains as well as in Corsica and the British Isles).

---

## 106 FRITILLARIA TUBIFORMIS Gren. et Godr.
Fritillary, Snakeshead
*F. delphinensis* Gren.

**Family** *Liliaceae*
**Description** A bulbous, herbaceous plant with an erect, leafy stem. Leaves alternate, lanceolate, ⅓–⅝ in (8–15 mm) wide and 2⅜–5 ins (6–12 cm) long, often close together on the upper third of the stem. Flower solitary, terminal, large, drooping, with 6 converging tepals, oblong or elliptical, 1¼–1¾ ins (30–45 mm) long, violet-coloured with an unusual chequered pattern (subspecies *tubiformis*) or yellow with red or purple markings (subspecies *moggridgei*). Stamens 6, always enclosed within the tepals; style non-protruding.
**Size** 6–12 ins (15–30 cm).
**Flowering period** (April–)June–July.
**Ecology and distribution** High altitude grasslands and grassy or stony pastures, usually on any type of subsoil although with a preference for limestone, from (2,625–) 4,920 to 6,560(–7,875) ft ((800–)1,500–2,000(–2,400) m). Quite rare, with only isolated examples in the Alps, especially the western zone; and in Corsica.
**Notes** Endemic to the Alps and Corsica. A protected plant.

## 107 GALIUM ANISOPHYLLON Vill.

**Family** *Rubiaceae*
**Description** A herbaceous, tufted, spreading plant, much branched at the base, with numerous erect or ascending stems. Leaves in whorls of 6–9, linear-lanceolate, or lanceolate-spatulate, ¼–⅝ in (7–16 mm) long and approx. ¹⁄₁₆ in (1–2 mm) wide with a mucronate-hyaline apex. Flowers white in a fairly compact sub-corymbose cymose inflorescence on short peduncles. Calyx minute. Corolla with a very short tube and flat, rounded limb, approx. ⅛ in (2–4 mm) wide, formed of 4 lobes ovate-lanceolate, acuminate-mucronate, spreading.
**Size** 2¾–6(–10) ins (7–15(–25) cm).
**Flowering period** July–September.

**Ecology and distribution** Pastures, meadows, woodland clearings, stony places and stabilized rubble, from (1,640–)3,935 to 6,560(–9,515) ft ((500–)1,200–2,000 (–2,900) m). Very common in the mountains of central Europe, from the Cevennes to the Alps, the Carpathians and mountains of the Balkan peninsula.
**Notes** A very variable polyploid species which easily crosses with related species such as *G. pumilum, G. pusillum* and *G. austriacum.*

## 108 GENTIANA ALPINA Vill.
Southern Gentian

**Family** *Gentianaceae*
**Description** A dwarf, more or less stemless plant, slightly tufted, with a rosette of basal leaves, oval-elliptical or oval, ⅝–1 in (1.5–2.5 cm) long, acute, a little longer than wide. Flower very large, dark blue, solitary, terminal, on a short peduncle or sessile. Calyx campanulate with widely spreading, triangular lobes. Corolla showy, 1⅜–1½ ins (3.5–4 cm) long, that is four-fifths or five-sixths of the whole plant, funnel-shaped-campanulate, a deeper blue towards the throat and a greenish-blue towards the base, spotted with blue; lobes 5, ovate-triangular, recurved.
**Size** 2–3⅛ ins (5–8 cm).
**Flowering period** July–August.

**Ecology and distribution** Pastures, alpine meadows and open grassy places, on a siliceous subsoil, from 5,905 to 8,860(–9,190) ft (1,800–2,700(–2,800) m). Found in the Sierra Nevada in Spain, the Pyrenees and western Alps, from Savoy to Lake Como.
**Notes** This species has, in the past, been confused with *G. kochiana* (see entry 111), *G. clusii* and *G. angustifolia.* All these species have been grouped together and given the composite name of *Gentiana acaulis*; nevertheless they are clearly separate and distinguishable one from another and also have different areas of distribution.

## 109  GENTIANA BAVARICA L.
Bavarian Gentian

**Family**  *Gentianaceae*
**Description**  A small, tufted perennial, branched at the base, with numerous sterile buds covered with small overlapping leaves, elliptical or obovate-lanceolate, yellowish-green, ½–⅝ ins (10–15 mm) long and ¼–⅓ in (5–8 mm) wide. Stem leaves similar to basals, often smaller, arranged in 3–4 pairs. Flowers dark blue, occasionally violet, solitary at the apex of each flowering stem. Calyx campanulate, angular, often shaded with violet, with triangular teeth. Corolla, cylindrical tube, ¾–1 in (20–25 mm) long and a flattened limb with spreading, oblong or obovate lobes.
**Size**  2–6 ins (5–15 cm) – in flower; ½–1½ ins (1–4 cm) in the subspecies *imbricata*.
**Flowering period**  July–August(–September).
**Ecology and distribution**  Peaty pastures, marshy and boggy places, moist heathlands and wetlands generally, on any type of subsoil (the subspecies *imbricata* on silica), from (4,265–)5,905 to 8,200(–10,500) ft ((1,300–)1,800–2,500(–3,200) m) and in exceptional cases up to 3,600 m (11,810 ft) – the subspecies *imbricata*. Quite frequent in the Alps and central Apennines. A protected plant.
**Notes**  The subspecies *bavarica* is widespread throughout its distribution area and can be distinguished from the subspecies *imbricata* which is more dwarfed, only grows on the highest peaks and has leaves closer together.

---

## 110  GENTIANA BURSERI Lapeyr.

**Family**  *Gentianaceae*
**Description**  A showy plant with a simple, erect stem. Leaves opposite, ovate-lanceolate, acute, on short petioles, with 5–7 clearly visible veins. Flowers pale yellow or golden-yellow, sometimes brown-spotted, sessile, in conspicuous heads or in 2–3 terminal whorls. Calyx membranous, split to the base on one side only. Corolla narrowly campanulate, with widely spreading lobes, up to 1½ ins (40 mm) long, with short membranous appendages among the 5–7 triangular, obtuse lobes.
**Size**  12–24(–40) ins (30–60(–100)) cm.
**Flowering period**  July–August.
**Ecology and distribution**  Pastures, woodland clearings and meadows, from (1,640–)4,920 to 8,860 ft ((500–)1,500–2,700 m). Endemic to the Pyrenees and south-western Alps.
**Notes**  Two subspecies are particularly noteworthy: the subspecies *burseri*, with pale yellow flowers, and acute appendages on the corolla limb, is exclusive to the Pyrenees while the subspecies *villarsii* Ronn., with truncate appendages on the corolla limb of the bright yellow flowers, is endemic to the south-western Alps. The illustration shows the subspecies *burseri*.

**111** **GENTIANA KOCHIANA** Perr. et Song.
**GENTIANA ACAULIS** L.
Trumpet Gentian
*G. excisa* Koch; *G. latifolia* Jak.

**Family** *Gentianaceae*
**Description** A small, more or less stemless plant with a basal rosette of leaves and 1–2 pairs of stem leaves. Basal leaves close to the soil, lanceolate or ovate-lanceolate, 2–6 ins (5–15 cm) long, about 3 times longer than wide, obtuse, opaque-green. Stem leaves oval, opposite. Flower dark blue, apical, solitary, pedunculate. Calyx campanulate with divergent teeth. Corolla very large, half or two-thirds the length of the entire plant, blue or violet-blue, green-spotted inside, conical-campanulate, limb consisting of 5 triangular lobes, recurved. Anthers golden-yellow.

**Size** 2–4(–6) ins (5–10(–15) cm).
**Flowering period** (May–)June–August.
**Ecology and distribution** Pastures, dry grassy places, debris and woodland clearings, on any type of subsoil, but with a preference for acid soils, from (2,950–)4,595 to 8,860(–9,840) ft ((900–)1,400–2,700(–3,000) m). Very common in all mountains of southern Europe (the Pyrenees, Alps, Apennines, Apuane Alps, Jura, and Carpathians) as well as the Balkan Mountains.
**Notes** The notes relating to *Gentiana alpina* (see entry 108) also apply. *G. kochiana* is a protected species.

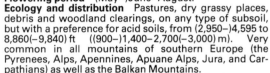

---

**112** **GENTIANA LUTEA** L.
Great Yellow Gentian

**Family** *Gentianaceae*
**Description** A sturdy, herbaceous plant, showy, with a simple hollow stem and thick, tuberous tap-root. Leaves large, basals elliptical, 8–12 ins (20–30 cm) long and 3¼–6 ins (8–15 cm) wide, on short petioles, glaucous-green, with convergent veins; stem leaves lanceolate, sessile, opposite. Flowers golden-yellow, united into 2–6 whorls in an elongate terminal inflorescence. Each whorl formed of 3–10 flowers, on short peduncles, emerging from the axil of two large leaf-like bracts. Corolla divided almost to the base into 5–9 lanceolate lobes which spread out like a wheel when the plant is in flower.

**Size** (16–)20–60(–80) ins ((40–)50–150(–200) cm).
**Flowering period** June–August.
**Ecology and distribution** Pastures, unmanured fields, detritus and stony places, on a calcareous subsoil, from (2,625–)3,280 to 8,200 ft ((800–) 1,000–2,500 m). Widespread, but sporadic, in the Iberian Mountains, Pyrenees, Jura, Vosges, Alps, Apennines, Carpathians and the mountains of Corsica, Sardinia, the Balkan peninsula and Asia Minor.
**Notes** The root is used for its medicinal properties and in the making of an aqua vitae. Indiscriminate picking has resulted in its rarity in many localities. A protected plant.

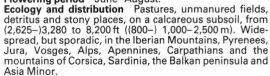

## 113 GENTIANA NIVALIS L.
Snow Gentian

**Family** *Gentianaceae*
**Description** A small, tufted annual, branched from the base into numerous slender, erect branches growing close together. Leaves fairly densely packed into a rosette at the base, oval, obtuse; stem leaves oval, acuminate, 3–5 veins, ¾–2 ins (2–5 cm) long. Flowers solitary at the branch ends, brilliant deep blue. Calyx tubular, angular, with long erect acuminate teeth. Corolla tubular with flat, circular limb, with a cylindrical tube ½–¾ in (12–18 mm) long, greenish below, limb ⅓ in (8 mm) in diameter, with 5 ovate-lanceolate, acute, spreading lobes.
**Size** ¾–6 ins (2–15 cm).
**Flowering period** June–August.
**Ecology and distribution** Pastures, moorlands, rocky ridges, from (2,625–)5,250 to 9,185(–9,840) ft ((800–)1,600–2,800(–3,000) m). Quite frequent in all European mountains (the Pyrenees, Alps, Apennines, Jura, Carpathians; the Balkan Mountains, in Scandinavia and the Scottish Highlands, as well as in Asia Minor and northeastern America.
**Notes** A protected species.

---

## 114 GENTIANA PANNONICA Scop.
Brown or Hungarian Gentian

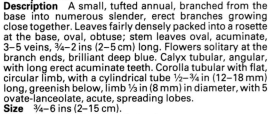

**Family** *Gentianaceae*
**Description** A showy, sturdy plant with an erect, hollow stem. Basal leaves oval or oblong, up to 8 ins (20 cm) long, opposite, sessile, with 5–7 clearly visible veins; stem leaves lanceolate. Flowers purple or deep purplish-red, tinged with yellow at the base, with numerous red spots, sessile in the axil of bract-like leaves, arranged in 2–3 terminal whorls. Calyx campanulate, divided into 5–8 unequal, recurved lobes, suffused with dark red. Corolla campanulate, with 5–8 broad, obtuse lobes.
**Size** 6–24 ins (15–60 cm).
**Flowering period** July–September.
**Ecology and distribution** Pastures, grassy places, screes, high altitude moorlands among dwarf pines, with a preference for a calcareous subsoil, from (2,625–)4,265 to 7,220(–7,545) ft ((800–)1,300–2,200(–2,300) m). Found in the central and eastern Alps, the Carpathians and Transylvanian Alps.
**Notes** A protected plant.

## 115  GENTIANA PUNCTATA L.
Spotted Gentian

**Family** *Gentianaceae*
**Description** A sturdy, herbaceous plant, erect, with opposite leaves, shiny, 2¾–4 ins (7–10 cm) long, ovate-elliptical, elliptical or broadly lanceolate, acute, conspicuously nerved. Flowers pale yellow with dark red, brown or black blotches and spots, sessile, arranged in 1–3 terminal whorls in the axils of leaf-like bracts. Calyx campanulate, one-third as long as the corolla, with 2–8 acuminate, unequal lobes. Corolla cylindrical-campanulate, flaring out at the top, with 5–8 short, obtuse lobes.
**Size** 8–24 ins (20–60 cm).
**Flowering period** July–September.
**Ecology and distribution** Pastures, stony alpine meadows, moraines, uncultivated places, on any type of subsoil although with a preference for acid soils, from (3,610–)4,595 to 8,530(–10,005) ft ((1,100–)1,400–2,600 (–3,050) m). Found in the Pyrenees, Alps, Carpathians and mountains of the Balkan peninsula.
**Notes** A protected species.

---

## 116  GENTIANA PURPUREA L.
Purple Gentian

**Family** *Gentianaceae*
**Description** An erect, herbaceous plant, sometimes sub-acaulescent, with a stiff, hollow stem. Leaves opposite, ovate-lanceolate or oblong-elliptical, large, up to 8 ins (20 cm) long, fairly keeled. Flowers purplish-red, sessile, in an apical head or in 2–3 terminal whorls. Calyx incised on one side. Corolla campanulate, violet-red on the outside and ridged with green at the base, yellowish and red-spotted on the inside, honey-scented, with 5–8 rounded or obtuse lobes, separated by short membranous appendages.
**Size** 8–24 ins (20–60 cm).
**Flowering period** July–September(–October).
**Ecology and distribution** Pastures, meadows, grassy places, woodland clearings, often on a siliceous subsoil, from (3,280–)5,250 to 8,860 ft ((1,000–)1,600–2,700 m). Quite frequent in the Alps, northern Apennines and Apuane Alps as well as in Scandinavia and eastern Asia (Kamchatka).
**Notes** Declared a protected species in some areas.

## 117 GENTIANA SAPONARIA L.

**Family** *Gentianaceae*
**Description** A herbaceous perennial with an erect, leafy stem. Leaves opposite, lanceolate or oblong, acute, attenuate or almost clasping the stem at the base, sessile, with three nearly parallel veins, hairless. Flowers dark blue, united into clusters in the axils of the upper leaves and in a terminal head. Calyx cylindrical-campanulate, green, with 5 teeth shorter than the tube. Corolla campanulate, its tube cylindrical at the bottom, greenish-blue shading to a deeper blue as the corolla opens outwards; limb campanulate at first then forming into 5 acute lobes which remain converging towards the apex for some distance. Throat of the corolla is equipped with 10 thread-like appendages alternating with the lobes of the limb.
**Size** 12–24 ins (30–60 cm).
**Flowering period** May–July.
**Ecology and distribution** Grassy places, damp woods and woodland clearings, from 1,640 to 4,920 ft (500–1,500 m). Found in the hills and mountains of the eastern United States and in the Appalachians, southwards as far as northern Florida and Louisiana.

---

## 118 GENTIANA SEPTEMFIDA Pallas
*G. freyniana* Bornm.

**Family** *Gentianaceae*
**Description** A tufted, herbaceous perennial, very branched at the base, with numerous erect or ascending stems. Leaves alternate, very close together, oval, ovate-lanceolate or even linear, slightly cordate at the base, sessile or sheathed, ⅝–1½ ins (15–40 mm) long. Flowers violet-blue united in the axils of the upper leaves into dense terminal inflorescences. Calyx approx. ½–1 in (12–24 mm) long, divided into 5 lanceolate, acute lobes. Corolla 1¼–1½ ins (30–40 mm) long, with a campanulate tube and limb formed of 5–6 ovate-triangular lobes, acute, approx. ¼ in (5–7 mm) long, furnished with the same number of shorter, subsidiary lobes, thickly fringed, around the throat.
**Size** 2–12 ins (5–30 cm).
**Flowering period** July–August.
**Ecology and distribution** Open grassy places, pastures, montane woods, from 5,905 to 10,500 ft (1,800–3,200 m). Found in the mountains of northern Anatolia, Armenia, northern Iran and Transcaucasia as well as the Caucasus.

## 119  GENTIANA TIBETICA  King
Tibetan Gentian

**Family**  *Gentianaceae*
**Description**  A herbaceous perennial, with an erect, simple, sturdy stem, leafless in the lower part. Leaves opposite, large, lanceolate, acuminate, with a wavy margin, bright green, 8–18 ins (20–45 cm) long and 1½–4 ins (4–10 cm) wide, with prominent, almost parallel, veins. Flowers united into a dense terminal umbel and a whorl in the axil of the last two leaves, on short peduncles. Calyx short, tubular, with a small-toothed margin. Corolla pale yellow or straw-coloured in the upper part and dark violet on the outside towards the base. Corolla tube cylindrical, ¾–1⅜ ins (20–35 mm) long, more than double the length of the calyx; open throat, with violet spots; limb flat, circular, with 5 oval lobes, acute, approx. ¼ in (5–6 mm) long. Stamens yellow, enclosed within the tube.
**Size**  12–20 ins (30–50 cm).
**Flowering period**  June–August.
**Ecology and distribution**  Open pastures and grassy places, at altitudes of 9,845 to 11,485 ft (3,000–3,500 m). Endemic to southern Tibet and the internal ranges of the Himalayas between the states of Sikkim and Bhutan.

---

## 120  GENTIANA VERNA  L.
Spring Gentian

**Family**  *Gentianaceae*
**Description**  A tufted, herbaceous perennial, in groups, with numerous closely-packed basal rosettes, from each of which emerges a solitary but showy flower. Basal leaves elliptical-lanceolate, oblong or ovate, up to 1¼ ins (3 cm) long; stem leaves alternate, in 1–3 pairs. Flowers brilliant blue, occasionally white, solitary at the apex of each flowering stem. Calyx very angular, almost winged, slightly inflated in the middle, with 5 acuminate, triangular teeth. Corolla ¾–1¼ ins (18–30 mm) in diameter, with a cylindrical tube and flat, circular limb with 5 spreading lobes, ovoid-rhomboidal, alternating with 5 blue, linear, scales divided into two.
**Size**  1¼–5 ins (3–12 cm).
**Flowering period**  (March–)April–July.
**Ecology and distribution**  Alpine pastures, grassy and stony places, moorlands and detritus of the lower slopes, on any type of subsoil, from (1,640–)2,625 to 8,860 (–11,485) ft ((500–)800–2,700(3,500) m). Very frequent in all European mountains (the Pyrenees, Alps, Apennines, Carpathians and Transylvanian Alps as well as the mountains of the Balkan peninsula and the British Isles.
**Notes**  This species is very variable; similar forms are also found in Scandinavia, Arctic Russia, Siberia, Asia Minor and the Himalayas. A protected species.

## 121 GERANIUM ARGENTEUM L.
Silvery Cranesbill

**Family** *Geraniaceae*
**Description** A more or less stemless, tufted plant with a thick basal rhizome, covered with greyish hairs that give the whole plant a silvery-silky appearance. Leaves all basal, rounded, ¾–1¼ ins (2–3 cm) in diameter, on long petioles, palmatisect, formed of 5–7 lobes each of which is divided into 3 segments. Flowers pink or pale red, 1–1¼ ins (25–30 mm) in diameter, open, solitary or united in pairs at the apex of the flower stem. Petals 5, broadly obovate, rounded or slightly retuse.
**Size** 2¾–5(–6) ins (7–12(–15) cm).
**Flowering period** July–August(–September).
**Ecology and distribution** Rocks, rocky pastures, ridges and crevices, on a mainly calcareous subsoil, from 4,920 to 7,220 ft (1,500–2,200 m). Found in the western Alps (Dauphiné) and in the eastern calcareous Alps (the Orobian – to the east of Lake Como – to the Julian), the Apuane Alps and the northern Apennines.
**Notes** Endemic to the Alps and Apennines. A protected plant.

## 122 GERANIUM CINEREUM Cav.
Ashy Cranesbill

**Family** *Geraniaceae*
**Description** A more or less stemless, tufted perennial covered with greyish hairs, with a thick vertical rhizome. Leaves all basal, ¾–1¼ ins (2–3 cm) wide, divided into 5–7 trifid or tridentate lobes. Flowers red or pale violet, usually in pairs on peduncles 2–4 ins (5–10 cm) long. Corolla 1–1¼ ins (2.5–3 cm) in diameter; petals 5, obovate, rounded at the apex or slightly retuse, with a very short claw.
**Size** 3¼–6 ins (8–15 cm).
**Flowering period** July–August.
**Ecology and distribution** Rocks and stony pastures, preferably on a calcareous subsoil, from 4,920 to 7,875 ft (1,500–2,400 m). Found in the eastern and central Pyrenees, central and southern Apennines as well as in the mountains of the western Balkan peninsula, Asia Minor and the Atlas Mountains of Morocco.
**Notes** Two subspecies are worth noting: subspecies *cinereum*, with shorter leaf segments, approx. 1/16 in (2 mm), and pale violet petals with darker veins, exclusive to the Pyrenees and subspecies *subaulescens*, with longer leaf segments ¼ in (5 mm) and red petals, widespread in all other zones. The illustration shows the latter subspecies.

## 123 GERANIUM GRACILE Ledeb.

**Family** *Geraniaceae*
**Description** A rhizomatose, herbaceous perennial, with a slender horizontal subterranean stem and pilose, ascending or erect, epigeal branches. Basal leaves sub-rounded, palmatifid, 3¼–6 ins (8–15 cm) wide, in broadly rhombic segments, crenate-dentate. Flowers violet-pink, with clearly visible dark red veins, at the apex of long peduncles in scant umbels of 2–4 flowers on short pedicels. Sepals approx. ⅓ in (8–9 mm) long, conspicuously pilose, with an apical awn approx. ⅛ in (2–3 mm) long. Petals 5, obovate-cuneate, with a long attenuate claw, slightly emarginate at the apex, ¾–⅞ in (18–22 mm) long. Stamens 10, close together to form a column, white at the base and red at the apex. Styles 5, spreading.
**Size** 12–28 ins (30–70 cm).
**Flowering period** June–July.
**Ecology and distribution** Montane woods and high altitude scrub, from (2,950–)4,595 to 5,575 ft ((900–)1,400 –1,700 m). Found in the mountains of north-eastern Anatolia, Transcaucasia and southern Caucasus.

---

## 124 GERANIUM SYLVATICUM L.
Crow Flower, Wood Cranesbill

**Family** *Geraniaceae*
**Description** A sub-acaulescent, herbaceous perennial with a thick, oblique, rhizome and pilose-glandular leafless epigeal stems. Basal leaves on long petioles, 2¾–5 ins (7–12 cm) wide, palmatisect, deeply divided into 5–7 ovate lobes, dentate or pinnatisect. Flowers violet-blue, in groups of 2–3 on long erect peduncles. Corolla cup-shaped, 1–1¼ ins (2.5–3 cm) wide. Petals 5, obovate, entire, rounded.
**Size** (8–)12–24(–32) ins ((20–)30–60(–80) cm)
**Flowering period** (May–)June–August.
**Ecology and distribution** Woods, damp uncultivated places and thickets, on any type of subsoil but with a preference for acid soils, from (2,295–)3,280 to 6,560 (–7,875) ft ((700–)1,000–2,000(–2,400) m). Very common in nearly all the mountains of Europe where, in the north, it grows almost down to the sub-montane zone; also common in the mountains of Asia and the eastern United States (it has been introduced more recently in the latter).
**Notes** A very variable species in which at least four subspecies have been identified, with flowers varying from bright red to violet, blue, pale sky-blue and white.

## 125 GEUM MONTANUM L.

Alpine Avens
*Sieversia montana* (L.) Spreng.

**Family** *Rosaceae*
**Description** A tufted, more or less stemless perennial, with a sturdy rhizome, without stolons. Basal leaves, 4–7 ins (10–18 cm) long, pinnate-compound with numerous oblong or elliptical leaflets, serrate-incised, pilose, gradually decreasing towards the base, with a much larger terminal sub-rounded and broadly ovate leaflet, lightly incised into finely serrate lobes. Flowers yellow, solitary at the apex of scapiform epigeal stems, often equipped with short leaf-like incised bracts immediately beneath the flower. Calyx formed of numerous sepals and surrounded by an outer calyx. Corolla 1¼–1½ ins (3–4 cm) wide, consisting of 6–7 broadly obovate petals, rounded or truncate at the apex. Fruit formed of numerous long achenes with feathery style.
**Size** 2–12(–16 ins (5–30(–40) cm).
**Flowering period** (May–)June–August(–September).
**Ecology and distribution** Pastures, alpine meadows, stony places and open woods, on any type of subsoil but with a preference for acid soils, from (2,295–)4,595 to 9,185(–10,500) ft ((700–)1,400–2,800(–3,200) m). Very common in all the central-southern mountains of Europe (the Pyrenees, Jura, Alps, Apuane Alps, Apennines and Carpathians as well as the mountains of Corsica and the Balkan peninsula).

## 126 GEUM REPTANS L.

Creeping Avens
*Sieversia reptans* L.

**Family** *Rosaceae*
**Description** A pilose, more or less stemless, prostrate plant with a creeping rhizome from which emerge reddish epigeal stolons, 4–32 ins (10–80 cm) long. Basal leaves pinnate-compound with numerous broadly rhomboidal, dentate-incised, pilose, lateral leaflets, and a terminal leaflet, a little larger than the laterals, palmate-incise, divided into 3 lobes. Flowers bright yellow, solitary at the apex of long peduncles. Calyx formed of numerous pilose sepals and covered by an almost similar epicalyx. Corolla 1¼–1½ ins (3–4 cm), consisting of 6–7 sub-rounded or broadly elliptical petals, entire or slightly emarginate at the apex. Fruit made up of numerous achenes with feathery styles.
**Size** 2–8 ins (5–20 cm).
**Flowering period** July–August.
**Ecology and distribution** Detritus, rubble, moraines, shifting stony ground and rocks, usually on a siliceous subsoil, from (4,920–)6,890 to 10,500(–12,465) ft ((1,500–)2,100–3,200(–3,800) m). Frequent throughout the Alps and also found in the Carpathians and mountains of the southern Balkan peninsula.
**Notes** A protected species in some areas.

## 127   GLAUCIDIUM PALMATUM   Sieb. et Zucc.

**Family** *Podophyllaceae*
**Description**   A herbaceous perennial with a sturdy tuberous rhizome from which emerge 1–2 epigeal stems. Leaves large, 2–3 on the upper half of each stem, with a long petiole 6–8 ins (15–20 cm), palmatifid, overall shape sub-rounded cordate, 4–12 ins (10–30 cm) wide, with oblong or rhomboidal lobes, sometimes trifid towards the apex, serrate margin. Bract leaflike, kidney-shaped or sub-rounded, lying close to the flower which is solitary, terminal. Sepals 4, petal-like, mauve or violet-pink, broadly ovate, 1⅜–2 ins (3.5–5 cm) long and ¾–1¾ ins (2–4.5 cm) wide, acute. Petals absent. Stamens numerous, pale yellow, ¼–½ in (5–10 mm) long.
**Size**   4–16 ins (10–40 cm).
**Flowering period**   April–May.
**Ecology and distribution**   Deciduous montane forests, damp and humid places, from 3,935 to 6,560 ft (1,200–2,000 m). Endemic to the mountains of Japan where it grows in the islands of Honshu (Hondo) and Hokkaido (Ezo).
**Notes**   The only species of the genus *Glaucidium*, it is related to the North American species *Hydrastis canadensis*.

---

## 128   GLOBULARIA CORDIFOLIA   L.
Matted Globularia

**Family** *Globulariaceae*
**Description**   A small, low-growing, creeping shrub much branched, with branches so close together that they form a thick mat. Leaves leathery, spatulate, slightly emarginate, closely grouped at the base of the flowering stems and forming dense rosettes. Flowering stems leafless or nearly so, erect, bearing an apical, globose head of ½–¾ in (1.2–2 cm) in diameter. Flowers sky-blue or violet-azure, dense, surrounded with short bracts, ovate-lanceolate or ovate; corolla two-lipped, the upper lip divided into two short segments and the lower lip trifid, consisting of 3 linear laciniae.
**Size**   3¼–6 ins (8–15 cm) – the flowering stems; 1¼–4 ins (3–10 cm) – the plant.
**Flowering period**   May–August.
**Ecology and distribution**   Crags, in rock fissures, stony places, dry slopes, on a calcareous subsoil, from (2,625–) 4,920 to 8,530(–9,190) ft ((800–)1,500–2,600(–2,800) m). Quite common in the mountains of central and southern Europe (the Pyrenees, Alps, Apennines, Jura, Carpathians and the Balkan peninsula).

### 129  GLOBULARIA INCANESCENS  Viv.
Apennine Globularia

**Family**  *Globulariaceae*
**Description**  A tufted, herbaceous plant, deciduous, with slender rhizomes and leafy epigeal stems. Leaves circular or oblong, occasionally obovate or oblanceolate, the basals lengthily attenuated and stalked, the stem leaves sub-sessile, greyish-green or mealy-white. Inflorescence in the form of a terminal head ⅝ in (1.5 cm) in diameter; involucral bracts 5, linear-lanceolate. Flowers pale sky-blue or violet-azure. Corolla two-lipped, the upper lip being entire and the lower trifid.
**Size**  1¼–2⅜ ins (3–6(–10) cm).
**Flowering period**  May–August.
**Ecology and distribution**  Rocks, rocky detritus and stony pastures, on a calcareous subsoil, from 4,920 to 6,560 ft (1,500–2,000 m). Widespread in the Apuane Alps and the nearby calcareous Tuscan-Emilian Apennines, where it is endemic.
**Notes**  A protected plant.

### 130  GLOBULARIA NUDICAULIS  L.
Leafless-stemmed Globularia

**Family**  *Globulariaceae*
**Description**  A low-growing, tufted, herbaceous plant, more or less stemless. Leaves in rosette form or nearly so, oblanceolate or obovate, lengthily attenuated into petiole, 2⅜–4(5) ins (6–10(–12) cm) long, apically rounded. Flowering stem leafless or with a few scales. Inflorescence in the form of a terminal head, 1.5–2.5 cm (⅝–1 in) in diameter, with numerous lanceolate or ovate bracts. Sky-blue or violet-azure flowers. Corolla two-lipped, the upper lip very short and the lower trifid.
**Size**  6–12 ins (15–30 cm).
**Flowering period**  May–July(–August).
**Ecology and distribution**  Stony pastures, stabilized rubble, rocky ground and rocky woodland clearings, on a calcareous subsoil, from (1,640–)2,625 to 8,530 ft ((500–)800–2,600 m). Quite common in the Pyrenees, the calcareous mountains of northern Spain and southern France, the Alps and northern Apennines.

## 131 GNAPHALIUM NORVEGICUM Gunn.
Highland Cudweed
*Omalotheca norvegica* (Gunn.) Sch. Bip.

**Family** *Compositae*
**Description** A herbaceous perennial with a creeping rhizome and erect stem. Leaves numerous or narrowly lanceolate, up to 3¼–4 ins (8–10 cm) long, ⅝–¾ in (1.5–2 cm) wide, pilose-arachnoid or tomentose-silky, sessile or gradually attenuate towards the base. Numerous heads, sessile, approx. ¼ in (6–7 mm) long, solitary or in groups of 2–3 to each bracteal leaf. Involucre formed of numerous lanceolate bracts, green at the centre with a dark or blackish margin. Flowers yellow or pale yellow.
**Size** 3¼–12 ins (8–30 cm).
**Flowering period** July–September.
**Ecology and distribution** Sparse woods, clearings, stony or grassy places and high altitude scrub, on an acid subsoil, from 4,265 to 8,860 ft (1,300–2,700 m). Found in the Pyrenees, Alps, Dinaric Alps, Carpathians, Caucasus, Urals and the Altai Mountains as well as central Europe (even at low altitudes), the Balkan peninsula, British Isles, Scandinavia, the Euro-Asian Arctic regions and north-eastern America.

---

## 132 GNAPHALIUM SUPINUM L.
Dwarf Cudweed
*Omalotheca supina* (L.) DC.

**Family** *Compositae*
**Description** A small, tufted plant with a creeping rhizome and numerous flowering stems, erect or prostrate. Leaves numerous, pilose-woolly, greyish-green, linear or narrowly lanceolate, ¾–1¼ ins (2–3 cm) long, very close together and under the inflorescence. Flowers arranged on 3–7 heads clustered on a short spike at the apex of the flowering stem. Head cylindrical or campanulate, ¼ in (6 mm) long, covered with an involucre of linear bracts, dark brown or blackish, arranged in 2–4 rows. Flowers all tubular, yellow.
**Size** ¾–4(–8) ins (2–10(–20) cm).
**Flowering period** (June–)July–September.
**Ecology and distribution** Pastures, damp meadows, moraines, stabilized rubble, snow-beds and stony places in general, on a mainly siliceous subsoil, from (2,625–)4,595 to 11,155(–12,140) ft ((800–)1,400–3,400(–3,700) m). Frequent and widespread in the Pyrenees, Alps, Apennines and Caucasus as well as in Sardinia, Corsica, the Balkan peninsula, Scottish Highlands, Scandinavia, central Asia and the Arctic regions of Europe and north-eastern America.

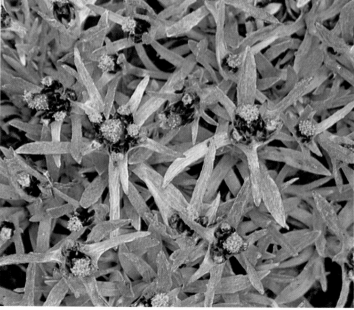

## 133  GYMNADENIA CONOPSEA  (L.) R. Br.
Fragrant Orchid

**Family** *Orchidaceae*
**Description** A showy, herbaceous plant, erect, with stout, two-lobed tubers. Epigeal stem with numerous alternate basal leaves, linear, 2⅜–8 ins (6–20 cm) long and ½–¾ in (1–2 cm) wide, and several short, erect, appressed stem leaves. Flowers pink or violet-pink, small, borne in the axil of a long linear bract, united in a terminal spiky inflorescence, rather dense, cylindrical shape, 2½–4 ins (6–10 cm) long. Perianth ½ in (1 cm) wide; a wide labellum, three-lobed, with a thread-like, incurved spur, double the length of the ovary which is inferior and sessile.
**Size** 6–24 ins (15–60 cm).
**Flowering period** May–July(–August).
**Ecology and distribution** Meadows, pastures, at the edge of woods, on any type of subsoil, from (2,295–)3,280 to 8,200 ft ((700–)1,000–2,500 m). Quite common in nearly all European mountains (the Pyrenees, Alps, Apennines, Carpathians and the Balkan Mountains as well as in Sicily, the British Isles and Scandinavia).
**Notes** This species often lives in association with the related *Gymnadenia odoratissima*, which can be distinguished from *G. conopsea* as it is smaller 6–16 ins (15–40 cm), its flowers are paler and smaller and it has a short spur the same length as the ovary.

---

## 134  GYPSOPHILA REPENS  L.
Creeping Gypsophila

**Family** *Caryophyllaceae*
**Description** A herbaceous perennial, much branched at the base, with numerous creeping stems from which emerge the ascending or erect epigeal branches. Leaves linear or lanceolate, often sickle-shaped, hairless, glaucous, fleshy, ½–1¼ ins (10–30 mm) long and ¹⁄₁₆–⅛ in (1–3 mm) wide. Flowering stems, branched at the top, with loose inflorescences of 5–30 flowers, pale pink or white. Calyx campanulate, approx. ⅛ in (2.5–3.5 mm) long, veined. Corolla ¼–⅓ in (6–8 mm) in diameter. Petals 5, obovate, emarginate, twice the length of the calyx. Stamens 10, more or less enclosed within the corolla; styles 2.
**Size** 2–10 ins (5–25 cm).
**Flowering period** May–September.
**Ecology and distribution** Stony places, detritus, stabilized rubble, dry gravelly river beds and high altitude moorlands, on a calcareous subsoil, from (1,970–)4,265 to 8,860(–9,185) ft ((600–)1,300–2,700(–2,800) m). Very widespread and frequent in the Pyrenees, Alps, Apuane Alps and Apennines as well as the mountains of central Europe (the Jura, Carpathians and Transylvanian Alps).

## 135 HABERLEA RHODOPENSIS Friv.

**Family** *Gesneriaceae*
**Description** A small, acaulescent perennial with a basal rosette of leaves, ovate-oblong or obovate, obtuse, crenate-serrate on the margin, softly hirsute, attenuate into a short petiole. Flower stems, one or more to each plant, each with 1–5 flowers. Overall colour, pale violet. Calyx tubular with 5 lobes. Corolla ⅝–1 in (15–25 mm) long, pilose inside, with a sub-cylindrical tube, fairly deep violet, longer than the limb; mouth open, with yellow and violet markings; limb slightly irregularly shaped, two-lipped with 5 broadly oval lobes, entire or retuse. Stamens 4, enclosed within the corolla tube.
**Size** 2⅜–4 ins (6–10 cm).
**Flowering period** April–August.
**Ecology and distribution** Cliffs and crags, rock fissures, rocky ravines, on a calcareous subsoil, from 4,920 to 8,860 ft (1,500–2,700 m). Found in the mountains of central and southern Bulgaria (Rhodope Mountains) and north-eastern Greece, where it is endemic.
**Notes** See also notes on *Ramonda myconi* (entry 217), also a member of the *Gesneriaceae*.

---

## 136 HIERACIUM AURANTIACUM L.
Orange Hawkweed, Grim the Collier, Devil's
Paintbrush, Dirty Dick

**Family** *Compositae*
**Description** A herbaceous perennial, acaulescent or nearly so, pilose-bristly with dark brown hairs. Basal leaves lanceolate-spatulate, dark green, lengthily attenuate at the base, obtuse or acute at the apex, pilose-bristly. Stem generally simple with sparse stem leaves, with a dense umbellate raceme of 2–12 heads on peduncles of varying length. Head ⅝–¾ in (1.5–2 cm) wide, with an ovoid involucre formed of numerous bristly bracts with glandular hairs on which tiny grains of dust and earth often stick. Flowers orange-red or bright orange, lighter in colour at the centre, all strap-shaped with linear-strap-shaped tongues, truncate and small-toothed at the apex.
**Size** 8–20 ins (20–50 cm).
**Flowering period** June–August.
**Ecology and distribution** Alpine meadows, pastures, on various types of subsoil such as schist, clay or limestone, from (2,950–)4,920 to 8,530 ft ((900–)1,500–2,600 m). Frequent in nearly all the central European mountains (the Alps, Jura, Vosges, Carpathians, Riesengebirge and mountains of the northern Balkan peninsula); also found in the hilly regions of central Europe. It has become naturalized in Scandinavia, North America and the British Isles.

## 137 HIERACIUM LANATUM (L.) Vill.
Woolly Hawkweed
*H. tomentosum* All.

**Family** *Compositae*
**Description** A herbaceous perennial, tufted, more or less stemless, cottony-white with long snow-white wavy hairs, frequently featherlike, with one or more simple or slightly branched stems. Leaves partly basal, a few stem leaves white-tomentose, oblong-lanceolate or nearly spatulate, acute. Heads 2–10 on each flowering stem, on fairly long branches, 1–1¼ ins (2.5–3 cm), with an involucre of linear bracts, woolly, approx. ½–¾ in (12–18 mm) long. Flowers yellow, all strap-shaped, with linear, strap-shaped florets, truncate and small-toothed at the apex, sometimes ciliate on the margin.
**Size** 4–20 ins (10–50 cm).
**Flowering period** June–July.
**Ecology and distribution** Rocks, stabilized rubble, rocky detritus, dry and stony woodland clearings, on any type of subsoil but with a preference for calcareous soils, from 4,920 to 6,560(–7,875) ft (1,500–2,000(–2,400 m). Quite frequent in the western Alps, from the Alpes Maritimes to the Leopontine Alps in north-western Italy, in the Jura and the Apuane Alps.

---

## 138 HIERACIUM VILLOSUM Jacq.
Hairy Hawkweed

**Family** *Compositae*
**Description** A herbaceous, tufted, acaulescent plant, sparsely covered with soft, whitish, hairs; rhizome short, stems numerous, leafless, simple or slightly branched. Basal leaves lanceolate, oblong or oblanceolate, attenuate, entire or small-toothed, wavy margined, acute. Heads terminal, generally one to each flowering stem, 1¼–1½ ins (3–4 cm) wide, with an ovoid involucre approx. ½–¾ in (14–20 mm) long, formed of linear bracts, acute, woolly. Flowers yellow, all strap-shaped, in the shape of a paintbrush or bell, with linear ligules, small-toothed, sometimes with a ciliate margin.
**Size** 6–16 ins (15–40 cm).
**Flowering period** July–August.
**Ecology and distribution** Rocks, stony pastures and stabilized rubble, on a calcareous subsoil, from (2,950–) 4,265 to 8,860 ft ((900–)1,300–2,700 m). Quite widespread in the Jura, Alps, Apennines, Carpathians and the mountains of the northern Balkan peninsula.

## 139 HOMOGYNE DISCOLOR (Jacq.) Cass.

**Family** *Compositae*
**Description** A herbaceous, acaulescent, perennial, with a basal rosette of sub-rounded or cordate leaves, ¾–1½ ins (2–4 cm) wide, dark green above and white-tomentose below, coarsely dentate, with a long pilose-tomentose petiole. Flower stem bearing one or two bract-like leaves, well-spaced, clasping, lanceolate, short. Head ½–⅝ in (10–15 mm) long, solitary at the apex of the flower stem, with a cylindrical involucre formed of numerous, linear, reddish bracts. Flowers pink or red, with a long, protruding style ending in a red stigma divided into two.
**Size** 4–12(–16) ins (10–30(–40) cm).
**Flowering period** June–August.
**Ecology and distribution** Pastures, damp meadows, by streams and in woodland clearings, on a calcareous sub-soil, from 4,590 to 7,875 ft (1,400–2,400 m). Endemic to the eastern Alps, from the Trentino region of Italy east-wards to the Karawanken Mountains and Mt. Schneeberg in Austria, and to the Dinaric Alps.
**Notes** There are two species of *Homogyne*, very closely related, that are typical of the alpine environment: *H. alpina*, with its leaves green on both sides and round-toothed margin, widespread in the Pyrenees, Alps, Apennines, Carpathians and Balkan Mountains, and *H. discolor* in which the lower side of the leaves is white, with teeth more coarsely cut and acute.

---

## 140 HORMINUM PYRENAICUM L.
Dragonmouth

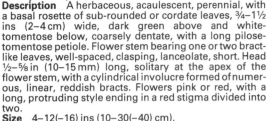

**Family** *Labiatae*
**Description** A sturdy, more or less stemless perennial, with a thick, woody, branched rhizome. Leaves in a basal rosette, oval or obovate, 1¼–2⅜ ins (3–6 cm) long and ¾–2 ins (2–5 cm) wide, stalked, semi-sheathed, dentate-serrate, hairless, with a puckered surface. Flower stem nearly always leafless, with numerous flowers gathered in groups of 2–4 in sessile clusters, giving them the false appearance of being whorled. Flowers violet, mostly uni-lateral, ⅝–1¼ ins (1.5–3 cm) long. Calyx tubular with 5 acuminate teeth. Corolla two-lipped with a slightly flared tube, wide, open throat, and upper lip of one nearly flat, rounded lobe, and lower lip three-lobed. Stamens 4, slightly protruding.
**Size** 4–12(–16) ins (10–30(–40) cm).
**Flowering period** June–August.
**Ecology and distribution** Pastures, grassy or stony places, dry meadows, sparse woods, on a calcareous subsoil, from (1,640–)3,280 to 7,875 ft ((500–)1,000–2,400 m). Widespread in the central Pyrenees, frequent in the central and eastern Alps, but very rare in the western Alps, from the Alpes Maritimes to the Lepontines in north-western Italy.

## 141 HUTCHINSIA ALPINA (L.) R. Br.
Chamois Cress
*Noccaea alpina* (L.) Reichb.

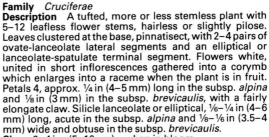

**Family** *Cruciferae*
**Description** A tufted, more or less stemless plant with 5–12 leafless flower stems, hairless or slightly pilose. Leaves clustered at the base, pinnatisect, with 2–4 pairs of ovate-lanceolate lateral segments and an elliptical or lanceolate-spatulate terminal segment. Flowers white, united in short inflorescences gathered into a corymb which enlarges into a raceme when the plant is in fruit. Petals 4, approx. ¼ in (4–5 mm) long in the subsp. *alpina* and ⅛ in (3 mm) in the subsp. *brevicaulis*, with a fairly elongate claw. Silicle lanceolate or elliptical, ⅙–¼ in (4–6 mm) long, acute in the subsp. *alpina* and ⅛–⅙ in (3.5–4 mm) wide and obtuse in the subsp. *brevicaulis*.
**Size** 2–4 ins (5–10 cm) – when in bloom.
**Flowering period** (May–)June–August.
**Ecology and distribution** Stony places, stabilized rubble, crags and precipices, wet debris; the subsp. *alpina* found mainly on limestone and the subsp. *brevicaulis* on any type of subsoil, from (3,610–)5,575 to 10,500(–11,155) ft ((1,100–)1,700–3,200(–3,400) m). Found in the Pyrenees, Alps, Carpathians and the Jura as well as the Apuane Alps and central-northern Apennines.

---

## 142 INCARVILLEA DELAVAYI Bur. et Franch.

**Family** *Bignoniaceae*
**Description** A showy, acaulescent, herbaceous plant, with a short, lobed rhizome, with 1–3 epigeal flowering stems and several erect basal pinnate-compound leaves 12–18 ins (30–45 cm) long. Leaflets opposite, lanceolate, crenate-dentate or sub-entire, acute, 4–5 ins (10–12 cm). Flower stem stout, erect, hairless, a little longer than the leaves, bearing a terminal raceme of 3–13 pedunculate flowers emerging from the axil of short linear bracts. Flowers pink or crimson-red, large, 2–3¼ ins (5–8 cm) long. Calyx tubular-campanulate, with 5 acuminate teeth. Corolla with a cylindrical tube, open throat, yellow inside and flat, circular limb, 2¾–4 ins (7–10 cm) wide, formed of 5 sub-rounded, slightly unequal lobes. Stamens 4, enclosed within the tube.
**Size** 16–28 ins (40–70 cm) – the flowering stem.
**Flowering period** March–June.
**Ecology and distribution** Pastures, open grassy places, from 7,875 to 11,485 ft (2,400–3,500 m). Endemic to the mountains of Yunnan province in southern China, where it is, however, relatively rare.

## 143 IRIS NEPALENSIS D. Don

**Family** *Iridaceae*
**Description** A tufted, herbaceous plant, with numerous slender rhizomes from which emerge several short, sub-acaulescent, epigeal stems. Leaves basal or nearly so, sheathed, narrowly sword-shaped, with clearly visible veins, bright green, with brown fibrous sheaths from old leaves at the base. Stem leaves alternate, short, sheathed. Flowers apical, solitary or 2–3, violet-blue. Bracts acuminate, herbaceous, equitant. Perianth with a short tube; limb 1½–1¾ in (4–4.5 cm) wide with 6 lobes of which the 3 narrowest (the standards) are oblong and the other 3 (the falls) are oblong-elliptical with white markings towards the base and an orange-yellow crest (the beard) inside, all reflexed. Stigmatic lobes, broad, erect, deeply bipartite, and in acuminate segments.
**Size** 6–8 ins (15–20 cm) – the flowering stems; 8–10 ins (20–25 cm) – the leaves.
**Flowering period** March–June.
**Ecology and distribution** Rocky pastures, open grassy places and cultivated ground, from 3,280 to 9,840 ft (1,000–3,000 m). Exclusive to the eastern Himalayas and the mountains of Yunnan province in southern China.

---

## 144 JOVIBARBA ALLIONII (Jord. et Fourr.)
### D.A. Webb
*Sempervivum allionii* (Jord. et Fourr.) Nym.

**Family** *Crassulaceae*
**Description** A fleshy, herbaceous plant with short stolons forming numerous groups of rosettes tightly packed against each other. Basal rosettes ¾–1¼ ins (2–3 cm) wide, almost spherical, formed of yellowish-green leaves, converging, oblong-lanceolate, ½–⅝ in (12–15 mm) long, acute, covered with short glandular hairs. Flowering stems erect with a branched terminal inflorescence in a dense head. Flowers greenish-yellow consisting of 6 fringed petals, ⅝ in (15 mm) long, converging almost to the extent of forming a tube.
**Size** 4–6 ins (10–15 cm).
**Flowering period** July–September.
**Ecology and distribution** Rocks, detritus of the lower slopes and stabilized rubble, preferably on a siliceous subsoil, from 4,595 to 7,875(–8,530) ft (1,400–2,400 (–2,600) m). Endemic to the Alps, more frequent in the western sector, from the Alpes Maritimes to the Graian Alps; also found, sporadically, in the Pre-Alps of Trentino in northern Italy.
**Notes** A protected species.

## 145 JUNCUS JACQUINII L.
Black Alpine Rush

**Family** *Juncaceae*
**Description** A tufted, herbaceous plant, sub-acaulescent, with erect stems and leaves emerging from a short rhizome. It is covered at the base by acuminate, brownish, leaf-sheaths. Leaves cylindrical, brilliant green, up to 8 ins (20 cm) long. Flower stems erect, with a dark brown or blackish head at the apex, pedunculate, with a peduncle emerging from a very long, linear bract, over-topping the inflorescence. Flowers sessile, from 4–12 in each head, distinguished by a black perianth, from which emerge yellowish-white anthers and a style branched into 3 pink or reddish stigmas, spirally twisted together.

**Size** 6–12 ins (15–30 cm).
**Flowering period** July–September.
**Ecology and distribution** Damp meadows, wet grassy places, stabilized rubble and water-sodden detritus, on an acid subsoil, from (4,920–)5,575 to 9,840(–10,500) ft ((1,500–)1,700–3,000(–3,200) m). Very frequent in the Alps and northern Apennines.

---

## 146 LEONTOPODIUM ALPINUM Cass.
Edelweiss

**Family** *Compositae*
**Description** A tufted, herbaceous plant, often with 2–5 stems emerging from the same base. Stem erect, pilose-woolly. Leaves alternate, lanceolate, oblanceolate or linear, greenish- or whitish-pilose. Inflorescence consisting of a dense corymb formed of 2–10 yellow heads surrounded by a rosette of 5–9 tightly packed bract-like leaves, woolly-white, almost snow-white, linear, longer than the corymb of heads, the whole giving the appearance of a single flower, 1⅜ ins (3.5 cm) in diameter. Head cylindrical-hemispherical, formed of numerous tubular yellow flowers.

**Size** 2–6(–8) ins (5–15(–20) cm).
**Flowering period** July–September.
**Ecology and distribution** Stony places, crevices in the rock faces, stony and exposed slopes, grassy bed-terraces and sometimes in the high altitude grasslands, mostly on calcareous subsoils, from (1,640–)5,575 to 10,500(–11,155) ft ((500–)1,700–3,200(–3,400) m). Quite common in the calcareous Alps, also widespread in the Pyrenees, siliceous Alps, Carpathians and mountains of the Balkan peninsula. Very similar species are also widespread in the Himalayas.
**Notes** A protected species which has almost disappeared from some areas as a result of over-picking.

## 147 LEONTOPODIUM NIVALE (Ten.) DC.
## LEONTOPODIUM ALPINUM Cass. subsp.
*nivale* (Ten.) Tutin
Snow Edelweiss

**Family** *Compositae*
**Description** A small, tufted, rhizomatous plant with 2–5 spreading stems arising from the base. Leaves closely packed, oblong-spatulate or obovate-lanceolate, woolly-white on both sides. Inflorescence formed of a corymb of 2–5 yellow heads, surrounded by a ring of short leaflike bracts, broadly lanceolate, unequal to or slightly longer than the corymb of heads. Head cylindrical, compact, short, with numerous tubular yellow flowers.
**Size** ¾–3¼(–5) ins (2–8(–12) cm).
**Flowering period** July–September.
**Ecology and distribution** Rocky ground, rocky debris, high altitude pastures and rocks, mostly on calcareous subsoils, from (5,905–)6,560 to 8,040 ft ((1,800–)2,000–2,450 m). Found in the central Apennines and the mountains of the Balkan peninsula, from southern Yugoslavia to western Bulgaria.
**Notes** Endemic to the Apennines and western Balkans, it is, unfortunately, indiscriminately picked by tourists, despite being a protected species.

---

## 148 LEUCANTHEMOPSIS ALPINA (L.) Heywood
Alpine Moon-daisy
*Chrysanthemum alpinum* L.; *Tanacetum alpinum* (L.) Sch. Bip.

**Family** *Compositae*
**Description** A small, tufted, acaulescent plant, with numerous ascending stems, each emerging from a basal rosette of oblong or oblanceolate leaves, somewhat incised or divided into 2–4 lobes according to the variety (from oblong-spatulate-dentate to spatulate-pinnatifid and almost to pinnatisect), slightly pilose. Stem leaves alternate, short, entire. Head solitary at the apex of the flower stem, ¾–1½ ins (2–4 cm) wide, with a flat involucre formed of numerous overlapping bracts. Disc-florets yellow, tubular; ray-florets white or occasionally pink, from 15 to 30, with lanceolate ligules, ⅓–½ in (8–12 mm) long, apically small-toothed.
**Size** 2–6 ins (5–15 cm).
**Flowering period** July–August.
**Ecology and distribution** Detritus of the lower slopes, moraines, stabilized rubble, debris, crags, precipices and dry grassy pastures, on a siliceous subsoil, from 5,905 to 9,840(–12,795) ft (1,800–3,000(–3,900) m). Very frequent in the Pyrenees, Alps, Apennines and Carpathians, in Corsica and the mountains of the central-western Balkan peninsula.

## 149 LEWISIA COTYLEDON (S. Wats.) Robinson

**Family** *Portulacaceae*
**Description** An acaulescent, herbaceous plant, with a short, robust rhizome. Leaves all basal, numerous, oblong-spatulate, fleshy, glandular on the margin when young, 1½–2½ ins (4–6 cm) long. Flower stems 1–3 to each plant, cylindrical; floral bracts small, ovate, ⅜ in (1 cm) long, margin fringed with glandular hairs. Flowers 1¼–1½ ins (3–4 cm) in diameter, 8–12 on each flowering stem, united in a lax corymbose inflorescence. Peduncle curved downwards before flowers open. Calyx formed of 2 broad, short sepals. Corolla open, consisting of 8–10 lanceolate-spatulate, entire or apically small-toothed petals, with pink lines running lengthwise along the centre and a clearly visible white margin. Stamens 7–10, shorter than the petals.
**Size** 4–5 ins (10–12 cm) – the flowering stems.
**Flowering period** May–June.
**Ecology and distribution** Dry rocky places, open stony areas and exposed slopes, from about 5,905 to 6,560 ft (1,800–2,000 m). Endemic to the Rocky Mountains where it is distributed in the north-western United States: Washington, Oregon and Idaho.

---

## 150 LEWISIA REDIVIVA Pursh

**Family** *Portulacaceae*
**Description** A dwarf, acaulescent plant with a short, fleshy rhizome from which emerge numerous leaves. Leaves linear-cylindrical, 1–2 ins (2.5–5 cm) long, fleshy, appearing as the snows melt and having almost completely disappeared when the flowers open. Flowers large, pink, 1¼–2½ ins (3–6 cm) in diameter, solitary at the apex of short leafless flowering stems, equipped with a short corona of bracts reaching half way up the petals. Sepals 6–8, greenish or coloured. Petals 12–18, oblanceolate, oblong or elliptical, acute or acuminate at the apex, frequently shading to white at the base. Stamens numerous, white, with orange anthers.
**Size** 1–3¼(–4) ins (2.5–8(–10) cm).
**Flowering period** May–July.
**Ecology and distribution** Crags and precipices, open stony places, rocky slopes and montane ridges, from (1,640–)2,625 to 8,200 ft (500–)800–2,500 m). Widespread in south-western Canada and the western states of North America, from British Columbia to Montana; also found in California.
**Notes** The roots have a bitter taste which accounts for the local name, ' Bitter-root '.

## 151 LIGUSTICUM MUTELLINOIDES (Crantz) Vill.

Small Alpine Lovage
*L. simplex* Vill.; *Gaya simplex* Gaud.

**Family** *Umbelliferae*
**Description** A more or less stemless tufted perennial with a thick rhizome, surrounded by the dry remains of old leaves, from which emerges a broad rosette of bipinnate or tripinnatisect basal leaves, 1¼–4 ins (3–10 cm) long, with linear lobes, constricted. Flowering stems, leafless or with one leaf at the most, terminating in a dense compound umbel, formed of 8–15 small pedunculate umbels. Involucre of 5–10 linear bracts, bifurcate or trifid; involucral bract formed of bracteoles the same length as the umbel which is ½–1¼ in (1–3 cm) wide. Flowers white or pink, minute.
**Size** 2–6(–10) ins (5–15(–25) cm.
**Flowering period** July–August(–September).
**Ecology and distribution** Stony places, dry pastures, stabilized rubble, rocky ridges, preferably on an acid subsoil, from 6,235 to 9,840(–11,155) ft (1,900–3,000 (–3,400) m). Frequent in the Alps, especially the central and eastern zones, the Dinaric Alps, Carpathians, Urals and Arctic Russia. Related species have also been recorded in the mountains of central Asia, Siberia and Alaska.
**Notes** This is the only umbellifer to be found at such a high altitude in Europe.

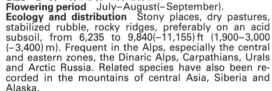

---

## 152 LILIUM CARNIOLICUM Bernh. ex Koch

*L. chalcedonicum* Jacq., non L.

**Family** *Liliaceae*
**Description** An erect, herbaceous plant with a tunicate bulb. Stem straight, not branched, with alternate, fairly sparse, lanceolate leaves, up to 3¼ ins (8 cm) long, with clearly visible veins, pilose on the veins on the lower surface. Flowers orange-red, drooping, in few-flowered lax inflorescences of 1–4 flowers. Sturdy peduncles; perianth formed of 6 tepals 1¼–2½ ins (3–6 cm) long, strongly recurved outwards and downwards, with brown or dark red spots. Stamens 6, erect, with long orange anthers.
**Size** 10–20(–32) ins (25–50(–80) cm).
**Flowering period** June–July.
**Ecology and distribution** High altitude pastures and clearings in the upland moors among shrubs, from 3,280 to 7,545 ft (1,000–2,300 m). Found in the south-eastern Alps, the mountains of the Balkan peninsula and the eastern Carpathians (Transylvanian Alps).
**Notes** Protected as a rare species.

## 153 LILIUM MARTAGON L.

Martagon Lily, Turk's-cap Lily

**Family** *Liliaceae*

**Description** A bulbous, herbaceous plant with a leafy erect stem. Leaves oblong-spatulate or broadly lanceolate, whorled at the lower part of the stem, sparse on the upper part. Flowers deep red, purple or pale pink, united in a lax racemose terminal inflorescence of 3–15 flowers. Peduncle incurved downwards; tepals 6, lanceolate, recurved, with deep purple spots. Stamens 6, convergent at first and then incurved towards the outside, projecting well out from the tepals, with red filaments and long vermilion anthers.

**Size** 8–36(–60) ins (20–90(–150) cm).

**Flowering period** June–August.

**Ecology and distribution** Quite frequent, usually found as isolated plants in alpine pastures, woodland clearings and upland moors, on fertile or damp ground, mainly on a calcareous subsoil, from (1,970–)2,625 to 8,860(–9,185) ft ((600–)800–2,700(–2,800) m). Sporadically, in the mountains of southern, central and eastern Europe (the Alps, Apennines and Carpathians), where it may even appear in the lowlands. Related species are found in eastern Asia (Siberia and Japan).

**Notes** A protected species throughout Europe.

## 154 LILIUM PYRENAICUM Gouan

Yellow Turk's-cap Lily

**Family** *Liliaceae*

**Description** An erect, sturdy, herbaceous plant, with a thick, tunicate bulb. Stem simple, with numerous alternate (especially on the lower part), erect-spreading, close together, linear-lanceolate leaves, 3¼–5⅛ ins (8–13 cm) long, ciliate on the margin, with clearly visible veins. Flowers orange-yellow, 1–8 in lax racemes, with long recurved peduncles. Perianth formed of 6 tepals 2–2¾ ins (5–7 cm) long, strongly incurved on themselves towards the outside, with a greenish band in the centre and brown-red spots.

**Size** 12–36(–52) ins (30–90(–130) cm).

**Flowering period** June–July.

**Ecology and distribution** Grassy places, woodland clearings and pastures, from 2,625 to 7,220 ft (800–2,200 m). Endemic to the Pyrenees, it is cultivated and allowed to grow wild in Europe, especially in the British Isles.

**Notes** A very rare protected species.

## 155 LINARIA ALPINA (L.) Mill.
Alpine Toadflax

**Family** *Scrophulariaceae*
**Description** A small, prostrate, much spreading perennial, glaucous-green, with creeping and ascending branches and a short branched rhizome. Leaves whorled in 3–4, glaucous-azure, oblong, lanceolate or ovate, sessile, in fleshy-spiky sections. Flowers violet-blue, occasionally white, or with an orange palate, united into short sparse terminal racemes, each one formed of 2–5 flowers. Calyx campanulate for a short distance, then with 5 lanceolate lobes. Corolla two-lipped, with a short tube prolonged into a cylindrical-conical, straight long spur. Upper lip divided into two, turned upwards or backwards; lower lip with palate to close the throat and a three-lobed limb with broadly ovate, rounded lobes.

**Size** 2–4(–8) ins (5–10(–20) cm – the flowering branches.
**Flowering period** June–August(–September).
**Ecology and distribution** Detritus of the lower slopes, screes, stabilized rubble and rocks, on any type of subsoil, from (3,935–)4,920 to 11,155(–12,465) ft ((1,200–)1,500 –3,400(–3,800) m). Very frequent in nearly all the mountains of central-southern Europe (the Iberian Mountains, Pyrenees, Jura, Alps, Apennines, Carpathians and Balkan Mountains).

---

## 156 LINNAEA BOREALIS L.
Twinflower

**Family** *Caprifoliaceae*
**Description** A small, evergreen, shrubby plant with creeping, woody branches from which emerge numerous delicate, ascending or erect leafy shoots. Leaves subrounded or broadly ovate, opposite, small-toothed, slightly pilose, suddenly narrowing into a short petiole. Flowers pale pink, drooping, arranged in pairs on long widely spreading V-shaped peduncles at the end of a leafless flower stem. Calyx short, more or less spherical. Corolla campanulate, with 5 short lobes, oval, rounded at the apex. Stamens 4.

**Size** 2–3¼(–6) ins (5–8(–15) cm) – the flowering stems.
**Flowering period** June–August.
**Ecology and distribution** Damp or wet meadows, coniferous woods, mossy or marshy places and grass-covered detritus, with a preference for a siliceous subsoil, from 3,935 to 6,560(–7,220) ft (1,200–2,000(–2,200) m). Not frequent in the Alps, it is particularly widespread in northern Europe (the Scottish Highlands and Norway), northern Asia and North America.

**Notes** This genus was named by Gronovius in honour of the Swedish botanist, C. Linnaeus né C. von Linné (1707–78). A protected plant.

## 157 LINUM ALPINUM Jacq.
### L. PERENNE L. subsp. *alpinum* (Jacq.) Ockendon
Alpine Flax

**Family** *Linaceae*
**Description** A herbaceous perennial, often branched at the base. Stems erect or ascending, delicate, leafy, not branched. Leaves alternate, close together, linear or lanceolate, ⅓–½ in (8–10 mm) long, sessile, with a single nerve. Flowers light sky-blue, terminal, in a lax inflorescence formed of 2–5 flowers on long erect peduncles. Corolla open, ⅝–1¼ ins (1.5–3 cm) in diameter. Petals broadly obovate, rounded, only just overlapping each other and very thin, soon falling after flowering. The fruit is a globose capsule.

**Size** 4–12(–20) ft (10–30(–50) cm).
**Flowering period** May–August.
**Ecology and distribution** Pastures, rocks, stony places and screes, preferably on a subsoil of basic rock, from (1,640–)4,595 to 7,220 (–7,545) ft ((500–)1,400–2,200 (–2,300) m). Quite common in the mountains of southern Europe (the Pyrenees, Alps, Apennines, Balkan Mountains) and the Urals.
**Notes** A species that is remarkably variable in habit and in the size of its parts.

---

## 158 LOBELIA KENIENSIS R.E.Fries et Th. Fries

**Family** *Campanulaceae*
**Description** A tree-like perennial, with a short, stumpy trunk, felty surfaced, hollow, covered almost from the base by numerous leaves arranged spirally, dense, linear-acuminate, channelled, erect-spreading, stiff and leathery 20–32 ins (50–80 cm) long; rainwater often collects in the axils of the leaves. Inflorescence a very dense terminal spike, 32–40 ins (80–100 cm) long and 6–12 ins (15–30 cm) wide, formed of a great many sessile flowers positioned in the axils of the conspicuous ovate bracts, incurved downwards. Flowers violet-blue, campanulate calyx with 5 acuminate teeth. Corolla tubular, two-lipped with 5 lobes, slightly longer than the calyx.

**Size** 6 ft 6 ins – 13 ft 4 ins (2–4 m) – the flowering plant.
**Flowering period** Almost all the year (December–January; May–October).
**Ecology and distribution** The high altitude grasslands of Mt. Kenya, especially in damp grassy areas; scrubby areas of heather, from (9,840–)11,155 to 14,105 ft ((3,000–)3,400–4,300 m).
**Notes** The giant lobelias are typical of African high mountains where about ten different species have been identified.

## 159   LOBIVIA CINNABARINA  (Hook.) Britton et Rose

**Family** *Cactaceae*
**Description** A succulent plant with a globose stem, slightly depressed and sunken in the centre. Surface of the stem formed of numerous dark green protuberances (or tubercles), very close together, distributed in a dense oblique spiral. Tubercle conical-prismatic, with a white woolly centre (areole), and, in the centre, 12 light-brown, robust needle-like spines, spreading, the central one being erect. Flowers fiery red, usually only a few on each plant although sometimes numerous, very large. Calyx green, woolly at the base, formed of numerous green sepals, overlapping, spatulate, continuing gradually to blend in with the petals. Corolla 2¾–3¼ ins (7–8 cm) wide, formed of numerous spatulate, obtuse, overlapping spreading petals. Stamens numerous, yellow.
**Size** The stem is 3¼–4 ins (8–10 cm) high and 6–7 ins (15–18 cm) wide.
**Flowering period** October–April.
**Ecology and distribution** Open pastures and high altitude steppes, around 8,200 to 11,485 ft (2,500–3,500 m). Endemic to the Bolivian Andes.
**Notes** The 75 species of the genus *Lobivia* – at one time included in the genus *Echinocactus* – are all examples of the succulent types of plants that grow in the arid, montane areas of the central-southern Andes.

---

## 160   LOISELEURIA PROCUMBENS  (L.) Desv.
Creeping Azalea
*Azalea procumbens* (L.)

**Family** *Ericaceae*
**Description** A low-growing, creeping, woody shrub, forming an intricate mat of branches. Leaves opposite, closely-packed, leathery, elliptical in shape, oblong or oval, ¼–⅓ in (5–8 mm) long. Flowers pink, united in groups of 2–5 at the end of the branches. Corolla approx. ¼–⅓ in (6–8 mm) in diameter, campanulate, quite deeply divided into 5 lanceolate lobes; stamens 5. Capsule ovoid, reddish.
**Size** 2–4(–8) ins (5–10(–20) cm) – the whole plant.
**Flowering period** (May–)June–August.
**Ecology and distribution** Grassy, humus-rich ground, among heather, in moraines and often in very windy places, on an acid subsoil, from (2,950–)4,920 to 8,860 (–9,840) ft ((900–)1,500–2,700(–3,000) m). As frequent in the European mountains (the Pyrenees, Alps, Carpathians, the Balkan Mountains and in Scandinavia) as in those of northern Asia and North America as far as the Arctic regions.

## 161 LOTUS ALPINUS (DC.) Schleich. ex Ram.
Alpine Birdsfoot Trefoil

**Family** *Papilionaceae*
**Description** A herbaceous perennial, prostrate spreading, much branched. Leaves imparipinnate with 5 obovate leaflets, oblanceolate or elliptical, approx. ¹⁄₁₆–¹⁄₃ in (2–8 mm) long and ¹⁄₁₆–¹⁄₈ in (1.5–4 mm) wide; stipules tiny, brown. Flowers bright yellow or orange yellow, often with red patches, united into inflorescences consisting of 2–3(–7) flowers. Corolla ½–⅝(–¾) in (10–16(–18) mm) long. Pod cylindrical, brownish or reddish, up to ¾–1 in (2–2.5 cm) long.
**Size** 2–4 ins (5–10 cm).
**Flowering period** (May–)June–September.
**Ecology and distribution** Pastures, stony places, stabilized rubble and detritus of the lower slopes, on any type of subsoil, from (5,905–)6,560 to 10,170 ft ((1,800–)2,000–3,100 m). Very common in all the mountains of southern Europe (the Pyrenees, Alps and Balkan Mountains).
**Notes** This is the high altitude relative of *Lotus corniculatus* L., which is common in sub-montane and montane zones; it is sometimes also referred to as a subspecies of the latter – *L. corniculatus* L. subsp. *alpinus* DC.

---

## 162 LYSICHITON AMERICANUM H. et S.

**Family** *Araceae*
**Description** A herbaceous, acaulescent, tufted plant, with a sturdy, vertical rhizome. Leaves basal, clustered large, erect, 10–32 ins (25–80 cm) long and 5–18 ins (12–45 cm) wide, with a long petiole and an oblong or ovate-lanceolate, undulate, shiny green blade. Flower stems one or two to each plant, emerging from the middle of the leaves, cylindrical, very sturdy. Flowers united into a dense spike (spadix) surrounded by a broad bract (spathe), bright yellow, concave, terminating in an acuminate green point. Spadix robust, cylindrical, 3¼–5 ins (8–12 cm) long, with many small green flowers.
**Size** 6–16 ins (15–40 cm).
**Flowering period** April–June.
**Ecology and distribution** Damp woods, swamplands, marshy pastures and montane regions and at low altitudes, from 4,920 to 6,560 ft (1,500–2,000 m). Widespread in western North America from Alaska to California and Montana.
**Notes** The root of this plant, baked and dried, was once used as food by the American Indians. During the summer the leaves and fruit are eaten by brown bears.

## 163 MIMULUS LEWISII Pursh

**Family** *Scrophulariaceae*
**Description** A small plant in dense, leafy tufts. Stems slim, pilose; leaves opposite, broadly lanceolate, small-toothed, acute or acuminate at the apex, with numerous veins. Flowers red or pinkish-red, bright, irregular, with a reddish tubular calyx. Corolla tubular-campanulate, two-lipped, with yellow throat inside and a limb formed of 5 broadly obovate lobes, spreading or reflexed, forming 2 opposite lips, one of 2 lobes and one of 3 lobes. Stamens 4, enclosed in the corolla tube.
**Size** 12–18(–40) ins (30–45(–100) cm).
**Flowering period** June–August.
**Ecology and distribution** Damp places, by streams and in marshy pastures, from 4,920 to 9,840 ft (1,500–3,000 m). Quite frequent in the Rocky Mountains, from British Columbia and Alberta in Canada to Utah and California in the western United States.

## 164 MINUARTIA GRAMINIFOLIA (Ard.) Jáv.
Apennean Sandwort

**Family** *Caryophyllaceae*
**Description** A herbaceous, prostrate-spreading, tufted plant, sometimes in a dense cushion. Flowering stems short, tomentose or hairless (according to the subspecies). Leaves lanceolate-linear or linear, stiff, ½–1½ ins (10–40 mm) long. Flowers white, solitary or in groups of 2–7 at the apex of the stems, ½ in (1 cm) diameter. Petals 5, obovate or elliptical, not quite equal to the sepals.
**Size** 1½–6 ins (4–15 cm).
**Flowering period** July–August.
**Ecology and distribution** Rocks, precipices, crags and screes on variable subsoils, with a preference for limestone, from 4,595 to 6,560 ft (1,400–2,000 m). Found in northern, central and southern Apennines, Sicily, Albania and southern Yugoslavia (subsp. *clandestina*).

**165** **MINUARTIA LARICIFOLIA** (L.) Schinz et Thell.
*M. striata* (L.) Mattf.

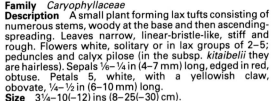

**Family** *Caryophyllaceae*
**Description** A small plant forming lax tufts consisting of numerous stems, woody at the base and then ascending-spreading. Leaves narrow, linear-bristle-like, stiff and rough. Flowers white, solitary or in lax groups of 2–5; peduncles and calyx pilose (in the subsp. *kitaibelii* they are hairless). Sepals ⅙–¼ in (4–7 mm) long, edged in red, obtuse. Petals 5, white, with a yellowish claw, obovate, ¼–½ in (6–10 mm) long.
**Size** 3¼–10(–12) ins (8–25(–30) cm).
**Flowering period** July–August.

**Ecology and distribution** Grassy and dry stony places, on siliceous rocks preferably serpentine or granite, from (4,265–)5,575 to 9,840 ft ((1,300–)1,700–3,000 m). Frequent in the Pyrenees, Alps, northern Apennines, Carpathians and other mountains of central and southern Europe.
**Notes** Several subspecies are distinguishable by their morphological variations. The subsp. *kitaibelii* is exclusive to the eastern Austrian Alps.

---

**166** **MINUARTIA RECURVA** (All.) Schinz et Thell.
Sickle-leaved Sandwort

**Family** *Caryophyllaceae*
**Description** A small plant with woody stems at the base forming dense leafy tufts. Leaves linear, dense, ⅙–½ in (4–10 mm) long. Flowers white, solitary or in groups of 2–3. Sepals with 5–7 veins, acute or acuminate. Petals 5, oblong or ovate-lanceolate, approx. ¼ in (5–6 mm) long, not quite equal to the calyx or slightly longer, constricted into a very short claw.
**Size** 2–4 ins (5–10 cm).
**Flowering period** June–August(–September).

**Ecology and distribution** Rocks, stony places, stabilized rubble, moraines and rocky ridges, on a siliceous subsoil, from 5,575 to 8,200(–10,170) ft (1,700–2,500(–3,100) m). Frequent in the Pyrenees and the Alps from the Graian to the Carnic and Salzburg Alps, in the central Apennines and the Carpathians.

### 167 MINUARTIA SEDOIDES (L.) Hiern
Mossy Cyphel
*Cherleria sedoides* L.; *Alsine cherleri* Fenzl.

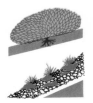

**Family** *Caryophyllaceae*
**Description** A small plant, very branched, forming dense cushions or compact mats, yellowish-green, sometimes as wide as 8–12 ins (20–30 cm). Stems short, erect, very close together, covered with short linear, closely overlapping leaves, approx. ¼ in (4–5 mm) long. Flowers greenish-yellow, solitary, numerous on every cushion, protruding a little from the cushion. Sepals lanceolate-linear or linear, approx. ⅛ in (2–5 mm) long. Petals very short or absent.
**Size** 2–3¼ ins (5–8 cm) – the flowering plant.
**Flowering period** July–August.
**Ecology and distribution** Rocks, stony places, stabilized rubble, detritus of the lower slopes and moraines, on any type of subsoil, from (4,920–)5,905 to 10,170 ft ((1,500–)1,800–3,100 m). Very frequent in the upper zones of the high alpine regions of the Pyrenees, Alps and Carpathians as well as the mountains of the western Balkan peninsula and the Scottish Highlands.

---

### 168 MINUARTIA VERNA (L.) Hiern
Vernal Sandwort

**Family** *Caryophyllaceae*
**Description** A herbaceous plant forming broad, lax tufts, often spreading, sometimes rather dense. Flowering stems, pubescent or tomentose. Leaves narrowly lanceolate, ½–¾ in (10–20 mm) long, fleshy. Flowers white, solitary or in small groups, with peduncles longer than the sepals. Sepals ovate-lanceolate, acuminate, with 3 veins. Petals 5, oval, obtuse, a little shorter than the sepals to slightly longer.
**Size** 2–6 ins (5–15 cm).
**Flowering period** May–August(–September).
**Ecology and distribution** Very frequent in stony places, rock faces, high altitude pastures and detritus, on any type of subsoil, from (3,935–)4,920 to 9,840(–10,500) ft ((1,200–)1,500–3,000(–3,200) m). Found in the mountains of central and southern Europe (the Pyrenees, Alps and Apennines); also common in the Caucasus and the mountains of Siberia, central Asia and North Africa.

## 169 MOLTKIA DOERFLERI Wettst.

**Family** *Boraginaceae*
**Description** A herbaceous perennial, branched at the base, with a sturdy horizontal rhizome. Stem epigeal erect, pilose-bristle-like with appressed hairs. Leaves lanceolate or lanceolate-linear, 1½–4 ins (4–10 cm) long, channelled, pilose-bristle-like with a ciliate margin. Flowers deep pink or purple tinged with violet in the axil of 2–3 linear bracts, united into dense few-flowered apical cymes. Calyx ½ in (10 mm) long, with 5 long linear pilose teeth. Corolla narrowly tubular, widening towards the middle and slightly contracted towards the throat, ¾–1 in (19–25 mm), with 5 short teeth, rounded, slightly spreading. Stamens enclosed within the corolla tube.
**Size** 12–20 ins (30–50 cm).
**Flowering period** June–August.
**Ecology and distribution** Craggy pastures, rocky areas and rock faces, from 4,920 to 6,560 ft (1,500–2,000 m). A Balkan species which is limited to the mountains of northern Albania and neighbouring areas.

---

## 170 MYOSOTIS ALPESTRIS Schmidt
Alpine Forget-me-not, Scorpion Grass
*M. pyrenaica* Pourr.

**Family** *Boraginaceae*
**Description** A small, rhizomatous perennial, tufted-spreading, covered with short, stiff, spreading hairs. Stems epigeal, numerous, radiate, with spatulate or oblong-lanceolate leaves, the lower stalked, the upper sessile and shorter. Flowers sky-blue, united into a compact scorpioid cyme, formed of numerous, close-growing flowers with very short peduncles. Calyx tubular with 5 teeth which are shorter than the corolla tube. Corolla ¼–½ in (6–10 mm) wide, with a cylindrical tube, ⅛–¼ in (3–5 mm) long, mouth circular, yellow, and a flattened-circular limb formed of 5 sub-rounded or broadly obovate sky-blue lobes, separated by short white markings. Stamens 5, arising in the corolla tube.
**Size** 2–8 ins (5–20 cm).
**Flowering period** (May–)June–September.
**Ecology and distribution** Meadows, grassy places, wet or damp areas, stabilized rubble, on any subsoil, from 4,590 to 9,840 ft (1,400–3,000 m), but as low as 2,625 ft (800 m) in Scotland. Frequent in nearly all the European mountains (the Pyrenees, Alps, Apennines, Carpathians, Balkan Mountains and in Corsica). Related species, found in the Arctic regions of Eurasia and North America, are sometimes identified as *M. alpestris*.

## 171 NIGRITELLA NIGRA (L.) Reichb. f.
Black Vanilla Orchid
*N. angustifolia* Rich.

**Family** *Orchidaceae*
**Description** A small, erect plant with a solitary stem emerging from a short digitate tuber. Stem epigeal angular, with decurrent leaf margins. Leaves 7–15, mostly basal, grasslike, 1¼–8 ins (3–20 cm) long, somewhat fleshy, channelled, small-toothed margin; stem leaves shorter. Flowers dark red or blackish (subsp. *nigra*) or bright red (subsp. *rubra*) or even whitish (subsp. *corneliana*), vanilla-scented, united into a dense ovoid, cylindrical or conical terminal spike. Tepals 6, slightly unequal; upward-turning, ovate-lanceolate or triangular labéllum. Spur bag-like, obtuse, short.
**Size** 3¼–6(–10) ins (8–15(–25) cm).
**Flowering period** (May–)June–August(–September).
**Ecology and distribution** Alpine grasslands and pastures, mostly on limestone, from (3,280–)4,265 to 8,530 (–9,185) ft ((1,000–)1,300–2,600(–2,800) m). Frequent in the Alps, Pyrenees, Massif Central, Jura, central Apennines, Carpathians, Balkan Mountains and in Scandinavia.
**Notes** Three subspecies of *Nigritella* have been identified; the commonest, sometimes described as separate species, are: *nigra* (*N. angustifolia*) and *rubra* (*N. rubra*; *N. miniata*: Rosy Vanilla Orchid, as illustrated). All *Nigritella* species are protected.

---

## 172 ONOBRYCHIS MONTANA DC.
Mountain Sainfoin
*O. viciifolia* Scop. subsp. *montana* (Pers.) Gam.

**Family** *Papilionaceae*
**Description** A tufted, herbaceous plant, prostrate-spreading, more or less stemless, branched at the base. Leaves imparipinnate, nearly all basal, slightly pilose with appressed hairs, a long petiole and 5–10 pairs of oval, oblong or elliptical, acute, mucronate leaflets. Flowers pink or purple, with the colours tending to merge into one another, numerous darker red veins, united in terminal spikes on long ascending scapiform stems, longer than the leaves. Raceme sub-conical, ¾–2¾ ins (2–7 cm) long. Calyx with a short pilose tube, 5 acuminate teeth much longer than the tube. Corolla, ½–⅝ in (10–14 mm) long, with a spreading standard, slightly shorter than the keel.
**Size** 2–8 ins (5–20 cm).
**Flowering period** July–August.
**Ecology and distribution** Grassy places, pastures, alpine meadows, stony or detritic places, on a calcareous or dolomitic subsoil, from 4,595 to 8,200 ft (1,400–2,500 m). Quite frequent in central-southern Europe (the Pyrenees, Jura, Alps, Apennines, Carpathians and the Balkan peninsula), the mountains of Asia Minor and the Caucasus.

## 173 OXYTROPIS CAMPESTRIS (L.) DC.

Meadow Milkvetch
*Astragalus campestris* (L.) DC.; *Phaca campestris*
Wald.

**Family** *Papilionaceae*
**Description** A tufted, acaulescent, herbaceous perennial, branched at the base. Leaves in a basal rosette, imparipinnate, with a long petiole and 10–15 pairs of leaflets, linear-lanceolate or oblong, acuminate, pilose-tomentose. Flowering stems ascending with a compact terminal ovoid raceme, 5–15 pale yellow flowers, sometimes whitish or pinkish. Peduncle very short. Calyx short, sub-cylindrical. Corolla with a standard, ⅝–¾ in (15–20 mm) long, obovate, spreading, slightly longer than the other petals.
**Size** 2–8 ins (5–20 cm).
**Flowering period** June–August(–September).
**Ecology and distribution** Pastures, grassy or stony places, detritus of the lower slopes, rocks, preferably on an acid subsoil, from 5,575 to 8,860(–9,840) ft (1,700–2,700(–3,000) m). Quite frequent in the Pyrenees, Alps, central Apennines, Carpathians, Caucasus and the mountains of the Balkan peninsula as well as Arctic Eurasia.
**Notes** A rather variable Arctic-alpine species of which several subspecies have been identified, such as *tiroliensis*, from the central-eastern Alps, and *sordida*, from the Eurasian Arctic.

---

## 174 PAEDEROTA LUTEA Scop.

Yellow Veronica
*Veronica lutea* (Scop.) Wettst., *P. egeria* L.

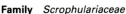

**Family** *Scrophulariaceae*
**Description** An erect, tufted herbaceous perennial, covered with short hairs. Leaves opposite, ovate-triangular, acuminate, margin closely serrate with at least 10 teeth on each side, hairless, ⅝–1¼ ins (15–30 mm) long and ¼–⅝ in (7–15 mm) wide. Flowers yellow, united into a short spiky terminal inflorescence, with short bracts. Calyx tubular, with linear teeth. Corolla irregular, ½–⅝ in (1–1.5 cm) long, with a long sub-cylindrical tube and two-lipped limb, shorter than the tube, with erect and slightly spreading lobes. Stamens 2, shorter than the corolla.
**Size** 2¾–8(–12) ins (7–20(–30) cm).
**Flowering period** May–August.
**Ecology and distribution** Cliff-faces and rock fissures, on a calcareous subsoil, from 3,280 to 7,220 ft (1,000–2,200 m). Endemic to the eastern Alps, from Trentino in northern Italy to the Salzburg Alps and Karawanken Mountains in Austria. A protected species.
**Notes** Closely related is *Paederota bonarota*, also of the south-eastern Alps, distinguishable from *P. lutea* by its violet-azure flowers and crenate leaves. These two species used to be included in the genus *Veronica* from which they differ by having a clearly two-lipped corolla.

## 175 PAPAVER BURSERI Crantz
Alpine Poppy
*P. alpinum* L. subsp. *alpinum*

**Family** *Papaveraceae*
**Description** A small, tufted perennial, acaulescent, slightly pilose. Leaves all basal, usually lanceolate, bipinnate- or tripinnate-divided, with 3–4 pairs of narrowly lanceolate or linear lobes, approx. 1/16 in (0.5–2 mm) wide. Flowers white, 5/8–3/4(–1¼) ins (1.5–2(–3) cm) wide. Calyx pilose-bristly, formed of two sepals which fall soon after opening. Corolla wide, cup-shaped, consisting of 4 petals sub-circular, with a yellow basal blotch.
**Size** 3¼–8 ins (8–20 cm) – the flowering stems.
**Flowering period** July–August.

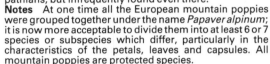

**Ecology and distribution** Stony places, crags and precipices, detritus of the lower slopes, moraines and gravelly ground flanking streams, mainly on a calcareous or dolomitic subsoil, from 3,935 to 6,560 ft (1,200–2,000 m). Indigenous to the north-eastern Alps and western Carpathians, but infrequently found even there.
**Notes** At one time all the European mountain poppies were grouped together under the name *Papaver alpinum*; it is now more acceptable to divide them into at least 6 or 7 species or subspecies which differ, particularly in the characteristics of the petals, leaves and capsules. All mountain poppies are protected species.

---

## 176 PAPAVER SUAVEOLENS Lapeyr.
Pyrenean Poppy

**Family** *Papaveraceae*
**Description** A small, acaulescent, tufted plant, bristly with persistent leaf bases. Leaves basal, irregularly incised or pinnatisect in lobes ovate-lanceolate, unequal, dentate or incised, approx. 1/8 in (2–4 mm) long. Flowers yellow, positioned apically on long, bristly stems, drooping in bud. Calyx formed of 2 rough, hairy sepals, falling soon after buds open. Corolla 1–1¼ ins (2.5–3 cm) wide, broad cup-shaped, consisting of 4 broadly obovate petals. Stamens numerous, yellow; ovary greenish.
**Size** 1¼–4 ins (3–10 cm).
**Flowering period** July–August.
**Ecology and distribution** Stony places, rocks and detritus, on a calcareous subsoil, from 5,905 to 8,200 ft (1,800–2,500 m). Endemic to the mountains of the Iberian peninsula: Sierra Nevada and Pyrenees.
**Notes** This species belongs to the large group of European mountain poppies. The most widespread is *P. rhaeticum* which usually has yellow flowers. Also important are: *P. kerneri*, also with yellow flowers, *P. sendtneri* and *P. burseri* (see entry 175) which have white flowers.

## 177 PARNASSIA PALUSTRIS L.
Grass of Parnassus

**Family** *Parnassiaceae*
**Description** A tufted, herbaceous plant, sub-acaulescent, with a short, branched rhizome from which emerge 2–5 flower stems. Leaves basal in a rosette, on long petioles, ovate-cordate, obtuse, entire, ¾–2½ ins (2–6 cm) long; stem leaves sparse (1–2), sessile, amplexicaul. Stems erect epigeal, each bearing a solitary terminal flower. Flowers white, ½–1¼ in (1–3 cm) wide, calyx with 5 short ovate lanceolate lobes. Corolla 5 petals, broadly ovate, rounded or obtuse, with delicate brownish veins running lengthwise. Stamens 5, about one-third the length of the petals, alternating with 5 fringed sterile staminodes.
**Size** 3–12 ins (8–30 cm).
**Flowering period** July–September(–October).
**Ecology and distribution** Wet places, marshlands, and raised bogs, from (2,625–)3,935 to 8,530(–9,840) ft ((800–)1,200–2,600(–3,000) m). Very common in all European mountains including the Caucasus, the mountains of central Asia, the colder regions of Europe, Asia and North America as well as the Atlas Mountains of North Africa.

---

## 178 PEDICULARIS KERNERI Dalla Torre
Rhaetian Lousewort
*P. rhaetica* A. Kerner; *P. rostrata* L.;
  *P. caespitosa* Sieb.

**Family** *Scrophulariaceae*
**Description** A low-growing, spreading-prostrate plant with short ascending stems. Leaves in a dense basal rosette, pinnatisect, oblong-lanceolate, on short petioles; stem leaves sparse or absent. Bracts similar to the leaves but shorter. Flowers deep pink with a purple upper lip, united into groups of 3–5 lax racemes. Calyx cylindrical with 5 leaflike, dentate sepals, recurved outwards. Corolla two-lipped, ¾ in (2 cm) long, with the tube slightly longer than the calyx. Upper lip helmet-shaped, laterally recurved and prolonged into an elongate conical beak, downwardly directed; lower lip three-lobed with ovate-broad lateral lobes, larger than the central one.
**Size** 2–4(–8) ins (5–10(–20) cm).
**Flowering period** July–August(–September).
**Ecology and distribution** Pastures, wet meadows, grassy places, natural debris, stabilized and grass-covered detritus, on an acid soil, from (3,935–)4,595 to 10,500(–11,155) ft ((1,200–)1,400–3,200(–3,400) m). Quite frequent in the Pyrenees and Alps, especially western and central ranges.

## 179 PEDICULARIS RECUTITA L.
Truncate Lousewort

**Family** *Scrophulariaceae*
**Description** A sturdy, herbaceous plant with a hollow, erect stem. Leaves partly basal, lanceolate, on long petioles, pinnatifid, with serrate lobes; stem leaves alternate, decreasing towards the tip, sessile, the upper lanceolate-linear. Flowers dark red or rust-coloured, sometimes tinged with green, united into a cylindrical terminal raceme which is dense at first, becoming more lax, with numerous flowers. Bracts pinnate-lobate or entire, linear, pilose. Calyx short, cylindrical. Corolla two-lipped with a short, cylindrical tube and limb consisting of a long upper lip, oblong, straight, helmet-shaped, and of a short lower one, three-lobed.
**Size** 8–24 ins (20–60 cm).
**Flowering period** July–August.
**Ecology and distribution** Wet pastures, swampy fields, marshy ground, grassy places and spinneys, from 4,920 to 8,200 ft (1,500–2,500 m). Endemic to the Alps, from Savoy to Austria and northern Yugoslavia although infrequent.

## 180 PEDICULARIS ROSTRATO-SPICATA
Crantz
Flesh-pink Lousewort
*P. incarnata* Jacq.

**Family** *Scrophulariaceae*
**Description** A herbaceous perennial with stiff, leafy, erect stem, hairless below, densely pubescent above. Leaves on long petioles, pinnatisect, with lanceolate segments, pinnate-lobed. Flowers pink with purplish-red upper lip, united into elongate racemes. Peduncles very short. Bracts short, three-lobed, woolly. Calyx cylindrical, woolly, with short teeth. Corolla two-lipped, cylindrical tube and a limb divided into two lips. Upper lip beak-shaped, ⅙ in (4 mm) long, recurved downwards, emarginate; lower lip three-lobed, spreading.
**Size** 6–18 ins (15–45 cm).
**Flowering period** July–August.
**Ecology and distribution** Montane pastures, dry meadows, damp grassy places, on any type of subsoil, from (4,920–)6,560 to 8,860 ft ((1,500–)2,000–2,700 m). Quite frequent in the Alps and also present, though very rare, in one particular area: Mt. Canigou, in the eastern Pyrenees.

## 181 PEDICULARIS TUBEROSA L.
Tuberous Lousewort

**Family** *Scrophulariaceae*
**Description** A small herbaceous, sub-acaulescent plant with an enlarged rhizome from which emerge one or two erect or ascending stems. Basal leaves on long petioles, pinnatisect with pinnatifid or deeply dentate segments; stem leaves short, sessile. Flowers yellow or pale yellow, united into a short sub-capitate compact terminal raceme, interspersed with short bracts. Calyx cylindrical, pilose, with 5 fringed lobes. Corolla two-lipped with a cylindrical tube, sub-equal to or slightly longer than the calyx; limb formed of an upper elongate lip, recurved like a beak, conical, emarginate, downwardly directed, and of a lower lip, spreading, expanded, slightly convex, three-lobed.
**Size** 4–10 ins (10–25 cm).
**Flowering period** June–August.
**Ecology and distribution** Pastures, alpine meadows and stony places, on any type of subsoil although with a preference for acid soils, from 3,935 to 8,860(–9,515) ft (1,200–2,700(–2,900) m). Occasionally found in the mountains of northern Spain, in the Pyrenees, Apuane Alps, northern and central Apennines and, more commonly, the Alps, especially in the interior, more protected, areas.

---

## 182 PEDICULARIS VERTICILLATA L.
Whorled Lousewort

**Family** *Scrophulariaceae*
**Description** A small, sub-acaulescent perennial with a short rhizome from which spring two or more erect stems. Leaves mostly basal, stalked, pinnatifid, with dentate or incised lobes; stem leaves in whorls of 3–4, a feature which makes it easy to distinguish this species from all the others. Flowers purplish-red or pink, mixed with short reddish bracts, united into whorls in a dense ovoid terminal raceme. Calyx short, swollen, pilose. Corolla two-lipped with cylindrical tube, 1½–2 times the length of the calyx, and a limb formed of two lips, the upper oblong and helmet-shaped, the lower one spreading, often variegated and veined, deeply divided into three lobes.
**Size** 2–10(–14) ins (5–25(–35) cm).
**Flowering period** June–August.
**Ecology and distribution** Stony pastures, damp grassy places and detritus, on a calcareous subsoil, from (2,950–)4,920 to 9,840 ft ((900–)1,500–3,000 m). Very common in all European mountains (the mountains of Iberia, the Pyrenees, Alps, Apennines, Carpathians, Balkan peninsula), the Caucasus and the mountains of central Asia as well as the Arctic regions of Eurasia and north-western America.

## 183  PENSTEMON RUPICOLA  (Piper) Howell

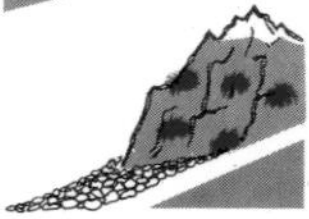

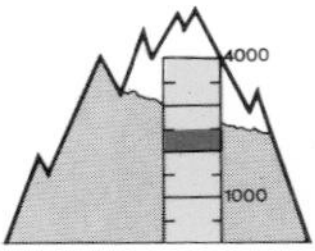

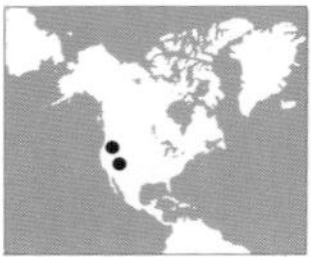

**Family** *Scrophulariaceae*

**Description** A small, shrubby plant, prostrate-spreading, very branched at the base, with the branches ascending at first and then drooping, fairly pilose. Leaves opposite, very close together in the sterile buds, ovate, acute, small-toothed margin, sessile, approx. ¼–⅓ in (7–8 mm) long and approx. ¼ in (5–6 mm) wide, fairly thick. Flowers pink, lilac-pink or light carmine-red, united in cymes at the apex of the flowering stems. Very short peduncles. Bracts small, clasped to the campanulate calyx with 5 acute-elliptical lobes, approx. ¼ in (6–7 mm) long. Corolla inflated, conical, conspicuously two-lipped, with a tube 1–1¼ ins (2.5–3 cm) long, gradually broadening; throat approx. ½ in (1–1.2 cm) long; limb ½–⅝ in (0.8–1.4 cm) long, with a bilobate upper lip, spreading, and a three-lobed lower lip with oblong, parallel lobes.

**Size** 3¼–6 ins (8–15 cm).

**Flowering period** May–July.

**Ecology and distribution** Rocks, exposed precipices and crags, rock faces, steep slopes, from 6,560 to 8,200 ft (2,000–2,500 m). Endemic to the Rocky Mountains and coastal ranges in the western United States.

**Notes** The genus *Penstemon*, at one time spelt 'Pentstemon', is typical of North America: more than 60 different species are to be found in the Rocky Mountains alone.

---

## 184  PETROCALLIS PYRENAICA  (L.) R. Br.
*Draba pyrenaica* L.

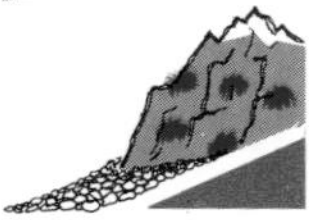

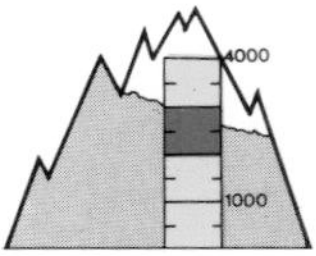

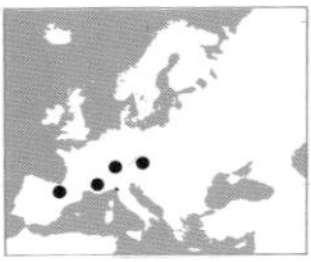

**Family** *Cruciferae*

**Description** A tufted, more or less stemless plant with dense rosettes of very closely-packed leaves. Rhizome short, branched. Leaves remaining close to the base of the stem, greyish, marginally pilose, spatulate, ⅙–¼ in (4–6 mm) long, cuneate at the base, digitate at the apex in 3–5 lobes. Flowers pink or pale lilac, sometimes with darker veins, united into dense racemose or corymbose inflorescences, at the apex of short leafless stems. Petals 4, ⅙–¼ in (4–6 mm) long, broadly obovate; yellow anthers. Silicule ovate or elliptical, ⅛–¼ in (3–6 mm) long.

**Size** 1¼–2 ins (3–5 cm) – the flowering plant.

**Flowering period** June–August.

**Ecology and distribution** Rocks and precipices, fissures and crevices, stabilized rubble and detritus of the lower slopes, preferably on limestone or dolomite, from 5,575 to 9,515(–11,155) ft (1,700–2,900(–3,400) m). Found throughout the entire alpine range, but especially in the northern and southern ranges, as well as in the Pyrenees and Carpathians.

**Notes** A protected species in some areas.

## 185 PHYTEUMA BETONICIFOLIUM Vill.
Blue-spiked Rampion

**Family** *Campanulaceae*
**Description** An erect, sub-acaulescent herbaceous plant
with a short rhizome from which emerge 1–3 flower
stems. Basal leaves oblong or lanceolate, cordate at the
base, on long petioles; stem leaves small, linear, sparse
or absent. Flower stem erect, often pilose on the lower
part, with a dense oblong or cylindrical terminal spike, up
to 1½ ins (4 cm) long. Flowers pale sky-blue or violet;
bracts linear, short. Calyx campanulate, with 5 linear
acuminate teeth. Corolla cylindrical, tubular, swollen and
split lengthwise in the middle to form 5 linear teeth which
come together towards the base and the apex. Style
passes through the corolla tube and emerges through the
top.
**Size** 8–28 ins (20–70 cm).
**Flowering period** June–August(–September).
**Ecology and distribution** Meadows, grassy or stony
pastures and sparse woods, preferably on a siliceous
subsoil, from 3,280 to 8,530 ft (1,000–2,600 m). Endemic
to the Alps and northern Apennines.
**Notes** Very closely related species are found in the
Pyrenees and northern Dinaric Alps.

---

## 186 PHYTEUMA HEMISPHAERICUM L.
Globe-headed Rampion

**Family** *Campanulaceae*
**Description** A small, sub-acaulescent plant, tufted-
spreading, with a short rhizome from which emerge one
or more ascending epigeal stems. Basal leaves numerous, closely packed, long, narrowly linear, sessile or with
an obscurely dentate margin; stem leaves sparse, alternate, linear. Flowers blue, arranged in a broad, globose
head, ⅝–¾ in (1.5–2 cm) wide, with lanceolate small-
toothed bracts, sub-equal to or shorter than the head.
Calyx, 5 teeth. Corolla narrowly tubular, arcuate, swollen
towards the base and split into thread-like lobes.
**Size** 2–4(–12) ins (5–10(–30) cm).
**Flowering period** July–August.
**Ecology and distribution** Grassy or stony pastures,
natural detritus, moraines and stabilized rubble, on an
acid humus-rich subsoil, from (1,970–)5,250 to 9,840
(–11,810) ft ((600–)1,600–3,000(–3,600) m). Found in the
mountains of central Spain, the Pyrenees, Alps and
Apennines.

## 187 PHYTEUMA ORBICULARE L.
Round-headed Rampion

**Family** *Campanulaceae*
**Description** A rhizomatous, herbaceous plant, tufted-spreading, with erect or ascending epigeal stems. Basal leaves on long petioles, cordate, triangular or oblong, crenate-dentate; stem leaves on short petioles, lanceolate-acuminate. Flowers dark blue, united into dense, more or less spherical heads with broad-based lanceolate bracts below. Calyx campanulate, with 5 lanceolate teeth. Corolla tubular, arcuate upwards, swollen in the middle and split lengthwise into 5 strap-shaped lobes. Stigma light-coloured, trifid, spreading.
**Size** 4–20 ins (10–50 cm).
**Flowering period** May–September(–October).
**Ecology and distribution** Pastures, meadows, grassy or stony places and rocks, on any type of subsoil although with a preference for limestone, from (985–)2,625 to 8,530 ft ((300–)800–2,600 m). Very common in almost all the mountains of central-southern Europe (the Jura, Vosges, Alps, Apennines, Carpathians – including the Tatra Mountains – Transylvanian and Dinaric Alps) and extending north into the lowlands of Belgium, northern Germany and Poland.

## 188 PHYTEUMA OVATUM Honck.
Dark Rampion
*P. halleri* All.

**Family** *Campanulaceae*
**Description** An erect, robust, more or less stemless herbaceous plant, with a short rhizome. Basal leaves on long petioles, obcordate, acuminate, irregularly serrate; stem leaves ovate-lanceolate, acute or acuminate, on short petioles or sessile. Flowers blackish-purple but pale violet or even white in the bud, united at the apex of the stem in a dense ovoid or cylindrical spike, 1½–2½ ins (4–6 cm) long, with long lanceolate-linear, spreading bracts at the base. Calyx with 5 linear teeth. Corolla cylindrical-tubular, strongly incurved upwards, slightly swollen and split lengthwise towards the middle, the pink style emerging from the top. Stigma bifid.
**Size** 12–32(–40) ins (30–80(–100) cm).
**Flowering period** (June–)July–August.
**Ecology and distribution** Montane woods, woodland clearings, thickets, damp meadows and stabilized rubble, from (1,970–)3,935 to 7,875 ft ((600–)1,200–2,400 m). Quite common in the Pyrenees, Alps, Apennines and Dinaric Alps.

## 189  PHYTEUMA VAGNERI A. Kerner

**Family** *Campanulaceae*
**Description** A robust perennial, erect, more or less stemless, with a swollen, fleshy rhizome. Basal leaves ovate-triangular or ovate-lanceolate, on long petioles, acuminate, dentate; stem leaves sparse, sub-sessile, linear. Flowers deep violet-blue to blackish, united into a short more or less spherical inflorescence to form a head at the base of which are linear-lanceolate bracts sub-equal to or longer than the head. Calyx with 5 linear or awl-shaped teeth. Corolla tubular, swollen and split lengthwise in the middle, prolonged into a darker tube at the end, incurved upwards. Style deep violet, emerging from the corolla tube.
**Size** 12–28 ins (30–70 cm).
**Flowering period** June–August.
**Ecology and distribution** Alpine pastures and montane grassy places, from 1,640 to 5,905 ft (500–1,800 m). Endemic to the eastern and southern Carpathians.

---

## 190  PINGUICULA ALPINA L.
Alpine Butterwort

**Family** *Lentibulariaceae*
**Description** An acaulescent plant with leaves in a basal rosette, broadly lanceolate or oblong, sessile, yellowish-green, with strongly inrolled margins, covered with sticky hairs and glands that secrete a proteolytic liquid which is capable of attacking and digesting any insects that may alight on the leaves. Flower stems 1–2 per plant, each with a solitary terminal flower. Calyx two-lipped, with 5 unequal lobes. Corolla white with two yellow spots, 1/3–1/2 in (8–10 mm) long, with a spur at the base approx. 1/8 in (2–4 mm) long and a two-lipped limb with 5 unequal lobes, generally 4 sub-rounded and one obcordate.
**Size** 2–4(–6) ins (5–10(–15) cm).
**Flowering period** June–July(–August).
**Ecology and distribution** Damp pastures, wet ground flanking streams, under dripping water and near springs, preferring a calcareous subsoil, from 3,280 to 8,530 ft (1,000–2,600 m). Quite frequent in the mountains of south-western and northern Europe (the Pyrenees, Alps, Jura, Scottish Highlands, Scandinavian Mountains) as well as the mountains of central Asia.
**Notes** Improperly labelled 'carnivorous', it is able to absorb nitrogen in protein form rather than as nitrates from the soil solutions. A protected plant.

## 191 POLEMONIUM COERULEUM L.
Jacob's Ladder

**Family** *Polemoniaceae*
**Description** An erect, herbaceous perennial, with simple stems or slightly branched at the base, slender. Leaves alternate, pinnate-compound, 4–16 ins (10–40 cm) long, in 6–12(–20) pairs of lanceolate or linear, acuminate leaflets. Flowers sky-blue, on short peduncles, united in dense terminal cymes. Calyx campanulate with 5 lobes. Corolla with a very short tube and an open, expanded limb of ¾–1 in (20–25 mm) in diameter, formed of 5 elliptical, broadly oval or rhombic lobes, slightly recurved outwards.
**Size** 12–28(–40) ins (30–70(–100) cm).
**Flowering period** (May–)June–August(–September).
**Ecology and distribution** Woods, damp meadows, pastures and wet ground flanking streams, on any type of subsoil, from (2,625–)3,935 to 7,545 ft ((800–)1,200–2,300 m). Sometimes found in the central Pyrenees, central Alps, Dinaric Alps, Carpathians and mountains of northern Europe; widespread in central-northern Russia and western Siberia.
**Notes** Frequently grown in gardens in temperate climates.

---

## 192 POLEMONIUM PULCHERRIMUM Hook.

**Family** *Polemoniaceae*
**Description** An erect perennial, with a simple or slightly branched, slender, pilose stem. Leaves large, pinnate-compound, basal leaves sub-rosetted; stem leaves alternate, erect-spreading, on widely-spaced nodes, with 30–40 linear-spatulate or oblong leaflets. Flowers violet-azure, on short peduncles, arranged in short few-flowered terminally cymose inflorescences. Calyx short, campanulate, pilose-hirsute. Corolla tube very short, white or yellowish throat and an open, expanded limb, consisting of 5 sub-rounded or broadly obovate lobes, round at the apex.
**Size** 6–8 ins (15–20 cm).
**Flowering period** June–August.
**Ecology and distribution** Rocks, craggy places and shaded rocky slopes, from 8,200 to 11,810 ft (2,500–3,600 m). Very widespread throughout the Rocky Mountains, from south-western Canada to the western United States (Arizona and Colorado).

## 193  POLYGALA CHAMAEBUXUS L.
Box-leaved or Shrubby Milkwort, Bastard Box

**Family** *Polygalaceae*

**Description** A low-growing, very branched shrublet, with prostrate and ascending branches. Leaves alternate, very close together, elliptical, oblong or lanceolate, sessile, leathery, with an entire margin, slightly mucronate at the apex, shiny green, ⅝–1¼ ins (15–30 mm) long and ¼–½ in (5–10 mm) wide. Flowers from white to yellow to red on short peduncles, borne in the upper leaf axils and forming a short terminal raceme. Calyx petal-like, formed of 5 sepals of which 3 very small ones are inside and 2 large (wings) are on the outside, oblong, often close together and spreading, almost giving the impression of the standard of a pea flower. Corolla, ½–⅝ in (10–14 mm), with a cylindrical tube and a limb formed of 3 lobes, the lower one of which (carina) is concave, entire or slightly lobed, and the two upper oval, converging on the carina. The commonest type has white wings and a yellow or orange carina with a white tube; another quite frequent type has carmine-red or pink wings and a red carina shading to yellow at the apex or completely yellow.

**Size** 2–6(–12) ins (5–15(–30) cm).

**Flowering period** (March–)April–July(–September).

**Ecology and distribution** Woods, dry pastures, high altitude scrub among dwarf pines and rhododendrons, pine-woods, dry grassy places and rocks, on mainly calcareous ground, from fairly low altitudes 985 to 1,970 ft (300–600 m) up to 7,545 to 7,875 ft (2,300–2,400 m). Endemic to the mountains of central and southern Europe, quite commonly found in the Alps, Jura, northern and central Apennines, Carpathians and the mountains of the north-western Balkan peninsula.

**Notes** A related species which grows exclusively in the Spanish eastern Pyrenees, is *Polygala vayredae*, easily distinguishable from *P. chamaebuxus* by its linear or linear-lanceolate leaves.

## 194 POLYGALA ALPESTRIS Reichb.
Mountain Milkwort

**Family** *Polygalaceae*
**Description** A small, prostrate-spreading plant with creeping branches, ascending or becoming erect. Leaves small, elliptical or oblong, alternate, sessile or nearly so, apically acute, sometimes tinged browny-red on the lower surface. Flowers violet-blue, occasionally white, irregular, forming simple, dense racemes, ⅝–1⅜ ins (1.5–3.5 cm) long, comprising 5–20 flowers. Petal-like calyx with 5 sepals, 3 of which are very small and 2 large (wings), lateral, oblong or ovate, ⅙–¼ in (4–6.5 mm) long. Corolla, approx. ¼ in (5–6 mm) long, with a sub-cylindrical, pale violet tube and a limb formed of 3 very short lobes, the lower one fringed (carina) and the upper two short, rounded.
**Size** 2¾–6 ins (7–15 cm).
**Flowering period** June–August.
**Ecology and distribution** Pastures, montane fields, grassy places, on any type of subsoil although with a preference for calcareous soils, from 3,280 to 8,860 ft (1,000–2,700 m). Frequent in the Pyrenees, Jura, Alps, Apennines and the mountains of the Balkan peninsula.

---

## 195 POLYGONUM VIVIPARUM L.
Viviparous Bistort

**Family** *Polygonaceae*
**Description** A herbaceous perennial with an erect, un-branched stem. Leaves alternate, lanceolate or oblong, entire, with a central vein, prolonged at the base into a sheath which clasps the stem at the height of the node. Flowers white or pink, united into a dense spike, narrow, cylindrical, ¾–2½ ins (2–6 cm) long. Lower flowers on the spike often replaced by red or brown fertile bulbils; upper flowers have a sub-cylindrical or almost urn-shaped perianth of 3–6 tepals, ⅛–¼ in (3–5 mm) long, with protruding stamens.
**Size** 2–12(–16) ins (5–30(–40) cm).
**Flowering period** June–August.
**Ecology and distribution** Pastures, alpine grasslands with *Carex curvula*, upland moors, snow-beds, grassy or stony places, on any type of subsoil, from (3,280–)4,920 to 10,498 ft ((1,000–)1,500–3,200 m). Common in nearly all European mountains (the Pyrenees, Auvergne, Jura, Alps, Apennines, Carpathians, Balkan and Caucasus Mountains, the mountains of central Asia (Altai Mountains and the Himalayas) and in Tibet, in the Rocky Mountains and in the Arctic regions of Eurasia and North America.

## 196  POTENTILLA ALCHIMILLOIDES (or ALCHEMILLOIDES) Lapeyr.
Alchemilla-leaved Cinquefoil

**Family** *Rosaceae*
**Description** A tufted, much branched, pilose, herbaceous perennial, woody at the base. Leaves palmatisect, with 5–7 leaflets, dark green above, silvery-white and tomentose below, oblanceolate or obovate, apically small-toothed. Inflorescence lax, branched, with linear or dentate bracts. Flowers pure white in lax, or sometimes dense, terminal groups. Calyx and epicalyx sub-equal, with lanceolate, acuminate, pilose lobes. Petals 5, ⅓–½ in (8–10 mm) long, almost twice the length of the sepals, obcordate or broadly obovate, emarginate.
**Size** 4–12 ins (10–30 cm).
**Flowering period** July–August.
**Ecology and distribution** Rocks, stony places and detritus of the lower slopes, from (2,625–)3,935 to 7,220 ft ((800–)1,200–2,200 m). Endemic to the Pyrenees.

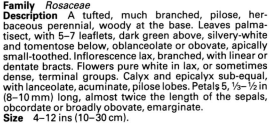

---

## 197  POTENTILLA AUREA L.
Golden Cinquefoil
*P. halleri* Ser.

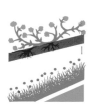

**Family** *Rosaceae*
**Description** A small, prostrate-spreading, tufted plant, often forming lax mats, branched at the base, with ascending branches. Leaves alternate, palmatisect, with 5 oblanceolate or spatulate leaflets, dentate at the apex, the apical tooth being shorter than the two flanking it, with appressed marginal hairs. Flowering stems with 1–5 flowers in loose inflorescences. Flowers bright yellow, ⅝–¾ in (1.5–2 cm) wide, with sepals and segments of the epicalyx lanceolate-linear, silvery-tomentose, shorter than the petals. Corolla 5–6 petals, ¼–½ in (7–11 mm) long, obcordate, with an orange patch at the base.
**Size** 2–8 ins (5–20 cm).
**Flowering period** June–September.
**Ecology and distribution** Arid pastures, stony places, rocks and sparse woods, on a siliceous subsoil, from (1,970–)3,935 to 9,515(–10,825) ((600–)1,200–2,900 (–3,300) m). A rather common species in all the mountains of central-southern Europe (the Cantabrians, Pyrenees, Jura, Alps, Apennines, Riesengebirge, Carpathians and mountains of the Balkan peninsula) and the high mountain ranges of Asia Minor.

## 198 POTENTILLA FRUTICOSA L.
Shrubby Cinquefoil

**Family** *Rosaceae*
**Description** A low-growing, woody shrub with reddish-brown branches. Leaves alternate, pinnate-compound, with 5 oblong or obovate leaflets, entire, apically retuse, ½–¾ in (1–2 cm) long. Flowers golden-yellow, ¾–1¼ ins (2–3 cm) wide, solitary or in small axillary or terminal groups. Epicalyx formed of 5 narrow bracts, as long as the sepals; calyx consists of 5 broadly ovate, greenish-yellow sepals. Corolla open, expanded, formed of 5 sub-rounded or slightly pointed petals, with a very short claw.
**Size** 8–40(–48) ins (20–100(–120) cm).
**Flowering period** June–August.
**Ecology and distribution** Rock faces, stony places and rocky ridges, from 6,560 to 7,875 ft (2,000–2,400 m). A rather rare species, it can be found in the Pyrenees, western Alps (Alpes Maritimes), central Apennines, Rhodope Mountains (Bulgaria), Urals, Caucasus, the mountains of central Asia and the Arctic regions of Eurasia and North America, where it grows as far south as the Rocky Mountains.

---

## 199 POTENTILLA GRANDIFLORA L.
Large-flowered Cinquefoil

**Family** *Rosaceae*
**Description** A tufted, sub-acaulescent, herbaceous plant, much branched at the base, with numerous ascending or erect stems, further branched, pilose. Leaves mostly basal, on long petioles, trifoliate, with obovate, coarsely dentate, leaflets, pilose-silky on the lower surface, ⅝–1½ ins (15–40 mm) long. Flowers golden-yellow, ⅝–1¼ ins (1.5–3 cm) wide, apical on each branch, on long peduncles. Bracts linear or trifoliate, sessile. Epicalyx and calyx with very similar lobes, lanceolate, shorter than the petals. Corolla 5 petals, broad, obcordate, spreading. Stamens numerous, yellow.
**Size** 6–16 ins (15–40 cm).
**Flowering period** June–August.
**Ecology and distribution** Dry pastures, meadows, rocks, stabilized rubble and craggy places, on an acid subsoil, from (3,280–)5,250 to 9,185(–10,170) ft ((1,000–)1,600–2,800(–3,100) m). Widespread in, and exclusive to, the eastern Pyrenees and the Alps.

## 200 POTENTILLA NITIDA L.
Pink Cinquefoil

**Family** *Rosaceae*
**Description** A prostrate-spreading, woody branched plant, forming dense silvery greenish-grey mats. Branches short, contorted, with short trifoliate leaves on short petioles. Leaflets obovate or obovate-lanceolate, golden-pilose, ¼–½ in (5–10 mm) long, acute or more often with 3 minute apical teeth. Flowers pink or pinkish-red, open, solitary or in groups of 2–3 at the apex of the branchlets. Epicalyx linear-lobed; calyx with 5 lanceolate, acuminate sepals. Corolla 5 petals, approx. ½ in (10–12 mm) long, sub-rounded or broadly obovate, entire or emarginate, with a short claw.
**Size** ¾–2(–4) ins (2–5(–10) cm).
**Flowering period** (June–)July–September.
**Ecology and distribution** Rocks, natural detritus and stabilized rubble, on a calcareous or dolomitic subsoil, from (3,935 to 10,500 ft (1,200–3,200 m). Fairly frequent in the calcareous Alps, especially in the outer northern and southern zones, and the northern Apennines.

## 201 POTENTILLA VALDERIA L.

**Family** *Rosaceae*
**Description** A tufted, spreading herbaceous plant, greyish-green, very branched at the base, with ascending, often apically incurved, branches. Leaves palmatisect, with 5–7 leaflets, oblanceolate or obovate-spatulate, apically small-toothed, often silvery-grey and tomentose on the underside. Inflorescences with few yellowish-white or creamy-white flowers on short peduncles. Bracts lanceolate, pilose with long spreading hairs. Calyx and epicalyx consisting of lanceolate-acuminate, conspicuously pilose, upwardly converging lobes. Petals 5, slightly shorter than the sepals, flask-shaped, being apically converging and then opening out. Stamens greenish-yellow.
**Size** 8–16(–20) ins (20–40(–50) cm).
**Flowering period** July–August.
**Ecology and distribution** Rocks, detritus of the lower slopes, stony and arid grassy places, on an acid subsoil, from 3,935 to 7,875 ft (1,200–2,400 m). Very rare and endemic to the Alpes Maritimes, on the granite massif of Argentera.

## 202  PRIMULA AURICULA L.

Bear's-ear, Auricula

**Family** *Primulaceae*
**Description** An acaulescent, herbaceous plant, with a short rhizome and a basal rosette of obovate or oblong-spatulate, fleshy leaves, sub-sessile or attenuate into a short petiole, entire or slightly dentate with a narrow cartilaginous margin, light-green or glaucous-green, sometimes mealy, 2–5 ins (5–12 cm) long. Flowering stem with a dense terminal umbel of 2–10(–15) yellow flowers, borne in the axil of a corona of small bracts. Calyx tubular. Corolla, ⅝–1 in (1.5–2.5 cm) wide, funnel-shaped, with a cylindrical tube, white throat inside and a spreading limb formed of 5 obovate, retuse lobes.
**Size** 2–6(–10) ins (5–15(–25) cm).
**Flowering period** (April–)May–July.
**Ecology and distribution** Crags, rock crevices, stony pastures, on a calcareous subsoil, from (2,625–)5,250 to 8,200(–9,515) ft ((800–)1,600–2,500(–2,900) m). Very common in the calcareous Alps, Jura, Vosges, Apennines, Dinaric Alps and Carpathians.
**Notes** This species shows a certain variability which has made it possible to identify several subspecies that differ in leaf shape and degree of pilosity. Nearly all primulas are protected plants, especially those with pink or red flowers.

## 203  PRIMULA CLARKEI Watt

**Family** *Primulaceae*
**Description** A small perennial, sub-acaulescent, tufted with numerous flowering stems. Leaves mostly basal, close together, petiolate, with a flat or nearly winged petiole; blade ½–¾ in (1–2 cm) long and wide, sub-rounded or almost kidney-shaped, cordate at the base and slightly emarginate at the apex, denticulate. Flowers pink, solitary at the apex of the flowering stems. Calyx tubular, approx. ¼ in (5–7 mm) long, covered with minute glands. Corolla funnel-shaped, with a tube twice as long as the calyx, divided into two parts, the lower one more constricted and the upper one wider, yellowish; limb open, circular, flattened, ½–¾ in (1–2 cm) wide, with yellow throat and obovate lobes, emarginate, white nearest the throat extending into pink.
**Size** 3¼–5 ins (8–12 cm).
**Flowering period** July–August.
**Ecology and distribution** Damp rocks, shaded craggy places, on a mainly acid soil, from 6,890 to 8,200 ft (2,100–2,500 m). Endemic to the western Himalayas.

## 204   PRIMULA CLUSIANA  Tausch.
*P. integrifolia* L. in part; *P. spectabilis* Mert. et Koch

**Family**  *Primulaceae*
**Description**  An acaulescent, herbaceous plant with a short rhizome. Leaves ⅝–3½ ins (1.5–9 cm) long and ½–1¼ ins (1–3 cm) wide, in a basal rosette, shiny, ovate-lanceolate, almost leathery, entire, obtuse, with a narrow cartilaginous margin. Floral stalk short with a very sparse umbel of 1–2 flowers, rarely more. Flowers pink or violet-red with white throats, borne on short peduncles. Calyx campanulate, ½–⅝ in (10–14 mm) long, incised; corolla 1–3¼ ins (2.5–8 cm) wide, with a short tube and expanded limb, formed of 5 obcordate deeply emarginate or sub-incised lobes.
**Size**  ¾–4¼ ins (2–11 cm).
**Flowering period**  May–July.
**Ecology and distribution**  Rocks, stony, craggy places, on a calcareous subsoil, from 5,575 to 7,220 ft (1,700–2,200 m). Exclusive to the calcareous eastern Alps (Austrian and German Alps).
**Notes**  This species is related to other primulas which are endemic to the eastern and southern Alps: *P. glaucescens* (see number 207), *P. wulfeniana*, *P. spectabilis*, which can be distinguished from each other by their leaves and inflorescence. A protected plant.

---

## 205   PRIMULA ELATIOR  (L.) Hill
Oxlip, Paigle

**Family**  *Primulaceae*
**Description**  An acaulescent, herbaceous plant with a thick short rhizome. Leaves all basal, 4–6 ins (10–15 cm) long, clearly puckered, ovate or oblong, irregularly dentate, greyish-green, with a long winged petiole. Flower stem cylindrical, erect, pilose, with an apical unilateral umbel of 5–18 pendent flowers; floral peduncles about ½ in (1 cm) long, incurved. Flowers pale yellow with orange throats. Calyx cylindrical-angular, ⅝ in (15 mm) long, with 5 lanceolate teeth, ⅙ in (4 mm) long. Corolla funnel-shaped, with a tube approx. ¾ in (18–20 mm) wide, with 5 elliptical or broadly obovate, retuse lobes.
**Size**  4–12 ins (10–30 cm).
**Flowering period**  March–July(–August).
**Ecology and distribution**  Woodland clearings, pastures, alpine meadows and open grassy places, on any type of subsoil but with a preference for limestone, from (2,625–)3,280 to 7,220(–8,530) ft ((800–)1,000–2,200(–2,600) m). Frequent in all the mountains of central-southern Europe, as far north as Denmark and as far east as central-southern Russia; also common in the Urals and mountains of central Asia.

## 206 PRIMULA FARINOSA L.
Bird's-eye Primrose

**Family** *Primulaceae*
**Description** A herbaceous plant with a short, robust rhizome. Leaves ¾–2½ ins (2–6 cm) long, in a basal rosette, oblong-lanceolate-spatulate, whitish-green, smooth above, mealy-white below, slightly small-toothed on the margin. Flowering stem mealy with a compact terminal umbel, nearly flat, comprising 5–25 flowers with short pedicels. Flowers pink or violet-pink; calyx tubular, ⅛–⅙ in (3–4 mm) long, mealy. Corolla ⅝ in (15 mm) wide with a cylindrical tube, throat constricted, yellowish, and a round, flattened limb formed of 5 obovate-obcordate lobes, deeply emarginate, almost bilobed.
**Size** 2–6(–8) ins (5–15(–20) cm).
**Flowering period** May–July(–August).

**Ecology and distribution** Damp meadows and pastures, moist stabilized rubble, on any type of subsoil but with a preference for acid soils, from (1,640–)2,625 to 8,200 (–9,515) ft ((500–)800–2,500(–2,900) m). Very frequent in all the mountains of northern and central Europe (the Pyrenees, Alps, Jura, Carpathians, in the British Isles and Scandinavia); in northern-central and eastern Asia (Japan), the mountains of North America and in the southern Andes as far south as Tierra del Fuego. A protected plant.

## 207 PRIMULA GLAUCESCENS Moretti
*P. calycina* Duby

**Family** *Primulaceae*
**Description** An acaulescent, herbaceous plant with a short thick rhizome. Leaves 1¼–4 ins (3–10 cm) long, in a basal rosette, glaucous-green, stiff, lanceolate or oblong-lanceolate, entire, apically acuminate, with a cartilaginous margin. Flower stem with a terminal umbel of 2–7 flowers, on very short pedicels, in the axil of a corona of pale-coloured, erect, linear bracts. Calyx tubular, ¼–¾ in (7–20 mm) long. Corolla pink or violet-red, ¾–1¼ in (2–3 cm) wide, funnel-shaped, with a tube ½–¾ in (10–20 mm) long and a limb formed of 5 oblanceolate-bilobate, sometimes irregularly small-toothed lobes.
**Size** 2–6 in (5–15 cm).
**Flowering period** May–July.

**Ecology and distribution** Grassy places, stony fields and rock crevices, on a calcareous subsoil, from 3,280 to 7,875 ft (1,000–2,400 m). Endemic to the southern Alps.
**Notes** This species is related to other primulas in the cycle of *Primula clusiana* (see entry 204). A protected plant.

## 208 PRIMULA HIRSUTA All.
Red Alpine Primrose
*P. rubra* Gmel.; *P. viscosa* Vill.

**Family** *Primulaceae*
**Description** An acaulescent, tufted, herbaceous plant, with a thick rhizome branched on the surface to form several leafy rosettes. Leaves sparse in broadly round rosettes, rhombic or cuneiform, 1¼–3¼ ins (3–8 cm) long and ½–1½ ins (1–4 cm) wide, glandular-pubescent, abruptly attenuate into a short petiole, coarsely dentate. Flower stem short, glandular with an umbel of 1–4 flowers just rising above the leaves. Flowers numerous in each cluster, pink with white throats, borne on peduncles ⅙–½ in (4–10 mm) long. Calyx campanulate, ⅛–¼ in (3–7 mm) long, with 5 spreading teeth. Corolla ⅝–1 in (1.5–2.5 cm) wide with a short, white tube and a limb formed of 5 obcordate lobes, deeply incised.
**Size** ¾–4 ins (2–10 cm).
**Flowering period** (April–)May–July.
**Ecology and distribution** Rocks, damp detritus and stabilized rubble, on a siliceous subsoil, from (2,295–)3,935 to 9,840(–11,810) ft ((700–)1,200–3,000(–3,600) m). Found in the central and eastern Pyrenees and the Alps, especially the central and eastern ranges. A protected plant.

## 209 PRIMULA MARGINATA Curtis
Marginate Primrose

**Family** *Primulaceae*
**Description** An acaulescent, herbaceous plant with a shrubby, often very long rhizome. Leaves in a basal rosette, ¾–4 ins (2–10 cm) long, spatulate, fleshy, attenuate into a short petiole, mealy-white on the underside, with a conspicuously dentate margin. Flower stem erect with a dense umbel of 3–20 violet or pink, occasionally whitish, flowers. Peduncles longer than the bracts, pilose-mealy. Calyx short, mealy. Corolla ¾–1⅛ ins (18–28 mm) wide with a cylindrical tube and a flared limb of 5 obcordate lobes, slightly emarginate.
**Size** 1¼–5 ins (3–12 cm).
**Flowering period** May–July.
**Ecology and distribution** Stony places, natural debris, rock crevices, on a calcareous subsoil, from 3,280 to 8,530(–10,825) ft (1,000–2,600(–3,300) m). Endemic to the western Alps, from the Ligurian to the Cottian. Quite frequent. A protected plant.

## 210 PRIMULA PEDEMONTANA Thomas ex Gremli
Piedmont Primrose

**Family** *Primulaceae*
**Description** A robust, rhizomatous, acaulescent herbaceous plant, with a basal rosette of spatulate or obovate-lanceolate leaves, ¾–4 ins (2–10 cm) long and ½–1¼ ins (1–3 cm) wide, attenuate into a short petiole, entire or slightly dentate at the apex, smooth, hairless, shiny green, often covered with red glands, at least on the margin. Flower stem short, glandular, with a dense umbel of 2–10 bright pink flowers with white throats. Peduncles short. Calyx tubular-campanulate, ⅛–¼ in (4–6 mm) long, covered with reddish glands. Corolla ¾–1 in (2–2.5 cm) wide, with a very long cylindrical tube and a flared expanded limb, formed of 5 broadly obcordate, emarginate lobes.
**Size** 1½–5 ins (4–12 cm).
**Flowering period** June–July.
**Ecology and distribution** Rocks, exposed stony places, arid rocky pastures and crevices in rock faces, on a siliceous subsoil, from 4,595 to 9,840 ft (1,400–3,000 m). Endemic to the western Alps, especially characteristic of the Gran Paradiso massif in the Graian Alps. A related subspecies (*Primula pedemontana* subsp. *iberica*) has been identified in the Cantabrian Mountains of northern Spain. A protected plant.

---

## 211 PRIMULA VIALII Delavay ex Franch.
*P. littoniana*

**Family** *Primulaceae*
**Description** A herbaceous, acaulescent perennial, with a robust rhizome. Leaves numerous in a basal rosette, diffuse-erect, lanceolate or oblong-spatulate, 6–8 ins (15–20 cm) long and 2½–2¾ ins (6–7 cm) wide, apically obtuse, lengthily attenuate at the base into a broad, flat petiole, decurrent, irregularly dentate, pilose-hirsute especially on the prominent veins on the underside. Flowers pale violet or pink, slightly drooping, united into a very dense terminal spike at the apex of the cylindrical and robust flower stem. Inflorescence 2¾–5 ins (7–12 cm) long and 1–1⅜ ins (2.5–3.5 cm) wide. Calyx campanulate with 5 ovate-lanceolate, flame-red lobes, ⅛ in (4 mm) long. Corolla with a tube ½ in (10 mm) long and a concave limb, ⅙–⅓ in (6–8 mm) in diameter, formed of 5 lanceolate lobes, paler inside. Stamens enclosed.
**Size** 12–24 ins (30–60 cm).
**Flowering period** April–June.
**Ecology and distribution** Open sites, high altitude rocky places, from 6,560 to 11,485 ft (2,000–3,500 m). This species is restricted to the eastern Himalayas and the Yunnan range in southern China.

### 212 PTEROCEPHALUS PERENNIS Coult.

**Family** *Dipsacaceae*
**Description** A tufted, sub-acaulescent perennial, woody at the base, with 3–7 ascending stems emerging from the same tuft. Leaves ¾–2 ins (2–5 cm) long and approx. ¹⁄₁₆ in (0.5–1.5 cm) wide, close together towards the base, greyish-green or tomentose, lyrate or oblong-spatulate, crenate or dentate, the terminal lobe ovate or oblong. Flowers pink or pale red, united into dense flattened heads, about 1¼ ins (3 cm) in diameter, surrounded by a corona of lanceolate bracts, ⅓–⅝ in (8–15 mm) long. Calyx ½–⅝ in (12–14 mm) long, with 12–18 small purple or dark red bristles. Corolla tubular-campanulate, ½–¾ in (12–20 mm).
**Size** 1¼–5 ins (3–12 cm).
**Flowering period** July–August.
**Ecology and distribution** Crags, rocky slopes and acid rocky areas in general, from 3,280 to 5,905(–6,560) ft (1,000–1,800(–2,000)) m). Found in the mountains of the south-western and southern Balkan peninsula: eastern Albania, north-western and south-eastern Greece.
**Notes** Endemic to the mountains of Albania and Greece.

---

### 213 PULSATILLA VERNALIS (L.) Miller

*Anemone vernalis* L.
Spring Pasque Flower

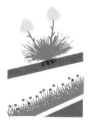

**Family** *Ranunculaceae*
**Description** A herbaceous, tufted, more or less stem-less, rhizomatous perennial, with basal evergreen leaves. Leaves on short petioles, slightly pilose or nearly hairless, pinnatifid with 3–5 dentate segments; stem leaves with linear segments, united to form a corona immediately under the flower, pilose-silky with yellowish-silver hairs. Flowers white inside and violet or pink outside, solitary, drooping then erect, consisting of a petal-like calyx (perianth), 1½–2½ ins (4–6 cm) wide. Perianth at first shaped like an incurving cup then broadening out, vil-lose outside, formed of 6 elliptical segments, ovate or obovate, briefly acuminate.
**Size** 2–6 ins (5–15 cm); up to 14 ins (35 cm) when plant is in fruit.
**Flowering period** April–June(–July) – flowering starts immediately the snow melts.
**Ecology and distribution** Pastures, grassy and stony places, on any type of subsoil, from (4,265–)4,920 to 8,860(–11,810) ft ((1,300–)1,500–2,700(–3,600) m). Fre-quent in all European mountains, from Scandinavia to the Sierra Nevada in Spain, and from the Apennines in Italy to Bulgaria; in central Europe it also grows at lower levels on the plains. A protected species.

## 214  PULSATILLA ALPINA  (L.) Delarbre
Alpine Anemone
*Anemone alpina* L.

**Family**  *Ranunculaceae*

**Description**  A more or less stemless, tufted perennial with a short, robust rhizome. Leaves mainly basal on long petioles, pubescent or nearly tomentose, bipinnatisect, with 2–3 pairs of segments, oblong-lanceolate, deeply incised, formed of lanceolate-acuminate lobes, often all incurved on one side. Stem leaves similar to basals and with short, wide-open petiole, united in a whorl to form a broad, showy corona under the flower. Flowers solitary at the apex of the stem, 1½–3¼ ins (4–8 cm) in diameter, more or less erect, colour variable from white to yellow according to the subspecies, formed of a solitary petal-like calyx (perianth); corolla absent. Perianth open, star-shaped, consisting of 6–7 hairless or silky, oval or rhombic, apically obtuse or acute segments. Stamens numerous, yellow. Infructescence showy, feathery.

**Size**  4–14 ins (10–35 cm); up to 18 ins (45 cm) when plant is in fruit.

**Flowering period**  May–July(–August).

**Ecology and distribution**  Pastures, alpine meadows, grassy places, woodland clearings, on variable subsoils according to the subspecies, from (3,280–)3,935 to 8,860 ft ((1,000–)1,200–2,700 m). Very widespread and frequent in all the mountains of central-southern Europe (the Pyrenees, Jura, Alps, Apennines, Carpathians, mountains of the Balkan peninsula and the Caucasus). Sometimes mistaken for a different species found in the Rocky Mountains, now identified as *P. occidentalis.*

**Notes**  Two subspecies, differing in the colour of their flowers and their ecology, are especially notable: subsp. *alpina* which is calcicole and has white or (rarely) red flowers (opposite, above), and subsp. *apiifolia* (or subsp. *sulphurea*), which lives on siliceous subsoils and has yellow flowers (opposite, below). *P. alpina* is a protected species.

**215  PULSATILLA RUBRA** (Lam.) Jord.
*Anemone rubra* Lam.

**Family**  *Ranunculaceae*
**Description**  A sub-acaulescent herbaceous perennial
with pubescent, stalked, basal leaves, usually tri-pinnate.
Leaf segments divided into narrow lobes. Stem leaves,
resembling the basals, sub-divided into about 20 lobes,
often forming a corona-like involucre borne at some
distance from the flower. The flowers are reddish-brown
or purplish-red, sometimes violet-coloured, pendulous
and carried terminally; they are formed of a petal-like
calyx consisting of 5–6 lanceolate segments 2-2½ times
longer than the stamens. There is no corolla.
**Size**  1¼–4 ins (3–10 cm); up to 18 ins (45 cm) when
plant is in fruit.
**Flowering period**  March–May (–June).
**Ecology and distribution**  Dry meadowlands, stony pastures, woodland glades; usually on a calcareous or sandy
subsoil, from 1,640 to 5,905 (500–1,800 m). Grows sporadically in the mountains of central and southern France
and central-eastern Spain as well as in the Pyrenees.
**Notes**  This species is closely related to *P. pratensis* and
*P. montana*, both of which are more commonly found in
the mountains of central and southern Europe. These two
species have between 25–30 lobes in their stem leaves
while *P. rubra* has fewer (see above).

## 215 (a)

## PULSATILLA HALLERI  (All.) Willd.
*Anemone halleri* All.

**Family**  *Ranunculaceae*
**Description**  A tufted, sub-acaulescent perennial with a
dense basal rosette of pinnatifid, pilose-woolly leaves.
Leaf blade divided into 3–5 segments which are sub-
divided into 2–3 oblong-lanceolate lobes. Stem leaves
sparse, usually joined to form a corona at some
distance from the flower. Pale violet or violet-coloured
flowers of erect habit, 2–3¼ ins (5–8 cm) in diameter,
growing singly at the apex of the stems; petal-like calyx
consists of 6 ovate-lanceolate or lanceolate wide-
spreading segments. There is no corolla.
**Size**  2–6 ins (5–15 cm); up to 16 ins (40 cm) when plant
is in fruit.
**Flowering period**  (May–) June–July.
**Ecology and distribution**  Meadowlands, pastures and
stony places, on a neutral or acid subsoil, from 3,280 to
9,840 ft (1,000–3,000 m). Grows sporadically in the Alps
and Carpathians as well as in the mountains of the Balkan
peninsula, the Crimea and Anatolia.
**Notes**  A montane species containing numerous subspecies, each localized within a very limited mountain
area. The commonest subspecies is *halleri* which is only
to be found in the south-western and central Alps.

## 216 PUYA RAIMONDII Harms

**Family** *Bromeliaceae*

**Description** An arborescent, perennial plant adapted to very dry areas. Characteristic habit represented by a single trunk, felty-woody, coarse, thick, 20–32 ins (50–80 cm) in diameter, very slow growing, covered at the bottom with the scales of fallen leaves from the preceding years. Leaves overlapping, dense, close together in a conspicuous, more or less spherical apical tuft, 6 ft 8 ins–8 ft 4 ins (2–2.5 m) from the ground in adult plants, linear-channelled or sword-like, spinose-dentate on the margin, leathery, erect and strongly acuminate at the apex, often with a divergent point, the lower leaves becoming more and more incurved downwards as they dry out, up to 3 ft 4 ins–5 ft (1–1.5 m) long. Flowers united in a very tall spike-like inflorescence, dense and compact, cylindrical-oblong, up to 10 ft–16 ft 8 ins (3–5 m) long, consisting of numerous floral racemes, equipped with long bracts protruding from the inflorescence. Flowers greenish-white, formed of a tubular flower with 6 oblanceolate lobes, up to 2 ins (5 cm) long, hairless.

**Size** 16 ft 8 ins–30 ft (5–9 m) – the flowering plant.

**Flowering period** Nearly all the year – October–March; May–June; and in other periods, too.

**Ecology and distribution** Found in the high montane steppes and high altitude dry pastures, from 11,485 to 14,765 ft (3,500–4,500 m). Exclusive to the Peruvian Andes, where it is comparatively rare.

**Notes** The genus *Puya* comprises 140 species, nearly all Andean. *P. raimondii* is a species that certainly deserves protection because of its rarity and scientific interest. Many species of *Puya* are characteristic of the high barren *páramos* and, in particular, of the bleak Andean *puna* where other forms of arborescent plants are quite frequent, such as the composites of the genus *Espeletia* and numerous *Cactaceae* (*Cereus, Echinocactus, Lobivia,* etc.).

## 217  **RAMONDA MYCONI** (L.) Reichenb.
*Ramonda pyrenaica* Rich.; *Verbascum myconi* L.

**Family** *Gesneriaceae*
**Description** An acaulescent perennial, with a flat basal rosette of strongly wrinkled, hirsute leaves, ¾–2½ ins (2–6 cm) long and ½–2 ins (1–5 cm) wide, rhombic-sub-rounded or oval, obtuse, crenate-dentate, on short petioles, covered with short white hairs above and with dense, long orange hairs beneath. Flower stems 2–5, each with one or more flowers. Flowers violet or violet-blue, with a circular, flattened corolla 1¼–1½ ins (3–4 cm) in diameter, a short white tube and yellow throat; corolla lobes 5, slightly unequal. Anthers yellow, mucronate, projecting.

**Size** 2½–5 ins (6–12 cm).
**Flowering period** June–August.
**Ecology and distribution** Rock crevices, shady crags, rocks in montane woods, on a calcareous subsoil, from (1,970–)2,625 to 5,905 ft ((600–)800–1,800 m). Endemic to the central and eastern Pyrenees as well as the mountains of north-eastern Spain.
**Notes** An interesting montane plant included in this book because it is one of the four European species of *Gesneriaceae*; this family consists almost exclusively of tropical and sub-tropical plants (e.g. *Gloxinia*).

---

## 218  **RAMONDA NATHALIAE** Pančić et Petrović

**Family** *Gesneriaceae*
**Description** A perennial acaulescent plant, with a flattened basal rosette of wrinkled, hirsute, leaves, 1¼–2 ins (3–5 cm) long and ½–1¼ ins (1–3 cm) wide, ovate or sub-rounded, truncate at the base, entire or slightly crenate, with short petioles. Flower stem glandular-pubescent, with 1–3 lilac or pale violet flowers. Corolla open and flattened-circular, 1¼–1⅜ ins (3–3.5 cm) in diameter, with a short, white tube, yellowish throat and a limb coloured as above; corolla lobes 4, occasionally 5, slightly unequal. Anthers obtuse, protruding slightly from the corolla, sometimes yellow with bluish shading.

**Size** 2½–3¼ ins (6–8 cm) – the flowering stem.
**Flowering period** May–July.
**Ecology and distribution** Shady rocks, crags and precipices and rock crevices, on a calcareous subsoil, from 4,920 to 8,200 ft (1,500–2,500 m). Endemic to the mountains of southern Yugoslavia and northern Greece.
**Notes** This plant is of interest for the same reasons as explained in the Notes to *Ramonda myconi* (see entry 217).

## 219 RANUNCULUS ALPESTRIS L.
Alpine Buttercup

**Family** *Ranunculaceae*
**Description** A small, perennial, tufted-spreading, plant, with a short rhizome and fibrous roots. Stems numerous, sub-acaulescent. Basal leaves numerous, petal-like, shiny green, small, generally sub-rounded, palmate-lobed divided into 3–5 crenate lobes, separated by rounded incisions. Stem leaves 1–2, tripartite or simple. Flowers white, 1–3 to each flowering stem, ¾ in (2 cm) wide. Calyx hairless. Corolla of 5–7 slightly emarginate, broadly obovate or obcordate petals, sometimes overlapping each other. Stamens numerous, yellow; achenes small, hairless on a hairless receptacle.
**Size** 1¼–5 ins (3–12 cm).
**Flowering period** June–September(–October).
**Ecology and distribution** Damp meadows, rocks, stabilized rubble, stony places in general, on a calcareous subsoil, from 4,265 to 8,530(–9,840) ft (1,300–2,600 (–3,000) m). Frequent in the Pyrenees, especially the eastern range, the Jura, Alps, northern and central Apennines and Carpathians.

---

## 220 RANUNCULUS GLACIALIS L.
Glacier Crowfoot

**Family** *Ranunculaceae*
**Description** A herbaceous, tufted-spreading, sub-acaulescent, hairless plant, with ascending stems. Leaves fleshy, petal-like, shiny green, palmate-tripartite; leaflets on small petioles, palmate-divided into 3–5 elliptical or oblong, acute segments. Stem leaves smaller, less divided. Flowers white or pink, 1–1⅜ ins (2.5–3.5 cm) wide, tending to redden after flowering. Sepals pubescent, covered with brown-red hairs. Corolla cup-shaped, persistent after flowering, with 5 petals broadly obovate, overlapping each other. Stamens numerous, yellowish-green.
**Size** 1½–10 ins (4–25 cm).
**Flowering period** July–September(–October).
**Ecology and distribution** Natural detritus, moraines, stabilized rubble, the pebbly ground flanking streams and wet stony places, preferably on a siliceous subsoil, from (4,920–)7,545 to 12,140 ft ((1,500–)2,300–3,700 m). In Switzerland it has been found at the summit of the Finsteraarhorn at 15,500 ft (4,275 m); this is the highest altitude at which a vascular plant has ever been seen in Europe. Quite frequent in the mountains of central and southern Europe (the Pyrenees, Sierra Nevada, Alps and Carpathians); especially widespread in the Arctic regions of Europe.

## 221 RANUNCULUS HYBRIDUS Biria
*R. pseudothora* Host

**Family** *Ranunculaceae*
**Description** A small, tufted perennial with fasciculate roots. Flowering stems, numerous, with several basal, greyish-green leaves, wider than long, kidney-shaped, coarsely dentate or nearly incised to the upper margin, on long petioles. Stem leaves sparse (1–3), smaller than the basal, sessile. Flowers yellow or golden-yellow, solitary or at most 2–3 at the apex of the flowering stems. Calyx, 5 short sepals, slightly shorter than the petals. Corolla ½–1 in (1–2.5 cm) wide, with 5 petals, obovate, concave, rounded. Stamens numerous, yellow; achenes small, with a short beak.
**Size** 4–6 ins (10–15 cm).
**Flowering period** June–August.
**Ecology and distribution** Stony places, detritus of the lower slopes, stabilized rubble and rock crevices, on a calcareous subsoil, from (3,280–)4,920 to 8,200 ft ((1,000–) 1,500–2,500 m). Quite common in the eastern calcareous and dolomitic Alps, from Lake Garda to Austria, the northern Dinaric Alps and central Apennines.
**Notes** This plant is highly poisonous.

---

## 222 RANUNCULUS MONTANUS Willd.
Mountain Buttercup
*R. geraniifolius* Pourr.

**Family** *Ranunculaceae*
**Description** A tufted, branched herbaceous plant, very variable in form and height, with a branched rhizome and numerous basal leaves on long petioles, sub-rounded, deeply divided into 3–5 obovate, dentate lobes, with ovate-obtuse teeth. Stem leaves smaller, deeply divided into 3–5 linear segments, entire or slightly dentate. Flowers yellow or pale yellow, solitary or in groups of 2–3. Calyx pubescent or tomentose. Corolla ¾–1⅜ ins (2–3.5 cm), with 5 obovate, concave petals.
**Size** (2–)4–12(–20) ins ((5–)10–30(–50) cm).
**Flowering period** May–August(–September).
**Ecology and distribution** Woods, pastures, detritus of the lower slopes and stabilized rubble, on any type of subsoil, from 3,280 to 9,185(–10,170) ft (1,000–2,800 (–3,100) m). Very common in all the mountains of central and southern Europe, the Caucasus, Anatolia and North Africa.
**Notes** A very variable species, now sub-divided into at least 13 related species, generally with very localized distribution, e.g. *R. gouanii* which is endemic to the Pyrenees, *R. venetus* to the eastern Alps and *R. croaticus* to the south-western Balkan peninsula.

## 223  RANUNCULUS PARNASSIFOLIUS L.

**Family** *Ranunculaceae*
**Description**  A herbaceous plant, acaulescent or nearly so, with a short, tufted rhizome. Basal leaves, stalked, greyish blue-green, with an elliptical, ovate-cordate or broadly lanceolate blade, with 5–7 almost parallel veins. Stem leaves sparse, narrow, sessile, amplexicaul. Flowers white, sometimes tinged with pink, borne terminally at the apex of the stem which may be simple or slightly branched. Flowers 1 to 10 on each stem, with a pubescent calyx, and corolla ¾–1 in (2–2.5 cm) wide. Petals 5, broadly obovate, concave, overlapping each other. Stamens yellow; achenes short, short-beaked.
**Size**  2–4(–12) ins (5–10(–30) cm).
**Flowering period**  July–August.
**Ecology and distribution**  Rocky places, stabilized rubble, moraines, rocky and earthy slopes, with a preference for limestone, from 6,235 to 9,515 ft (1,900–2,900 m). Sometimes found in the Pyrenees, the mountains of northern Spain and northern Alps; it is very rare in the western Alps, Rhaetian Alps and Dolomites.

## 224  RANUNCULUS PYRENAEUS L.
Pyrenean Buttercup

**Family** *Ranunculaceae*
**Description**  A tufted, herbaceous, more or less stemless plant with a thick, vertical, fibrous rhizome. Leaves mostly basal, linear, linear-spatulate or narrowly lanceolate, sessile, parallel-veined. Stem leaves sparse, linear, short. Flowers white, solitary, in groups of up to 10. Peduncles pubescent near the top. Calyx with 5 whitish, hairless sepals. Corolla ½–¾ in (1–2 cm) wide, with 5–6 petals, concave, obovate, sometimes overlapping each other. Stamens numerous, yellow, short; achenes rhomboidal, swollen, smooth.
**Size**  2–6(–8) ins (5–15(–20) cm).
**Flowering period**  May–July.
**Ecology and distribution**  Pastures, damp meadows, grassy and earthy slopes, on any type of subsoil although most frequently on limestone, from 5,250 to 8,860 (–9,840) ft (1,600–2,700(–3,000) m). Very common in the mountains of the Iberian peninsula (Sierra Nevada, Cantabrian Mountains), the Pyrenees and in Corsica.

## 225 RANUNCULUS SEGUIERI Vill.

**Family** *Ranunculaceae*
**Description** A tufted, spreading, pubescent or nearly hairless, herbaceous plant, with numerous sub-acaulescent ascending stems. Leaves mostly basal, stalked, palmatifid with 3–5 lobes deeply incise-flabellate and segments lanceolate or linear, acuminate; main incisions broad, secondary incisions very narrow, acute. Stem leaves 1–2, smaller than the basals. Flowers white, ¾–1 in (2–2.5 cm) wide, solitary at apex of the flowering stems. Calyx hairless. Corolla with 5 concave petals, entire or slightly notched at the apex. Stamens numerous; achenes small, ovoid, borne on a pubescent receptacle.
**Size** 3¼–8 ins (8–20 cm).
**Flowering period** June–July.

**Ecology and distribution** Stabilized rubble, detritus of the lower slopes, on a calcareous subsoil, from 5,905 to 8,200(–11,155) ft (1,800–2,500(–3,400) m). Quite frequent in the Cantabrian Mountains and western Alps but slightly less so in the calcareous central and eastern Alps, central Apennines and Dinaric Alps.

---

## 226 RAOULIA GLABRA Hook. f.

**Family** *Compositae*
**Description** A prostrate-spreading herbaceous plant, with numerous ascending, slender branches forming a fairly dense carpet. Leaves very close together, almost overlapping, growing up the stem to just below the head, linear or oblong, acute, hairless, often outwardly incurved, approx. ¼ in (4–5 mm) long. Flowers pure white in heads ¼–½ in (7–10 mm) wide, borne apically on the fertile stems. External involucral bracts similar to the leaves; internal bracts white, linear. Ray-florets female; disc-florets tubular, bisexual, numerous, approx. ¼ in (5 mm) long. Achenes small, oblong, pubescent, with a pappus of up to ¼ in (5 mm).
**Size** 2–10 ins (5–25 cm).
**Flowering period** November–February.

**Ecology and distribution** Stony or rocky places, open pastures and dry detritus, from (1,970–)2,625 to 4,920 ft ((600–)800–1,500 m). Endemic to the mountains of New Zealand.
**Notes** The genus *Raoulia* comprises scarcely more than 20 species, nearly all of which are endemic to New Zealand.

## 227 RHINANTHUS SUBALPINUS Wettst.
Yellow-rattle

**Family** *Scrophulariaceae*
**Description** An annual, erect, herbaceous plant, stem, angular, simple or slightly branched. Leaves opposite, broadly lanceolate, shorter than the internodes, crenate-dentate. Flowers yellow in a dense terminal inflorescence consisting of whorls of 2–4 flowers at each node. Bracts shorter than the leaves, ovate, oblong or triangular, dentate, with basal teeth longer than the apicals, lengthily acuminate and almost aristate. Calyx hairless, somewhat urn-shaped, laterally compressed, with 5 acute teeth. Corolla bilabiate, with a cylindrical tube and a two-lipped limb: upper lip helmet-shaped terminating at the top in two violet teeth; lower lip three-lobed.
**Size** 2–12(–20) ins (5–30(–50) cm).
**Flowering period** June–July(–August).
**Ecology and distribution** Pastures and grassy slopes on any type of subsoil, from 5,905 to 8,200 ft (1,800–2,500 m). Frequent in the Alps, especially in the central and eastern ranges.
**Notes** There are numerous species of the genus *Rhinanthus* in the Alps which are very similar to each other, hybridizing easily.

## 228 RHODODENDRON FERRUGINEUM L.
Alpenrose or Alpine rose

**Family** *Ericaceae*
**Description** A bushy, evergreen, much branched shrub. Leaves hairless, oblong or lanceolate, 1¼–2 ins (3–5 cm) long, ½–¾ in (1–2 cm) wide, upper surface dark green and shiny, under surface rust-coloured with glandular scales. Flowers pink or violet-red, pedunculate, united into a terminal raceme. Corolla tubular at first, then funnel-shaped-campanulate, slightly irregular, ½–⅝ in (1–1.5 cm) long, divided into 5 obtuse lobes, often almost at right-angles to the peduncle.
**Size** (8–)20–40(–48) ins ((20–)50–100(–120) cm).
**Flowering period** May–July(–August).
**Ecology and distribution** High altitude moorlands, sparse woods, pastures and stony places, preferably on a siliceous subsoil, from (1,640–)4,920 to 9,840(–10,500) ft ((500–)1,500–3,000(–3,200) m). Very common in all the mountains of southern Europe (the Pyrenees, Jura, Alps, northern Apennines and Dinaric Alps).
**Notes** A very slow-growing, protected species.

## 229 RHODODENDRON HIRSUTUM L.
Hairy Alpenrose or Hairy Alpine Rose

**Family** *Ericaceae*
**Description** An erect, evergreen, much branched, pilose shrub. Leaves oblong, ciliate on the margin, similar to those of *R. ferrugineum* but green on the underside with reddish glands. Flowers light pink or deep pink in terminal racemes. Corolla funnel-shaped campanulate, approx. ⅝ in (1.3–1.5 cm) long, and then as for previous species.
**Size** (8–)12–40(–48) ins ((20–)30–100(–120) cm).
**Flowering period** (May–)June–August.
**Ecology and distribution** Stony places, pastures, rocky debris, bed terraces and exposed crags, on a calcareous subsoil, from (1,640–)3,935 to 7,875(–8,530) ft ((500–)1,200–2,400(–2,600) m). Common in the central and eastern Alps (but rarer in Savoy), the Jura, Carpathians and mountains of the north-western Balkan peninsula.
**Notes** A protected plant.

## 230 RHODOTHAMNUS CHAMAECISTUS
(L.) Reichb.
Dwarf Alpenrose or Dwarf Alpine Rose
*Rhododendron chamaecistus* L.

**Family** *Ericaceae*
**Description** A much-branched, dwarf shrub, with densely leafy branches. Leaves leathery, hairless, ciliate on the margin, ovate or oblong-lanceolate, ⅓–½ in (8–10 mm) long and approx. ⅛ in (2–4 mm) wide, green on both sides. Flowers pale pink or red, in groups of 2–3 in terminal inflorescences. Corolla regular, open, with a very short tube and 5-lobed, broadly ovate, limb. Stamens 10 with red anthers, lengthily protruding and spreading.
**Size** 4–12(–16) ins (10–30(–40) cm).
**Flowering period** (May–)June–July(–August) – the flowers often open before the snow has completely thawed.
**Ecology and distribution** Rocks, stabilized rubble, stony places and shady screes, on a calcareous or dolomitic subsoil, from (2,625–)4,265 to 6,890(–8,530) ft ((800–)1,300–2,100(–2,600) m). Widespread in the eastern Alps, the southern peripheral zones to the east of Lake Como and north to the east of the Allgäuer Alps as far as Carinthia in Austria.
**Notes** Endemic to the eastern Alps; a protected plant.

## 231 ROSA PENDULINA L.
Alpine Rose, Wild Rose of the Alps
*R. alpina*

**Family** *Rosaceae*
**Description** A small, usually erect, much branched shrub, generally spiny with short straight prickles which are sometimes absent on the upper branches. Leaves alternate, pinnate-compound, hairless, green or yellowish-green, consisting of 7–11 leaflets, elliptical, serrate, ¾–2 ins (2–5 cm) long. Flowers deep pink or purplish-red, solitary or in groups of 2–3. Calyx formed of 5 lanceolate sepals, prolonged by a long point, tomentose inside. Corolla 1¼–2½ ins (3–6.5 cm) wide, consisting of 5 broadly obovate or irregularly sub-rounded, truncate petals. Stamens numerous, yellow. Fruit ovoid-oblong, red.
**Size** 12–60(–80) ins (30–150(–200) cm).
**Flowering period** (May–)June–August.
**Ecology and distribution** Pastures, open grassy places, sparse woods and rocky places, on any type of subsoil, from (1,640–)2,625 to 8,530 ft ((500–)800–2,600 m). Quite common in the Pyrenees, Alps, Apennines, Auvergne, Vosges, Jura, Carpathians and mountains of the Balkan peninsula.
**Notes** The petals and fruit (hips), which contain a tannic substance, are used for their astringent properties in home-made medicines.

---

## 232 SALIX HERBACEA L.
Least Willow

**Family** *Salicaceae*
**Description** A small, prostrate plant with rooting, creeping, underground stems, branched below ground, from which emerge short epigeal branchlets. Leaves sparse, ¼–¾ in (0.5–2 cm) long and ⅓–1 in (0.8–2.5 cm) wide, sub-rounded or almost kidney-shaped, serrate, bright green, hairless, with clearly visible veins. Flowers united in very short axillary or terminal catkins, ¼–⅝ in (0.5–1.5 cm) long, greenish-yellow, with 2–12 sessile flowers.
**Size** ¾–1½ ins (2–4 cm) – the flowering plant.
**Flowering period** June–August.
**Ecology and distribution** Damp meadows, moist detritic slopes, snow-beds, on a mainly siliceous granite or diorite subsoil, from 5,905 to 9,185(–11,155) ft (1,800–2,800(–3,400) m). Common in all European mountains (the Pyrenees, Alps, Apennines, Carpathians, Balkan Mountains, Scottish Highlands, and in Scandinavia); also widespread in the Arctic regions of Asia and North America.
**Notes** This species often forms very extensive uniform populations (*Salicetum herbaceae*) typical of the higher altitudes.

## 233 SALIX RETICULATA L.
Netted Willow, Reticulate Willow

**Family** *Salicaceae*
**Description** A dwarf, woody plant with very branched, creeping, underground stems. Branchlets short, erect, with a few leaves ¾–1¼ ins (2–3 cm) long, alternate, oval, obovate or sub-rounded, entire, leathery, often cordate at the base, dark green above and whitish beneath, with a clearly visible, intricate network of veins. Male flowers united in short, erect or ascending catkins, sub-cylindrical, reddish, ⅝–1¼ ins (1.5–3 cm) long; female flowers in greenish-grey catkins.
**Size** ¾–2 ins (2–5 cm) – the flowering plant.
**Flowering period** June–August.
**Ecology and distribution** Rocky slopes, boulders, rocks and stony detritus, mainly on a calcareous subsoil, from (4,265–)5,905 to 9,840(–11,155) ft ((1,300–)1,800–3,000 (–3,400) m). Very common and frequent in the mountains of central Europe (the Pyrenees, Alps and Carpathians), rarer in the mountains of northern Europe; also found in the Urals, the Altai Mountains in central Asia and the Arctic zones of Asia and North America.
**Notes** This is a typical colonizing species of detritic sites and rocky slopes where it forms, in company with *Salix retusa*, a typical vegetal pioneer association (*Salicetum retusae-reticulatae*).

---

## 234 SALIX RETUSA L.
Blunt-leaved Willow

**Family** *Salicaceae*
**Description** A dwarf, creeping plant with very branched prostrate stems forming lax carpets. Leaves alternate, very close together, green on both sides, ½–¾ in (1–2 cm) long, oblong or oblanceolate, hairless, on short petioles, apically truncate or emarginate. Flowers united in short terminal, erect or ascending catkins, ovoid or oblong, greenish-yellow, ⅝–¾ in (1.5–2 cm) long, with 8–10 flowers. Stamens long, with reddish anthers protruding.
**Size** ¾–1½ ins (2–4 cm) – the flowering plant.
**Flowering period** (June–)July–August.
**Ecology and distribution** Pastures, rocky places, detritus and stabilized rubble, from (3,935–)4,920 to 9,840(–11,155) ft ((1,200–)1,500–3,000(–3,400) m). Very common and frequent in all European mountains (the Pyrenees, Alps, Jura, Apennines, Carpathians, Balkan Mountains and the Scottish Highlands). Similar species are also found in the Altai Mountains of central Asia.
**Notes** This is a very common species on high altitude rocky detritus and stabilized rubble, where it forms a typical association with *Salix reticulata*.

## 235 SAPONARIA CAESPITOSA DC.
Tufted Soapwort

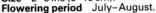

**Family** *Caryophyllaceae*
**Description** A small plant forming dense, leafy tufts with several erect, unbranched stems, each of which has 2–4 pairs of stem leaves. Basal leaves closely packed, linear-lanceolate. Flowers deep pink, sub-sessile, in dense apical cymes. Calyx cylindrical, greenish at first then dark red, densely pilose. Corolla open, almost circular-flattened, ⅓–⅝ in (8–14 mm) in diameter; petals 5, broadly ovate, rounded or apically sub-truncate, with slender arcuate scales on throat.
**Size** 2–6 ins (5–15 cm).
**Flowering period** July–August.
**Ecology and distribution** Rocks, natural debris and detritus of the lower slopes, from 5,905 to 8,200 ft (1,800–2,500 m). An uncommon plant, endemic to the central Pyrenees.

## 236 SAPONARIA LUTEA L.
Yellow Soapwort

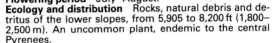

**Family** *Caryophyllaceae*
**Description** A herbaceous plant with a rhizomatous, slightly branched stem; branches erect, pilose, simple, with a dense tuft of linear leaves at the base, often arching outwards; leaves ¼–½ in (6–12 mm) long. Stem leaves opposite, in 2–3 pairs. Flowers pale yellow, in a terminal head, sessile or sub-sessile. Calyx pilose, cylindrical. Corolla ⅓–½ in (8–10 mm) in diameter. Petals 5, with a deep violet claw and a yellow or golden-yellow limb, obovate or oblanceolate, often spatulate. Stamens and styles well protruding from the throat; filaments dark at first, becoming white; anthers yellowish-white.
**Size** 2–6 ins (5–15 cm).
**Flowering period** (June–)July–August.
**Ecology and distribution** Rocks, cliff faces, stony places and rocky pastures, on calcareous soil, from (4,920–)6,560 to 8,530 ft ((1,500–)2,000–2,600 m). Endemic to the western Alps, from the Graian Alps and Alpes du Dauphiné to the cantons of Valais and Ticino. Rather rare and relatively frequent only in the Gran Paradiso Mountains in the Valle d'Aosta, Italy.

## 237 SAUSSUREA ALPINA (L.) DC.
*Serratula alpina* L.

**Family** *Compositae*
**Description** A perennial plant with basal leaves in a lax rosette. Stem erect, basal leaves numerous, narrowly ovate or lanceolate, on short petioles, dark green on the upper surface and woolly-white on the underside; stem leaves, sparse, linear, sessile, entire or slightly dentate. Flowers violet-pink in shortly pedunculate heads, 4–12, in a compact corymb at the apex of the stem. Heads ovoid-sub-cylindrical, ⅝–¾ in (1.5–2 cm) long and ¼–⅓ in (7–8 mm) wide, covered with white linear, long-hairy-tomentose bracts. Flowers with dark purplish-red anthers; style white with pink stigma, divided into two, well protruding from the flower.
**Size** 2–12(–20) ins (5–30(–50) cm).
**Flowering period** July–September.
**Ecology and distribution** Pastures, meadows, grassy and stony places, on any type of subsoil, from 4,920 to 9,840(–10,825) ft (1,500–3,000(–3,300) m). Quite wide-spread in all central European mountains (the Pyrenees, Alps, Carpathians, the mountains of the Balkan peninsula, Scottish Highlands and mountains of Scandinavia), the Urals and Arctic regions of Eurasia and North America.

## 238 SAXIFRAGA AIZOIDES L.
Yellow Mountain Saxifrage

**Family** *Saxifragaceae*
**Description** A tufted plant forming lax carpets. Basal shoots prostrate, branched, with numerous ascending or erect flowering stems. Leaves spreading, ½–1 in (1–2.5 cm), linear, aculeate-acuminate, fleshy, slightly small-toothed. Flowers yellow in a lax, frond-like inflorescence, glandular-pilose, with 3–8 flowers. Petals 5, ⅛–¼ in (3–6 mm) long, oblong-spatulate or elliptical, spreading, well-distanced, longer than the sepals and alternating with them, varying in colour from bright yellow to orange or red, often red-spotted.
**Size** 2–6(–12) ins (5–15(–30) cm).
**Flowering period** June–September(–October).
**Ecology and distribution** Damp rocks, shingle and stream shores, wet debris and by springs, on any type of subsoil although with a preference for limestone, from (2,625–)3,280 to 9,185(–10,170) ft ((800–)1,000–2,800 (–3,100) m). Found in the Pyrenees, Jura, Alps, northern and central Apennines, Carpathians, mountains of the Balkan peninsula, northern Europe and North America.

## 239 SAXIFRAGA ANDROSACEA L.
Scree Saxifrage

**Family** *Saxifragaceae*
**Description** A small, more or less stemless tufted plant with a branched rhizome forming numerous leafy rosettes close together at the base. Rosette composed of numerous leaves, ½–¾ in (1–2 cm), oblong-lanceolate, sometimes spatulate, very tightly packed, acute or obtuse, long pilose; several varieties have tridentate leaves or are apically lobed. Flower-stem pilose, leafless or sometimes with 2–3 leaves, alternate, linear, short. Flowers white, solitary or in a short apical raceme of 2–3 flowers. Calyx campanulate, short, with 5 teeth. Corolla flared, 5 oblong or ovate petals, attenuate at the base, entire or slightly emarginate at the apex, approx. ¼ in (5–7 mm) long.
**Size** ¾–3¼ ins (2–8 cm).
**Flowering period** (May–)June–August.
**Ecology and distribution** Moraines, stabilized rubble, damp detritus and snow-beds, on a fairly calcareous subsoil, from (4,920–)5,905 to 11,485 ft ((1,500–)1,800–3,500 m). Common in the Pyrenees, Alps, Auvergne, Carpathians and central (the Altai Mountains) and northeastern Asia.

---

## 240 SAXIFRAGA AQUATICA Lapeyr.
(Pyrenean) Water Saxifrage

**Family** *Saxifragaceae*
**Description** An evergreen, tufted, herbaceous perennial, with lax basal leaves and erect branches forming a large, loose cushion. Leaves palmate-semicircular, shiny, fleshy, up to 1½ ins (4 cm) long. Flowering stems, thick ⅛–⅙ in (3–4 mm) diameter, with numerous sessile stem leaves. Flowers white in a short, dense inflorescence, with short linear bracts. Petals 5, ¼–⅓ in (6–9 mm) long, oblong-obovate, much longer than the sepals.
**Size** (8–)10–24 ins ((20–)25–60 cm).
**Flowering period** July–August.
**Ecology and distribution** Damp places, along the banks of streams, from 4,920 to 7,220 ft (1,500–2,000 m). Endemic to the central and eastern ranges of the Pyrenees.
**Notes** This species has sometimes been confused with *Saxifraga adscendens*, a biennial species found widely in all the mountains of Europe.

## 241 SAXIFRAGA BRYOIDES L.
Moss Saxifrage

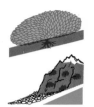

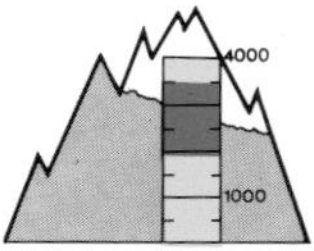

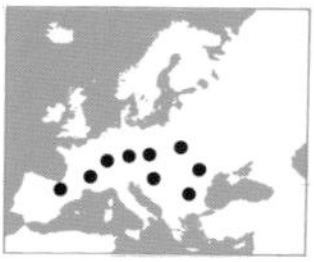

**Family** *Saxifragaceae*
**Description** A small, creeping plant with prostrate branches bearing numerous compact, leafy, ovoid-oblong rosettes, forming dense mats. Prostrate branches ¾–2 ins (2–5 cm) long. Basal leaves small, linear, ⅙–⅓ in (4–8 mm) long, incurved. Flowering stems erect or ascending with linear or lanceolate stem leaves, ⅙–¼ in (4–6 mm) long, ciliate. Flowers white, united in groups of 2–5 in a short terminal inflorescence. Petals 5, white, spotted with orange or bright yellow near the base, oval or oblong, rounded, 2–3 times the length of the sepals.
**Size** 1½–3¼(–4) ins (4–8(–10) cm) – the flowering stems.
**Flowering period** July–August(–September).
**Ecology and distribution** Rocks, stabilized rubble, stony and craggy places, on a siliceous subsoil, from 6,560 to 11,810(–13,125) ft (2,000–3,600(–4,000) m). Quite widespread in the Pyrenees, Auvergne, Alps, Carpathians and Balkan Mountains.

## 242 SAXIFRAGA BURSERANA L.
One-flowered Cushion Saxifrage

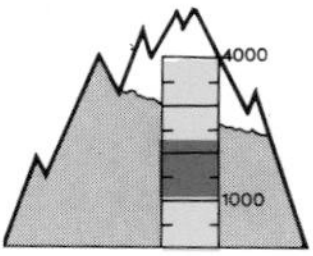

**Family** *Saxifragaceae*
**Description** A low-growing, mat-forming plant consisting of dense cushions of short frond-like branches. Leaves linear, stiff, erect, almost needle-like, very dense, bluish-grey, approx. ¼–½ in (5–12 mm) long and little more than approx. ¹⁄₁₆ in (1 mm) in width. Flowering stems erect, covered with reddish glands. Flowers large, white, solitary, with short, reddish sepals. Petals 5, obovate, ¼–½ in (7–12 mm) long and ¼–⅓ in (5–9 mm) wide. Stamens short, yellow.
**Size** ¾–2½ ins (2–6 cm) – the flowering stems.
**Flowering period** March–April(–July).
**Ecology and distribution** Rocks, crags and precipices, detritus of the lower slopes, on a calcareous or dolomitic subsoil, from (985–)4,920 to 6,890(–8,200) ft ((300–)1,500–2,100(–2,500) m). Quite common in the calcareous-dolomitic, eastern Alps.
**Notes** Endemic to the calcareous eastern Alps where it inhabits two parallel zones, one to the north, the other to the south of the main watershed.

## 243  SAXIFRAGA CAESIA L.
Blue Saxifrage, Bluish-grey Saxifrage

**Family**  *Saxifragaceae*
**Description**  A low-growing, mat-forming plant consisting of dense cushions of short frond-like stems, each with a flat apical rosette made up of short grey-blue, oval oblong or elliptical leaves, ⅛–⅓ in (3–8 mm) long and approx. ¹⁄₁₆ in (1–2 mm) wide, arching towards the outside, with 5–7 calcareous scales. Flowers white, united in groups of 2–6 in a short terminal inflorescence. Short sepals, greenish. Petals 5, ⅙–¼ in (4–6 mm) long, obovate, wide, flaring outwards. Anthers yellow.
**Size**  1½–5 ins (4–12 cm) – the flowering stems.
**Flowering period**  July–September.
**Ecology and distribution**  Stony places, rocks, stabilized rubble and gravelly pastures, on a calcareous or dolomitic subsoil, from (2,625–)4,920 to 9,185(–9,840) ft ((800–) 1,500–2,800(–3,000) m). Frequent in the Pyrenees, the calcareous regions of the Alps, the Apuane Alps, central Apennines, Carpathians and the Dinaric Alps.
**Notes**  A protected plant.

## 244  SAXIFRAGA CLUSII Gouan
French Saxifrage

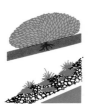

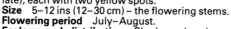

**Family**  *Saxifragaceae*
**Description**  A more or less stemless, herbaceous plant with leafy rosettes at the base formed of erect leaves, ¼–⅝ in (6–15 mm) long, spatulate, attenuate into a long and broad petiole, irregularly dentate, pilose. Flowering stems, erect, slender, branched in the upper half, with bracts larger below and smaller above. Inflorescence broad, open, of numerous white flowers. Sepals recurved. Petals 5 unequal (2 shorter and 3 longer, spatulate), each with two yellow spots.
**Size**  5–12 ins (12–30 cm) – the flowering stems.
**Flowering period**  July–August.
**Ecology and distribution**  Shady rocks, damp craggy places and along the banks of streams, on an acid subsoil, from 4,920 to 8,530 ft (1,500–2,600 m). Endemic to the Pyrenees, Cevennes and the mountains of northern Spain.

## 245 **SAXIFRAGA CUNEIFOLIA** L.
Spoon-leaved Saxifrage

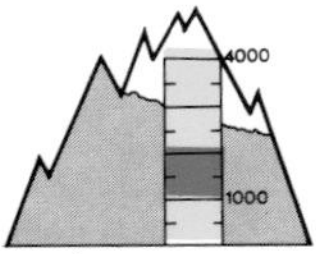

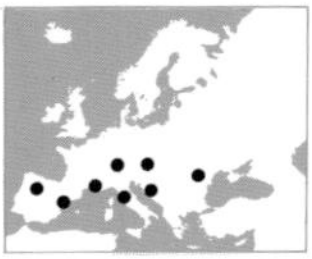

**Family** *Saxifragaceae*
**Description** A small, herbaceous, acaulescent or more or less stemless plant, with a lax rosette of sub-leathery, fleshy leaves, orbicular-spatulate, entire or dentate in the upper half, attenuate into a broad petiole, slightly ciliate. Flowers white in sparse inflorescences. Peduncles up to 6 ins (15 cm) long, slender, glandular-pubescent. Sepals reflexed; petals 5, approx. ⅛–⅙ in (2.5–4 mm) long.
**Size** 2½–10 ins (6–25 cm).
**Flowering period** June–August.
**Ecology and distribution** Shady crags and precipices, damp rocks in woods, preferably on a siliceous subsoil but on other ground-types, too, from (1,310–)3,280 to 5,575(–7,545) ft ((400–)1,000–1,700(–2,300) m). Very common in the Pyrenees, Cevennes, Alps, northern Apennines, eastern Carpathians and the north-western Balkan peninsula.

## 246 **SAXIFRAGA EXARATA** Vill.
Furrowed Saxifrage

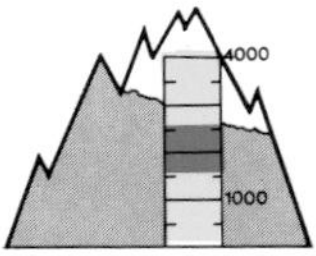

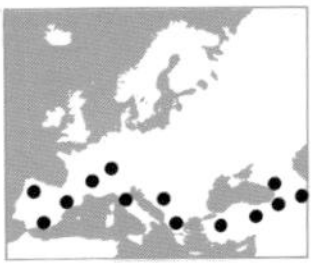

**Family** *Saxifragaceae*
**Description** A tufted, herbaceous, more or less stemless plant, forming fairly lax, dense cushions. Leaves, ⅙–⅝ in (4–15 mm) long, in dense basal rosettes, cuneate, divided into 3–7 linear lobes, pilose. Flowering stems, erect, pilose, with short, sparse, linear stem leaves, and 3–10 flowers in a short raceme. Flowers white, occasionally pink, with 5 short sepals half the length of the petals, and with 5 petals ⅙ in (4 mm) long and approx. ¹⁄₁₆ in (2 mm) wide.
**Size** 2–6 ins (5–15 cm) – the flowering stems.
**Flowering period** (June–)July–September.
**Ecology and distribution** Crags and precipices, stabilized rubble, rocky places and open stony pastures, on a siliceous subsoil from (2,625–)5,905 to 8,860(–11,810) ft ((800–)1,800–2,700(–3,600) m). Quite frequent in the Iberian Mountains, Pyrenees, Alps, Apennines, Caucasus and the mountains of the Balkan peninsula and Armenia.
**Notes** A protected species which, although easily confused with the similar species *Saxifraga moschata*, found mainly on calcareous subsoil, is distinguished by its petals – sub-equal to its sepals, and by its yellowish or greenish-yellow colouring.

## 247 SAXIFRAGA GERANIOIDES L.

Geranium-like Saxifrage

**Family** *Saxifragaceae*
**Description** A tufted, herbaceous plant with a woody rhizome from which arise several sterile stems with dense leafy rosettes and a number of fertile flowering stems. Basal leaves sub-circular in outline, ⅝–1¼ in (1.5–3 cm) wide, deeply incised into 9–27 acute, triangular-lanceolate, acuminate segments, very close together but not overlapping, with short glandular hairs. Stem leaves sparse. Flowers white in short compact inflorescences, sub-campanulate. Petals 5, oblanceolate, approx. ½ in (10–12 mm) long.
**Size** 2¾–8 ins (7–20 cm).
**Flowering period** July–August.
**Ecology and distribution** Rocks, stony places and detritus of the lower slopes, on a siliceous or acid subsoil, from (3,935–)4,920 to 6,890(–9,680) ft ((1,200–)1,500–2,100(–2,950) m). Exclusive to the central and eastern Pyrenees and mountains of north-eastern Spain.

---

## 248 SAXIFRAGA HIRSUTA L.

Kidney Saxifrage

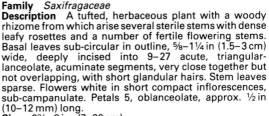

**Family** *Saxifragaceae*
**Description** A tufted, herbaceous, more or less stemless plant, with a rosette of slightly leathery, kidney-shaped, orbicular or ovate-oblong leaves, crenate or serrate-dentate with 7–25 teeth, fairly bristly, usually red on the underside, ⅓–1¼ ins (8–30 mm) long. Petiole slender, pilose, ¾–2½ ins (2–6 cm) long. Flowers white in a sparse inflorescence. Petals 5, white with a few pale red spots near the base and one yellow spot, ¼ in (4–5 mm) long.
**Size** 5–12 ins (12–30 cm).
**Flowering period** May–July.
**Ecology and distribution** Shady, damp places and along the banks of streams, from (1,640–)3,280 to 8,200 ft ((500–)1,000–2,500 m). Present, but not frequent, in the central and western Pyrenees, northern Spain and south-western Ireland.
**Notes** This species has a very wide distribution area, identifiable with two subspecies: *hirsuta*, which is widespread in the mountains of the north-western Iberian peninsula and south-western Ireland, and *paucicrenata* (Gillot) D.A. Webb, which is calcicole and limited to the western Pyrenees. It crosses easily with such similar species as *S. umbrosa*, to produce hybrids which are widespread throughout central and western Europe, e.g. *S. polita, S. geum.*

## 249  SAXIFRAGA JUNIPERIFOLIA  Adams

**Family** *Saxifragaceae*
**Description** A small, tufted plant forming dense cushions consisting of tightly packed, compact leafy rosettes. Leaves ¼–⅝ in (7–14 mm) long, linear-lanceolate, strongly mucronate or apiculate with a narrow translucent margin, small-toothed in the upper half. Flowering stems short, leafy, with a short dense apical inflorescence of 3–11 light yellow, sub-sessile flowers. Petals 5, approx. ¼ in (5–6 mm) long, obovate or cuneate, acute, sub-erect, shorter than the stamens.
**Size** ¾–1½ ins (2–4 cm) – the flowering stems.
**Flowering period** May–July.
**Ecology and distribution** Shady crags and precipices and damp rocky places, from 4,920 to 6,890 ft (1,500–2,100 m). Found in the mountains of central and northern Greece, southern Bulgaria, western Asia Minor and the Caucasus.
**Notes** Two subspecies are identifiable: *juniperifolia* with 6–11 flowers and an ovoid inflorescence, found in Bulgaria and the Caucasus, and *sancta* with only 3–7 flowers and a globose inflorescence, which is known from Greece and Asia Minor.

## 250  SAXIFRAGA MARGINATA  Sternb.

**Family** *Saxifragaceae*
**Description** A small plant forming a dense cushion of short, erect stems, closely covered with leaves partly in rosette form and partly alternate. Leaves stiff, ¼–½ in (5–12 mm) long, obtuse, with whitish margins. Flowers white or pale pink, apical, in groups of 2–8 on the flowering stems. Sepals reddish, short. Petals 5, broadly ovate or elliptical, ⅓–½ in (8–11 mm) long; stamens short, with yellow anthers.
**Size** 2¾–4 in (7–10 cm) – the flowering stems.
**Flowering period** May–July.
**Ecology and distribution** Rocks, precipices and crags, on a calcareous subsoil, from 5,905 to 6,890 ft (1,800–2,100 m). Found in the central and southern Apennines, southern Carpathians and the mountains of the Balkan peninsula, from southern Yugoslavia to Bulgaria and Greece.
**Notes** Endemic to south-eastern Europe.

## 251 SAXIFRAGA OPPOSITIFOLIA L.
Purple Saxifrage

**Family** *Saxifragaceae*

**Description** A herbaceous plant with creeping stems that form lax cushions or sparse carpets. Stems erect, covered with small, opposite, oval or oblong leaves, green or bluish-green, ⅛–¼ in (2–5 mm) long and ¹⁄₁₆–⅛ in (1–3 mm) wide, tightly packed to resemble 4 rows, with a thickened tip carrying lime-secreting pits. Flowers red or pink, occasionally white, solitary at the apex of short stems. Calyx campanulate with ciliate lobes. Corolla approx. ¼–½ in (6–12 mm) diameter, campanulate-flared. Petals 5, obovate, ¼–⅝ in (5–15 mm) wide. Stamens shorter than the petals.

**Size** ½–1¼(–2) ins (1–3(–5) cm) – the flowering stems.

**Flowering period** May–August.

**Ecology and distribution** Rocks, stony places, stabilized rubble, moraines and detritus of the lower slopes, on any type of subsoil, from (2,625–)5,905 to 12,465 ft ((800–)1,800–3,800 m). A typical Arctic-alpine species, frequent in all European mountains (the Sierra Nevada, Pyrenees, Auvergne, Jura, Alps, Apennines, Carpathians and Balkan Mountains) and widespread in Arctic regions, from Scandinavia to Siberia, Alaska and Canada.

**Notes** A very variable species; numerous geographical races have been identified as distinct subspecies.

---

## 252 SAXIFRAGA PANICULATA Miller
Livelong Saxifrage
*S. aizoon* Jacq.

**Family** *Saxifragaceae*

**Description** A small plant formed of numerous densely-packed leafy rosettes, some fertile, others sterile. Each rosette consists of spatulate leaves, incurved upwards, ½–1½ ins (1–4 cm) long, fleshy, small-toothed, apically obtuse or acuminate and with dense marginal lime-pits. Flowering stems reddish, with a few leaves. Inflorescence short, loosely racemose, with 7–14 pedunculate flowers. Flowers white, sometimes yellowish, often red-spotted. Petals 5, oval.

**Size** (1½–)5–10(–12) ins ((4–)12–25(–30) cm) – the flowering stems.

**Flowering period** June–August.

**Ecology and distribution** Stony and steep places, rocks, stabilized detritus and rubble, arid pastures, from (2,625–)3,935 to 8,530(–10,170) ft ((800–)1,200–2,400(–3,100) m). Very common in all the mountains of Europe, Greenland and North America.

**Notes** A protected species in some areas.

## 253　SAXIFRAGA POROPHYLLA　Bertol.

**Family** *Saxifragaceae*
**Description** A herbaceous plant consisting of numerous flattened rosettes, often closely packed to form a dense cushion. Leaves numerous, lanceolate, acute, ⅓–½ in (8–11 mm) long, in rosettes of ¾–3¼ ins (2–3 cm) diameter. Flowering stem emerging from the centre of the rosette, reddish, with small, sparse, lanceolate leaves. Flowers red or pink, in an elongate, often apically recurved, raceme, with 6–12 flowers. Calyx urn-shaped-campanulate, pink, pilose, with 5 teeth recurved outwards. Corolla red, formed of 5 petals, approx. ⅛ in (2–2.5 mm) long, equal to or slightly projecting from the calyx.
**Size** 2–4(–6) ins (5–10(–15) cm) – the flowering stems.
**Flowering period** June–August.
**Ecology and distribution** Precipices and crags, rock crevices and steep stony slopes, mainly on limestone, from 4,265 to 8,200 ft (1,300–2,500 m). Present, but not frequent, in the central-southern Apennines.
**Notes** Endemic to the Apennines and strictly protected because of its rarity.

---

## 254　SAXIFRAGA RETUSA　Gouan

**Family** *Saxifragaceae*
**Description** A dwarf plant forming dense and compact mats or cushions. Stems small, stiff, with closely-packed, opposite, ovate-lanceolate, bluish-green leaves, in 4 rows, approx. ⅛ in (2–4 mm), recurved outwards, with 3–5 lime-pits. Flowers purplish-red, arranged apically on the flowering stem in groups of 2–5. Corolla open, expanded. Petals 5, approx. ¼ in (4–5 mm) long, approx. 1/16 in (2 mm) wide, with an ovate limb and well-defined, narrow, linear claw. Stamens erect, with purple filaments, showy, longer than the petals; anthers orange.
**Size** ¾–2 ins (2–5 cm) – the flowering stems.
**Flowering period** June–July(–August).
**Ecology and distribution** Exposed rocks, stabilized rubble, detritus and moraines, on a basic or acid subsoil, from 6,560 to 9,840(–11,810) ft (2,000–3,000(–3,600) m). Found in the Pyrenees, western Alps, (from the Alpes Maritimes to the Simplon Pass), eastern Alps (Taurus Mountains, Salzburg Alps), Carpathians and Balkan Mountains.
**Notes** The most widespread subspecies is *retusa*, which is calcifuge; the only subspecies in the western Alps is *augustana*, which is calcicole.

## 255 SAXIFRAGA SEDOIDES L.
Eastern Saxifrage

**Family** *Saxifragaceae*
**Description** A small prostrate plant forming a loose mat consisting of numerous small, branched stems. Basal leaves linear-lanceolate, acuminate, fleshy, with an expanded petiole, ⅓–½ in (8–12 mm) long, entire or three-lobed, united into lax rosettes. Flowering stems sometimes leafy, with 1–2 yellow flowers. Sepals greenish. Petals 5, yellow or greenish-yellow, approx. ⅛ in (2–3 mm) long, spreading, narrowly lanceolate, well-spaced, sub-equal to the sepals and alternating with them. Stamens equal to the petals, with yellow anthers. Ovary broad, flattened, green.
**Size** ⅝–2 ins (1.5–5 cm) – the flowering stems.
**Flowering period** June–September.
**Ecology and distribution** Rocks, stabilized rubble and detritus of the lower slopes, snow-beds and shady screes where the snow remains for a long time, on a calcareous-dolomitic subsoil, from 5,250 to 9,840(–13,125) ft (1,600–3,000(–4,000) m). Found in the eastern Pyrenees, eastern calcareous Alps and central Apennines.

---

## 256 SAXIFRAGA STELLARIS L.
Starry Saxifrage

**Family** *Saxifragaceae*
**Description** A tufted plant with a short, creeping stem and more or less dense basal rosette. Basal leaves ½–2 ins (1–5 cm), fleshy, spatulate or attenuate, glossy, with a few apical teeth. Flowering stems, one or more to each rosette, reddish, pilose, branched near the top, with small bracts. Petals 5, narrowly lanceolate, acute, well-spaced, with pink anthers. Ovary large, two-celled, pink shading to red.
**Size** 2–8(–10) ins (5–20(–25) cm).
**Flowering period** June–August.
**Ecology and distribution** Damp rocky places, along the banks of streams, wet pastures, marshes and near springs, on any type of subsoil, from (1,970–)3,935 to 9,185(–10,825) ft ((600–)1,200–2,800(–3,300) m). Frequent in all the mountains of Europe and north-eastern America.

## 257  SCUTELLARIA ALPINA L.
### Alpine Skullcap

**Family** *Labiatae*
**Description** A perennial plant with creeping stems, branched at the base then with ascending, pilose branches. Leaves opposite, small, oval, sub-sessile, apically obtuse, crenate or slightly serrate. Flowers in whorled inflorescences, arranged in 4 rows in the 2 or 3 terminal whorls. Bracts similar to the leaves, green or violet. Calyx short, pilose-glandular. Corolla ¾–1 in (20 –25 mm) long, pale violet or azure-violet in the upper part with a whitish tube and lower lip; tube cylindrical, two-thirds the length of the whole corolla; upper lip of limb helmet-shaped, concave, and lower lip broadened, more or less three-lobed, spreading.
**Size** 4–12 ins (10–30 cm).
**Flowering period** June–August(–September).
**Ecology and distribution** Rocks, detritus of the lower slopes and stony places in general, on a calcareous sub-soil, from 3,280 to 7,875(–8,200) ft (1,000–2,400(–2,500) m). Quite common and widespread in the Pyrenees, Alps, central Apennines, Carpathians (subsp. *alpina*) and Balkan Mountains; it also grows in the open plains of European Russia and central-northern Asia (subsp. *supina*).

---

## 258  SEDUM ATRATUM L.
### Dark Stonecrop

**Family** *Crassulaceae*
**Description** A small succulent plant, tufted, annual, red-dish or brownish-red, sometimes quite dark, very branched at the base forming numerous short branches, erect or ascending. Leaves alternate, ⅙–¼ in (4–6 mm) long, oblong or club-shaped, flattened near the base, green or reddish. Flowers small, pink or yellowish, in dense, short terminal inflorescences on flowering stems. Petals 5–6, lanceolate-acute, erect or nearly converging, with a darker line of colour (red or greenish-yellow) down the centre. Stamens and ovary the same colour as the petals, often deeper.
**Size** 1¼–4 ins (3–10 cm).
**Flowering period** June–August.
**Ecology and distribution** Rocks, detritus of the lower slopes, stabilized rubble and stony places, usually on a calcareous subsoil, from (3,280–)4,595 to 10,500 ft (1,000–)1,400–3,200 m). A very widespread species, common in the Pyrenees, Jura, Alps, Apennines, Carpathians and the mountains of the Balkan peninsula.

**259 SEMPERVIVUM ARACHNOIDEUM** L.
Cobweb Houseleek

**Family** *Crassulaceae*
**Description** A small, fleshy plant with a basal rosette, ¼–1 in (0.5–2.5 cm) wide, with a thick covering of fine white threads like a cobweb especially over the upper part. Basal leaves oblong or lanceolate, tightly-packed, converging, varying from red to pink to a greenish colour, woolly. Stem erect, covered by alternate, broadly lanceolate, reddish leaves. Flowers pink, clustered at the apex of the stem into a compact umbel of 5–10 flowers. Corolla consisting of 8–10 pink petals with a purple midvein, ¼–½ in (7–10 mm) long and ⅛ in (3 mm) wide. Stamens with red filaments; ovaries numerous, reddish or purple, arranged in a corona.
**Size** 1½–6 ins (4–15 cm).
**Flowering period** (June–)July–September.
**Ecology and distribution** Rocks, stony pastures, rock crevices, detritus of the lower slopes and cliff faces, with a preference for acid soils although sometimes present on other types, from (1,640–)5,575 to 9,840 ft ((500–)1,700–3,000 m). Very common in the Pyrenees, Alps and Apennines.
**Notes** All *Sempervivum* species are protected plants.

---

**260 SEMPERVIVUM MONTANUM** L.
Mountain Houseleek

**Family** *Crassulaceae*
**Description** A stolon-bearing, succulent, herbaceous plant, with a basal rosette of more or less flat, open leaves, ⅝–1½ ins (1.5–4 cm) wide. Basal leaves, ⅓–½ in (8–10 mm) long, oblanceolate, oblong-spatulate or obovate, convergent towards the centre of the plant, opaque green, often with a dark red or brownish tip, pubescent and ciliate on the margin. Flowering stems reddish, with alternate, lanceolate leaves. Flowers pink or violet-red, in dense terminal umbels of 2–5(–8). Petals 11–13, ½–¾ in (12–20 mm) long and approx. ¹⁄₁₆ in (2 mm) wide. Stamens numerous with pink or red filaments; ovaries arranged in a corona, greenish-yellow.
**Size** 2–4(–8) ins (5–10(–20) cm).
**Flowering period** July–August(–September).
**Ecology and distribution** Rocks, rocky slopes and stony places, on an acid subsoil, from (2,295–)3,935 to 10,500 (–11,155) ft ((700–)1,200–3,200(–3,400) m). Quite frequent in the Pyrenees, Alps (especially the central range), northern Apennines, Carpathians and in Corsica.
**Notes** Like other *Sempervivum* species, a protected plant.

**261 SEMPERVIVUM WULFENII** Hoppe ex Mert.
et Koch

**Family** *Crassulaceae*
**Description** A succulent herbaceous plant with an erect stem, basal rosette, 1½–2½ ins (4–6 cm) wide and long robust stolons with terminal offset rosettes. Basal leaves oblong-spatulate, sharp-pointed, marginally ciliate, bluish-green tending to reddish towards the base, often convergent near the centre. Flowering stems, erect, with alternate, reddish leaves. Flowers yellow, in dense compact umbellate inflorescences. Corolla formed of 12–18 linear petals, with a red mark near the base, ½ in (10 mm) long and approx. ¹⁄₁₆ in (1–2 mm) wide, woolly on the outside. Stamens numerous, with purple filaments; ovaries numerous, arranged in a corona, yellow or greenish.
**Size** 6–10 ins (15–25 cm).
**Flowering period** July–August.

**Ecology and distribution** Rocks, crags and precipices, stony places and stabilized rubble, on a siliceous subsoil, from 5,575 to 8,860 ft (1,700–2,700 m). Endemic to the Alps, especially the central and eastern ranges, but not frequent.
**Notes** Like other *Sempervivum* species, a protected plant.

---

**262 SENECIO DORONICUM** (L.) L.
Chamois Ragwort

**Family** *Compositae*
**Description** A herbaceous perennial with an erect, robust stem, pilose or more often tomentose-woolly. Leaves lanceolate, oblong or nearly linear, the basals being wider and longer, attenuate into a short petiole, stem leaves sessile, amplexicaul, shorter and well-spaced on the stem. Heads in groups of 2–3, rarely more, at apex of stem, showy, 1½–2½ ins (4–6 cm) across. Involucre hemispherical at first then flattened; disc small, flat, yellow. Ray-florets yellow, numerous (from 15–18 to 25), with lanceolate ligules, usually longer than the disc diameter.
**Size** 8–24 ins (20–60 cm).
**Flowering period** July–August.

**Ecology and distribution** Arid pastures, meadows, stabilized rubble, grassy and stony places, sparse woods, on any type of subsoil although with a preference for limestone, from (3,280–)4,920 to 8,200(–10,170) ft ((1,000–)1,500–2,500(–3,100) m). Frequent in the Pyrenees, Alps, Apennines, Carpathians and mountains of the Balkan peninsula.

**263 SENECIO HALLERI** Dandy
One-flowered Alpine Groundsel
*S. uniflorus* All.

**Family** *Compositae*
**Description** A herbaceous perennial, acaulescent or nearly so, with a basal rosette of lanceolate, obovate-lanceolate or nearly spatulate leaves, attenuate into a long petiole, entire, slightly dentate or almost pinnatifid with rounded lobes, white-silky or tomentose. Stem leaves few, lanceolate, almost entire, smaller, sessile. Heads ¾–1¼ in (2–3 cm) wide, solitary at the apex of the ascending stems. Involucre hemispherical, with a row of linear bracts and a few shorter bracts outside. Disc- and ray-florets bright yellow or golden yellow. Disc flat or slightly swollen, with tubular flowers; ray consisting of 7–15 flowers with ligules broadly lanceolate or oblong.
**Size** 2–6 ins (5–15 cm).
**Flowering period** July–October.
**Ecology and distribution** Stony or rocky places and arid pastures, on an acid subsoil, from (6,235–)8,200 to 11,810 ft (1,900–)2,500–3,600 m). An endemic alpine species, its distribution area limited to the western Alps (Graian Alps and Italian Pennines) where it is not frequent.

---

**264 SENECIO INCANUS** L.
Grey Alpine Groundsel

**Family** *Compositae*
**Description** A small, tufted, sub-acaulescent perennial, with a basal rosette and ascending flower stems. Leaves basal, narrowly lanceolate or lanceolate-spatulate, attenuate into a long petiole, pinnatifid or lobed into rounded segments, lobed, white-silky; stem leaves sparse or absent, smaller. Heads in groups of 4–10 to form lax terminal corymbs. Head ½–⅝ in (12–15 mm) wide, consisting of a hemispherical involucre with 6–10 bracts in one row and a few shorter ones. Disc-florets yellow, tubular; ray-florets 6–8, yellow, with lanceolate or obovate ligules.
**Size** 1¼–6 ins (3–15 cm).
**Flowering period** July–September.
**Ecology and distribution** Rocks, moraines, detritus and stony places in general, on a siliceous subsoil, from (4,265–)6,560 to 11,155(–11,485) ((1,300–)2,000–3,400 (–3,500) m). Widespread in the Alps, Carpathians and northern Apennines.
**Notes** Three subspecies are particularly distinctive: *incanus* is widespread in the western Alps, from the Alpes Maritimes to the Lepontine Alps and northern Apennines; *insubricus* is found in the central Alps (in Switzerland and to the north of Bergamo, Italy); and *carniolicus* in the eastern Alps and Carpathians.

## 265 SENECIO KENIODENDRON R.E. Fries et Th. Fries

**Family** *Compositae*

**Description** An arborescent perennial, with a stocky trunk, felty-woody, covered with the remains of old dry leaves. Leaves large, overlapping, densely packed at the apex of the stem in a more or less spherical rosette, showy, which can be over 3 ft 4 ins (1 m) diameter. Leaves elliptical, oblong or lanceolate-spatulate, incurved upwards, acute or acuminate, pilose, small-toothed. Flowers in a terminal inflorescence up to 4 ft 4 ins (1.3 m) long, branching out into dense, oblong panicles formed of numerous pedunculate heads. Head yellowish, surrounded by an involucre of light-coloured bracts.

**Size** 13–20 ft (4–6 m) – the flowering plant.

**Flowering period** Nearly all the year: October–February; May–July.

**Ecology and distribution** In the montane savannahs and grasslands of the high tropical mountains, especially in stony places, from (11,485–)12,465 to 15,420 ft ((3,500–)3,800–4,700 m). Exclusive to Mt. Kenya in central East Africa.

**Notes** This species belongs to the so-called 'Senecio giants', the subgenus *Dendrosenecio*, which are plants with tree-like habit typical of the high African mountains. The genus *Senecio* is widespread throughout the world and comprises about 1,500 species of which, however, only about 10 are from the subgenus *Dendrosenecio*.

---

## 266 SENECIO LEUCOPHYLLUS DC.
White Alpine Groundsel

**Family** *Compositae*

**Description** A robust, tufted, sub-acaulescent, white-tomentose, herbaceous perennial, with ascending stems. Basal leaves numerous, white-silky, thick, oval or oblong pinnatifid, with more or less cuneate or dentate, apically rounded lobes; stem leaves equally pinnatifid, shorter. Flowers all yellow, in heads in corymbs at the end of the stems. Heads 12–16 to each plant, large, surrounded by 12–15 involucral bracts with 2–4 supplementary bracts at the base. Disc-florets numerous; ray-florets sparse, generally from 5 to 7, well-spaced, with lanceolate or oblong ligules.

**Size** 4–8 ins (10–20 cm).

**Flowering period** August–September.

**Ecology and distribution** Arid pastures, open stony and rocky places, generally on an acid subsoil, from 4,920 to 8,860 ft (1,500–2,700 m). Endemic to the Pyrenees and Cevennes.

**Notes** Sometimes regarded as a species close to *S. incanus*, it is distinguishable by its greater height, more robust habit and greater number of bracts on the flower head.

## 267 SIDERITIS ENDRESSII Willk.

**Family** *Labiatae*
**Description** A shrubby plant, woody at the base, very branched below with epigeal ascending stems, spreading. Leaves elliptical, obovate or oblanceolate, opposite, sub-sessile, ½–1½ (1–4 cm) long and ¼–¾ in (5 –20 mm) wide, entire or crenate-dentate, more or less pilose. Flowers pale yellow, in short compact inflorescences, formed of 5–10 whorls of 6 flowers each, interspersed with dentate, ovate-cordate bracts, ⅓ in (8–9 mm) long. Calyx ⅓–⅔ in (9–17 mm) long, with 5 radiate teeth. Corolla two-lipped, very short, ⅓–½ in (8 –10 mm) (subsp. *endressii*), or long, ⅔–¾ in (18–20 mm) (subsp. *laxispicata*), with a short, cylindrical tube, open throat often brown, and a limb consisting of an entire or emarginate upper lip and a three-lobed lower one with an oblong or obovate central lobe and narrow, linear lateral lobes.
**Size** 3¼–6(–12) ins (8–15(–30) cm).
**Flowering period** July–August.
**Ecology and distribution** Stony places and arid pastures, often on a calcareous subsoil, from (1,640–)3,280 to 5,905 ft ((500–)1,000–1,800 m). Endemic to the Pyrenees (subsp. *endressii*) and the mountains of south-western Spain (subsp. *laxispicata*).
**Notes** These two subspecies are identifiable by the length of the corolla, calyx and leaves.

---

## 268 SILENE ACAULIS (L.)Jacq.
Moss Campion, Cushion Pink

**Family** *Caryophyllaceae*
**Description** A dwarf, herbaceous plant forming dense cushions or compact mats. A short stem with small, opposite, linear leaves, ¼–½ in (5–12 mm) long, with a rigid, ciliate margin. Flowers pink, violet-pink or wine-red, solitary at apex of stem, emerging very slightly from the cushion, with a dark red or violet tubular calyx, up to ½ in (1 cm) long. Corolla open, ⅓–½ in (8–12 mm) diameter. Petals 5, slightly spatulate, elliptical, oblong or obovate, sometimes small-toothed.
**Size** ¼–¾ in (5–20 mm).
**Flowering period** June–August(–September).
**Ecology and distribution** Rocks, damp rubble, stony slopes, detritus of the lower slopes, screes and moraines, preferably on calcareous soil, from 5,250 to 9,840 (–11,810) ft (1,600–3,000(–3,600) m). Very common in the Pyrenees, Alps, Apennines, Carpathians, in the British Isles, Scandinavia, Balkan peninsula, the Urals and mountains of Asia and North America.
**Notes** A protected plant.

## 269 SILENE ELISABETHA Jan
*Melandrium elisabethae* (Jan) Röhrh.

**Family** *Caryophyllaceae*
**Description** A small, tufted plant with a dense basal rosette of lanceolate, oblanceolate or nearly spatulate, acute leaves, almost hairless, 3¼–5 ins (8–12 cm) long. One or two stems emerging from the basal rosette, erect or ascending, with 2–3 pairs of small leaves. Flowers pink or violet-red, solitary or 2–3 at the apex of the stem, large, with a tubular, pilose, calyx ¾ in (20 mm) long, with 10 clear veins. Corolla 1¼–1½ ins (30–40 mm) diameter; petals 5, with a linear claw, throat with fringed scales and a broadly spatulate limb, bilobed, sub-dentate.
**Size** 2–8(–10) ins (5–20(–25) cm).
**Flowering period** (June–)July–August(–September).
**Ecology and distribution** Rocks, crags and precipices, stony places in general, on a calcareous or dolomitic subsoil, from 4,265 to 8,200 ft (1,300–2,500 m). Endemic to the calcareous and dolomitic southern Alps; quite rare and limited to the area between Lake Como and Lake Garda in northern Italy.
**Notes** A protected species because of its rarity.

---

## 270 SILENE RUPESTRIS L.
Rock Campion

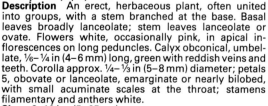

**Family** *Caryophyllaceae*
**Description** An erect, herbaceous plant, often united into groups, with a stem branched at the base. Basal leaves broadly lanceolate; stem leaves lanceolate or ovate. Flowers white, occasionally pink, in apical inflorescences on long peduncles. Calyx obconical, umbellate, ⅙–¼ in (4–6 mm) long, green with reddish veins and teeth. Corolla approx. ¼–⅓ in (5–8 mm) diameter; petals 5, obovate or lanceolate, emarginate or nearly bilobed, with small acuminate scales at the throat; stamens filamentary and anthers white.
**Size** 2–10 ins (5–25 cm).
**Flowering period** (May–)July–August(–September).
**Ecology and distribution** Rocks, dry stony places and natural detritus, generally on an acid subsoil, from 5,250 –9,840 ft (1,600–3,000 m). Frequent in the Pyrenees, Alps, northern Apennines, the mountains of Scandinavia and Corsica as well as the mountains of central and northern Europe (Carpathians and Transylvanian Alps).

## 271  SILENE VALLESIA  L.

**Family**  *Caryophyllaceae*
**Description**  A pilose-glandular, sticky, tufted plant with herbaceous stems. Leaves oblong-lanceolate or spatulate, short, pilose. Flowers pink or pinkish-white, solitary or 2–3 apical on the branches. Calyx tubular-club-shaped, with reddish veins. Corolla large, ⅝ in (15 mm) diameter, petals 5, with a reddish claw, limb bifid with oblong lobes, often curled upwards, lighter shades of pink on the upper surface and darker on the lower.
**Size**  2–6 ins (5–15 cm).
**Flowering period**  July–August.
**Ecology and distribution**  Rocks, stony places and detritus of the lower slopes, on an acid soil, from (3,610–) 4,920 to 9,840(–10,170) ft ((1,100–)1,500–3,000(–3,100) m). Found in the western Alps, Mt. Ventoux, the Alpes du Dauphiné, central Apennines and mountains of the western Balkan peninsula. Infrequent.

## 272  SILENE ZAWADZKII  Herbich

**Family**  *Caryophyllaceae*
**Description**  A tufted, herbaceous perennial, with a woody rhizome, branched into 2 or more ascending epigeal branches, spreading, pubescent. Basal leaves oblong or elliptical, up to 5 ins (12 cm) long, hairless, acute; stem leaves, opposite, in 3–5 pairs, smaller than the basals. Flowers white, large, solitary or in short cymes of 2–4 flowers. Calyx tubular at first, becoming swollen, ⅝–⅔ in (15–17 mm), pilose, with 10 lengthwise veins. Corolla ⅞–1¼ ins (22–30 mm) wide, consisting of 5 petals with an erect linear claw; limb spreading, broadly obovate, emarginate.
**Size**  4–12 ins (10–30 cm).
**Flowering period**  May–July.
**Ecology and distribution**  Sparse woods and clearings, pastures, from 3,935 to 6,560 ft (1,200–2,000 m). Endemic to the eastern Carpathians (northern Romania and southwestern Russia).
**Notes**  Similar to two other European montane *Silene* species with a very restricted distribution area: *S. lanuginosa* is localized in the Apuane Alps and *S. auriculata* in the mountains of Greece.

## 273 SOLDANELLA ALPINA L.
Alpine Snowbell

**Family** *Primulaceae*
**Description** A small, acaulescent perennial with a short rhizome and a basal rosette of kidney-shaped or cordate, sub-rounded leaves, ⅝–1 in (1.5–2.5 cm) wide, almost leathery, entire, on fairly long petioles. Flower stems, 1–2 on each plant, erect or ascending, with 2–3 violet-blue, occasionally white, drooping, shortly stalked flowers, apical. Calyx broadly campanulate, deeply divided into 5 lobes. Corolla conical-campanulate, ⅓–½ in (8–13 mm) long, fringed to half its length into numerous linear lobes.
**Size** 2–6 ins (5–15 cm).
**Flowering period** April–August; the first flowers are often already opening as the snow thaws.
**Ecology and distribution** Damp meadows, grassy or stony places, on any type of subsoil although with a preference for limestone, from (1,640–)3,280 to 8,860 (–9,840) ft ((500–)1,000–2,700(–3,000) m). Quite common in the Pyrenees, Jura, Alps, Apennines and Dinaric Alps.
**Notes** Sometimes recognized as a protected plant.

---

## 274 SOLENANTHUS APENNINUS (L.) Fisch. et Mey.

**Family** *Boraginaceae*
**Description** A robust, ashy-green, erect, herbaceous plant, covered with bristly hairs. Basal leaves large, elliptical or broadly lanceolate, 12–20 ins (30–50 cm) long; stem leaves smaller, ovate-elliptical, obovate or lanceolate, gradually narrowing to cuneate or auriculate at the base. Flowers violet-red or purple-azure, in a dense, terminal, scorpioid cyme which becomes enlarged after flowering. Calyx bristly, ⅓–½ in (8–10 mm) long. Corolla cylindrical or funnel-shaped, sub-equal to the calyx, with 5 obovate, obtuse lobes; throat almost closed by 5 small internal scales.
**Size** (12–)24–40(–48) ins ((30–)60–100(–120) cm).
**Flowering period** (April–)May–July.
**Ecology and distribution** Sparse woods, pastures, high altitude grassy places, from (1,970–)2,625 to 5,905 (–6,560) ft ((600–)800–1,800(–2,000) m). Common in the southern and central Apennines and Sicily; unsubstantiated sightings have been made in northern Greece and Albania.
**Notes** Endemic to southern Italy and Sicily.

## 275 STACHYS MACRANTHA (C. Koch) Stearn
*S. grandiflora* (Willd.) Benth.

**Family** *Labiatae*
**Description** A herbaceous perennial, sparsely branched at the base, with one or two epigeal, erect, simple, hirsute stems. Leaves opposite, in 2–3 pairs on the stem, broadly ovate or ovate-triangular, crenate, cordate at the base, ¾–6 ins (2–15 cm) long and ⅝–4 ins (1.5–10 cm) wide, stalked with petioles 1¼–12 ins (3–30 cm) long. Floral bracts leaflike, sessile. Flowers deep pink or purple-red, in dense apical false-whorls of 10–15 flowers, not very close together; bracteoles linear. Calyx ½–⅔ in (11–17 mm) long, with 5 sub-spinescent teeth. Corolla two-lipped, 1¼–1⅜ ins (30–35 mm) long, with a tube longer than the calyx; limb consists of an upper lip, expanded, concave, and a lower lip, three-lobed.
**Size** 4–24 ins (10–60 cm).
**Flowering period** June–September.
**Ecology and distribution** Meadows, clearings in pine and beech woods, rocky slopes, from 5,250 to 10,825 ft (1,600–3,300 m). Endemic to the mountains of north-eastern Anatolia, Transcaucasia, the southern Caucasus and north-western Iran.

---

## 276 STACHYS MONIERI (Gouan) P. W. Ball
Alpine Betony
*S. densiflora* Benth.

**Family** *Labiatae*
**Description** A herbaceous perennial, woody at the base. Stem erect, covered with long yellow hairs, bristly. Basal leaves in rosette, oval or oblong, on long petioles, cordate at the base, ¾–3¼ ins (20–80 mm) long and ½–1¼ ins (10–30 mm) wide; stem leaves opposite, sub-sessile. Flowers deep pink or purple, in closely packed false-whorls forming compact spikes, in the axil of two leaflike bracts. Calyx campanulate, ½–⅝ in (10–15 mm) long, with 5 acuminate teeth about half as long as the tube. Corolla with cylindrical tube, longer than the calyx, often pale pink, and a two-lipped limb with upper lip entire, concave, and lower lip three-lobed.
**Size** 4–12(–16) ins (10–30(–40) cm).
**Flowering period** July–August.
**Ecology and distribution** Alpine meadows, arid pastures, on a calcareous subsoil, from 3,935 to 7,875 ft (1,200–2,400 m). Widespread in the Pyrenees, Alps, northern and central Apennines and Dinaric Alps.

## 277 THLASPI ROTUNDIFOLIUM (L.) Gaud.
Round-leaved Pennycress

**Family** *Cruciferae*
**Description** A small plant in sparse compact tufts, with a robust root and creeping stems branched at the base. Leaves mostly dense at the base and some on the stem, all oval, oblong or sub-rounded, fleshy, entire or sub-crenate; basals attenuate into short petioles, azure-green; stem leaves auriculate, glossy green. Flowers deep pink or violet-red, in short compact inflorescences forming a hemispherical, honey-scented corymb. Petals 4, approx. ¼ in (6–7 mm). Silicule elliptical or oval with a short apical style.
**Size** 2–6 ins (5–15 cm).
**Flowering period** (May–)June–September.
**Ecology and distribution** Detritus, unstabilized screes and rubble, preferably on limestone (although several subspecies will only grow on a siliceous subsoil), from (2,625–)4,920 to 9,185(–11,155) ft ((800–)1,500–2,800 (–3,400) m). Very common in the Alps, especially subsp. *rotundifolium*, calcicole; related species also found in the Sierra Nevada, Pyrenees, Apennines, Carpathians and the Balkan Mountains.
**Notes** This species is a typical colonizer and consolidator of detrital material.

---

## 278 TOLPIS STATICIFOLIA (All.) Sch. Bip.
*Hieracium staticifolium* All.

**Family** *Compositae*
**Description** A herbaceous perennial with a short rhizome from which emerge several subterranean stolons at the ends of which new leaf rosettes are formed as well as a number of simple or slightly branched leafless stems. Leaves all basal, in rosettes, oblanceolate or lanceolate-spatulate, lengthily attenuate, entire or small-toothed, acute, 1½–4 ins (4–10 cm) long. Terminal heads at apex of stem and branches. Involucre approx. ½ in (9–11 mm) long, formed of two rows of linear bracts, some very long and others short, pilose or woolly. Flowers bright yellow or golden-yellow, all ligulate, with linear strap-shaped ligules, truncate and small-toothed at the apex.
**Size** 4–20 ins (10–50 cm).
**Flowering period** July–September.
**Ecology and distribution** Stony pastures, rubble, limestone quarries, dry grassy places and rocks, on a mainly calcareous subsoil, from 3,280 to 8,200 ft (1,000–2,500 m). Frequent in the Alps, Jura, western and central Carpathians and mountains of the north-western Balkan peninsula, as far as Albania and Macedonia.

### 279 TRIFOLIUM ALPINUM L.
Alpine Clover

**Family** *Papilionaceae*
**Description** A herbaceous, tufted, sub-acaulescent, prostrate-spreading perennial, with short stems creeping at first then ascending or erect. Leaves mostly basal, on long petioles, trifoliate, with leaflets lanceolate or linear, acute, ½–1½ ins (10–40 mm) long, with showy stipules. Flowers pink or purple-violet, fragrant, in a dense apical head composed of 3–12 flowers. Calyx cylindrical, deeply divided into 5 teeth of which the lowest is much longer than the others. Corolla ¾–1 in (18–25 mm) long, with petals enclosed within the standard which is lanceolate or oblong-lanceolate and slightly arching.
**Size** 2–6(–8) ins (5–15(–20) cm).
**Flowering period** June–August.
**Ecology and distribution** Pastures, alpine meadows, grassy or stony places, on acid soils, from (3,935–)5,250 to 10,170 ft ((1,200–)1,600–3,100 m). Common in the mountains of northern Iberia, the Pyrenees, Cevennes, Alps and northern and central Apennines.

---

### 280 TROLLIUS EUROPAEUS L.
Globe Flower

**Family** *Ranunculaceae*
**Description** An erect, herbaceous perennial, with a simple, sturdy, unbranched or slightly branched stem. Basal leaves on long petioles, palmatifid, with 3–5 lobes, each of which is deeply incised into 2–3 dentate-serrate, lanceolate segments. Stem leaves smaller and less incised, sessile. Flowers yellow, solitary at the apex of the stem, more or less spherical, 1½–2 ins (4–5 cm) in diameter. Sepals petal-like, 10–12, converging, giving the appearance of a closed flower; petals 5–15, small, functioning as nectaries. Stamens numerous; fruit of several follicles.
**Size** 4–28 ins (10–70 cm).
**Flowering period** May–August.
**Ecology and distribution** Damp meadows, pastures and montane woodland clearings, on variable subsoils, from 3,280 to 8,860(–9,185) ft (1,000–2,700(–2,800) m). Very common in all European mountains (the Pyrenees, Alps, northern Apennines, Carpathians, Balkan Mountains, the British Isles and Scandinavia); it also comes down into the lowlands of eastern and northern Europe. Similar species are found in the Caucasus and the mountains of North America.
**Notes** A protected plant.

## 281 TROPAEOLUM POLYPHYLLUM Cav.

**Family** *Tropaeolaceae*
**Description** A herbaceous annual or perennial, stem prostrate at first then ascending, swollen, almost fleshy, leafy. Leaves alternate, on petioles of 1½–2½ ins (4–6 cm) long; blade sub-rounded, peltate, deeply divided almost to the centre into 7–9 oblong-spatulate, lanceolate or linear, entire or sinuate-dentate, glaucescent lobes. Flowers yellow, solitary, borne on long peduncles from the leaf axils on the upper part of the stem. Calyx tubular, with 5 lobes broadly ovate, prolonged into a long greenish-yellow spur. Corolla formed of 5 obcordate petals, longer than the sepals, with a long, attenuate claw, the two superior ones being wider and marked with red.
**Size** 12–24 ins (30–60 cm).
**Flowering period** October–April.
**Ecology and distribution** Woods, montane pastures and grassy or stony places, from 5,905 to 8,200 ft (1,800–2,500 m). Found in the Andes to the south of Peru, through Chile and Argentina, where it is an endemic species.
**Notes** The genus *Tropaeolum* (nasturtium) comprises about 80 species, all localized in the Andean range, from Colombia to Bolivia and Chile, widespread from the rain forest to the arid montane steppes.

---

## 282 UVULARIA GRANDIFLORA Pursh

**Family** *Liliaceae*
**Description** A rhizomatous, herbaceous plant with a simple or slightly branched stem, with incurved terminal branches, spreading-ascending, erect, with scale-like leaf sheaths near the base. Leaves on the upper part of the stem, alternate, perfoliate, flexuous, delicate, limp, ovate-lanceolate, pale green, lighter on the underside. Peduncles short, slender. Flowers yellow, solitary at the apex of the branches, drooping, campanulate or cylindrical. Perianth formed of 6 lanceolate tepals, lightly attached at the base and with a slight green raised area, with a central green marking, 1¼–1⅜ ins (3–3.5 cm) long. Stamens shorter than the perianth, yellow.
**Size** 12–16 ins (30–40 cm).
**Flowering period** May–June.
**Ecology and distribution** Montane woods, woodland clearings and damp places, from 1,640 to 4,920 ft (500–1,500 m). Widespread from southern Canada to Georgia and Carolina in the south-eastern United States, through the Appalachian Mountains.

## 283 **VACCINIUM VITIS-IDAEA** L.

Cowberry, Red Whortleberry, Mountain Cranberry

**Family** *Ericaceae*

**Description** A low-growing, much branched, evergreen shrub with prostrate branches and ascending branchlets at the top. Leaves close together, leathery, ½–1½ ins (1–4 cm) long, obovate or spatulate, with strongly revolute margins, lengthily attenuate into the petiole. Inflorescence a dense raceme, drooping, consisting of 3–6 white or whitish flowers (sometimes tinged with pink), with an inferior ovary. Corolla campanulate with 5 obtuse lobes, sometimes recurved. Berry red, edible.

**Size** 4–12(–32) ins (10–30(–80) cm).

**Flowering period** May–August.

**Ecology and distribution** Woodland clearings, high altitude heathlands, grassy or stony places, on a siliceous subsoil, from (1,970–)3,280 to 8,860(–9,840) ft ((600–) 1,000–2,700(–3,000) m). Found in all the European mountains (the Pyrenees, Alps, northern Apennines, the mountains of the British Isles, Scandinavia and Balkan peninsula), northern Asia and North America.

**Notes** There are other species of Cowberry which belong to the genus *Vaccinium: V. uliginosum*, Bog Whortleberry and *V. myrtillus*, Bilberry, which are equally common in the mountains of Eurasia and North America.

---

## 284 **VALERIANA MONTANA** L.

Mountain Valerian

**Family** *Valerianaceae*

**Description** A herbaceous, more or less stemless perennial, with a short, robust, woody rhizome. Epigeal stem erect, with a cluster of ovate basal leaves, on long petioles, undulate, glossy, coarsely dentate on the margin; stem leaves opposite, narrowly ovate, with a short petiole. Flowers pink, pale pink or white, in a dense terminal corymb, formed of more shortly pedunculate corymbs in the axils of the linear bracts. Calyx short, minute. Corolla tubular, slightly pouched at the base, with a limb consisting of 5 short, unequal lobes. Stamens 3, protruding from the corolla; style elongate. Fruit crowned with a feathery pappus.

**Size** 8–20 ins (20–50 cm).

**Flowering period** May–August.

**Ecology and distribution** Woods, woodland clearings, stabilized rubble, detritus and stony places, generally on a calcareous subsoil, from (1,970–)3,280 to 8,530 ft ((600–) 1,000–2,600 m). Frequent in the mountains of central and southern Europe (the Pyrenees, Alps, Jura, Apennines, Carpathians and the mountains of Sardinia, Corsica and the northern Balkan peninsula).

## 285 VALERIANA SUPINA L.
Dwarf Valerian

**Family** *Valerianaceae*
**Description** A small, tufted-spreading, prostrate, plant with a creeping woody stem and ascending branches forming a dense leafy mat. Basal leaves ovate, acute, entire or dentate, shortly stalked; stem leaves opposite in one or two pairs, sessile. Flowers pink in dense short terminal corymbs, with numerous short linear bracts at the base. Calyx very short. Corolla tube short, cylindrical, and a limb formed of 5 rounded, open lobes. Style lengthily projecting, bifid. Fruit crowned with a long feathery pappus.
**Size** 1¼–4(–6) ins (3–10(–15) cm).
**Flowering period** July–August.
**Ecology and distribution** Stony places, stabilized rubble, damp detritus, snow-beds, and along the banks of streams, on a calcareous subsoil, from 5,905 to 9,515 (–9,840) ft ((1,800–2,900(–3,000) m). Endemic to the central and eastern Alps, from the Rhaetian to the Carnic Alps, but most frequent in the western sector of its distribution area.

## 286 VERATRUM ALBUM L.
White False Helleborine

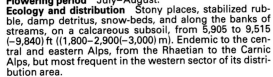

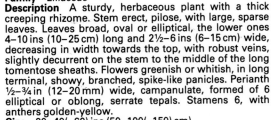

**Family** *Liliaceae*
**Description** A sturdy, herbaceous plant with a thick creeping rhizome. Stem erect, pilose, with large, sparse leaves. Leaves broad, oval or elliptical, the lower ones 4–10 ins (10–25 cm) long and 2½–6 ins (6–15 cm) wide, decreasing in width towards the top, with robust veins, slightly decurrent on the stem to the middle of the long tomentose sheaths. Flowers greenish or whitish, in long terminal, showy, branched, spike-like panicles. Perianth ½–¾ in (12–20 mm) wide, campanulate, formed of 6 elliptical or oblong, serrate tepals. Stamens 6, with anthers golden-yellow.
**Size** 20–40(–60) ins (50–100(–150) cm).
**Flowering period** June–August.
**Ecology and distribution** Fertile meadows, damp pastures and farm animal tracks, from 2,295 to 8,860 ft (700–2,700 m). A nitrophilous plant, common in the Pyrenees, Alps, Apennines, Jura, Vosges, Carpathians and Balkan Mountains. Related species are found in the Arctic regions of north-eastern Europe and eastern Asia.
**Notes** A highly poisonous species with a narcotic and paralyzing action due to the presence of alkaloids. The leaves can be mistaken for those of the *Gentiana lutea* (see entry 112), but differ in the hairiness of the basal sheaths.

## 287 VERONICA ALPINA L.
Alpine Speedwell

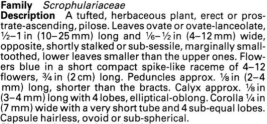

**Family** *Scrophulariaceae*
**Description** A tufted, herbaceous plant, erect or prostrate-ascending, pilose. Leaves ovate or ovate-lanceolate,
½–1 in (10–25 mm) long and ⅙–½ in (4–12 mm) wide,
opposite, shortly stalked or sub-sessile, marginally small-
toothed, lower leaves smaller than the upper ones. Flowers blue in a short compact spike-like raceme of 4–12
flowers, ¾ in (2 cm) long. Peduncles approx. ⅛ in (2–4
mm) long, shorter than the bracts. Calyx approx. ⅛ in
(3–4 mm) long with 4 lobes, elliptical-oblong. Corolla ¼ in
(7 mm) wide with a very short tube and 4 sub-equal lobes.
Capsule hairless, ovoid or sub-spherical.
**Size** ¾–6(–10) ins (2–15(–25) cm).
**Flowering period** July–August.
**Ecology and distribution** Stony places, stabilized rubble, detritus and moraines, preferably on an acid subsoil,
from (4,920–)5,905 to 9,840(–11,485) ft ((1,500–)1,800–
3,000(–3,500) m). Quite frequent in the mountains of central and southern Europe (the Iberian Mountains,
Pyrenees, Alps, Apennines, Carpathians, Balkan Moun-
tains, in Corsica, the British Isles and Scandinavia) and in
Arctic regions of north-eastern Asia and North America.

## 288 VERONICA APHYLLA L.

**Family** *Scrophulariaceae*
**Description** A dwarf, sub-acaulescent plant with creeping stolons from which emerge the epigeal stems. Leaves
obovate or elliptical-oblong, rounded, ½–⅝ in (10–15
mm) long and ¼–½ in (5–10 mm) wide, sessile, in rosettes at the base of the flowering stems. Flower stems
erect or ascending, generally leafless, with a small compact apical umbel of 2–5 flowers in the axils of short
oblong sessile bracts. Flowers violet, sometimes tinged
with pink, ¼–⅓ in (5–8 mm) wide. Calyx ⅛ in (3 mm)
long, with 4 sub-equal lobes. Corolla flattened-circular
with a very short tube and a limb of 4 unequal lobes, one
of which is quite large, two medium-sized and one small.
**Size** ½–1½(–2½) ins (1–4(–6) cm).
**Flowering period** June–August (–September).
**Ecology and distribution** Rocks, alpine pastures, stabilized rubble and snow-beds, on a calcareous subsoil, from
3,935 to 9,840 ft (1,200–3,000 m). Found in the Pyrenees,
Jura, Alps, Apennines, Carpathians and mountains of the
Balkan peninsula. Endemic to the mountains of central-
southern Europe.
**Notes** Related species are also found in the Altai Moun-
tains of central Asia and in North America.

## 289 VERONICA FRUTICANS Jacq.
Rock Speedwell
*V. saxatilis* Scop.

**Family** *Scrophulariaceae*
**Description** A prostrate-spreading plant, with woody creeping branches, ascending at the end. Leaves opposite, oblong or lanceolate, sessile, hairless or slightly pubescent, ⅓–¾ in (8–20 mm) long and ¹⁄₁₆–¼ in (2–7 mm) wide. Flowers dark blue with reddish or purple throats, united into short dense racemes, up to 1½–2½ ins (4–6 cm) long, of 4–10 flowers. Peduncles ¼ in (6 mm) long at first, becoming ⅝–¾ in (15–20 mm) when in fruit. Calyx ¼ in (5 mm) long, pilose. Corolla ½–⅝ in (10–15 mm) wide, with a very short tube and a limb of 4 sub-equal lobes.
**Size** 2–4(–6) ins (5–10(–15) cm).
**Flowering period** June–August(–September).
**Ecology and distribution** Stony places, detritus, rocks and stony pastures, on any type of subsoil, from 3,935 to 9,185(–9,840) ft (1,200–2,800(–3,000) m). Found sporadically in the Pyrenees, Vosges, Alps, Apennines, Carpathians and the mountains of the northern Balkan peninsula, in Corsica, the British Isles, Scandinavia and Arctic Europe (northern Russia, Iceland).

---

## 290 VERONICA PEDUNCULARIS Bieb.

**Family** *Scrophulariaceae*
**Description** A herbaceous, rhizomatous perennial, very branched at the base, with numerous ascending or erect, pubescent, epigeal stems. Leaves opposite, ⅓–1¹⁄₁₆ ins (8–27 mm) long and ⅙–¾ in (4–18 mm) wide, shortly stalked, broadly ovate or lanceolate, apically obtuse, truncate or slightly ciliate at the base, marginally incisedentate or serrate. Inflorescences in terminal racemes of 2–5 on each stem, each consisting of 10–25 very densely packed flowers. Flowers white, pinkish-white or pale sky-blue, veined in purplish-red. Calyx approx. ⅛ in (3–4 mm) long, 4-lobed. Corolla ⅓–½ in (8–13 mm) wide, with a very short tube and flattened-circular limb formed of 4 slightly unequal lobes, the smallest of which is ovate and the others sub-rounded.
**Size** 2½–12 ins (6–30 cm).
**Flowering period** April–July.
**Ecology and distribution** Alpine pastures, meadows, rocky slopes and woodland clearings, from (330–)2,950 to 8,860 ft ((100–)900–2,700 m). Widespread in the mountains of north-eastern Anatolia, Transcaucasia and the Caucasus.
**Notes** Related species are also found in the Crimean and south Ukrainian lowlands, for example, *V. umbrosa* Bieb.

## 291 VERONICA PONAE Gouan
Spiked Pyrenean Speedwell
*V. gouani* Mor.

**Family** *Scrophulariaceae*
**Description** A tufted perennial with an erect or ascending stem. Leaves opposite, oblong-lanceolate or broadly ovate, more or less cordate at the base, acute, sub-sessile, finely serrate, pubescent. Flowers sky-blue or violet-blue, pedunculate in the axils of short linear bracts, arranged in lax terminal racemes, up to 6 ins (15 cm) long. Peduncles ⅓–¾ in (8–20 mm) long, longer than the bracts. Calyx approx. ⅛ in (3.5–4 mm) long, with 4 sub-equal lobes. Corolla approx. ½ in (10 mm) diameter, with a very short tube and a flattened-circular limb of 4 unequal lobes.
**Size** 4–20 ins (10–50 cm).
**Flowering period** June–August.
**Ecology and distribution** Shady rocks, moist grassy places and damp woods, from 3,935 to 8,200 ft (1,200–2,500 m). Found in the Pyrenees and mountains of northern Spain; endemic to the Iberian peninsula.

---

## 292 VERONICA SATUREJOIDES Vis.

**Family** *Scrophulariaceae*
**Description** A tufted, herbaceous perennial, woody and leafless at the base, with prostrate-ascending, densely leafy branches. Leaves opposite, sub-rounded or oblanceolate, entire, slightly fleshy, ¼–½ in (6–10 mm) long, erect or almost appressed to the stem, finely pilose on the margin. Flowers pale violet or sky-blue, in short compact racemes up to 1¼ in (3 cm) long, with 6–12 sub-sessile flowers in the axils of short oblanceolate bracts. Calyx approx. ⅛ in (2.5–3 mm) long with 4–5 teeth. Corolla ¼ in (7 mm) wide, with a very short white tube and a limb of 4 unequal lobes. Stamens 2, and the style projecting well out of the tube.
**Size** 4–12 ins (10–30 cm).
**Flowering period** June–August.
**Ecology and distribution** Rocks, crags and precipices, rocky detritus and alpine meadows, from 5,575 to 7,220 ft (1,700–2,200 m). Endemic to the mountains of the southern Balkan peninsula, from south-western Bulgaria to Macedonia and northern Albania.

### 293 VICIA PYRENAICA Pourr.
Pyrenean Vetch

**Family** *Papilionaceae*
**Description** A hairless, herbaceous perennial, prostrate-spreading, stolon-bearing, branched at the base. Leaves compound-pinnate with a short terminal tendril and 4–6 pairs of oblong or sub-rounded leaflets, truncate or emarginate, mucronate; lower leaves without tendrils. Flowers violet-red or purple, large, solitary in the leaf axils. Calyx tubular campanulate, hairless, slightly irregular, with 5 short teeth. Corolla ⅝–1 in (16–25 mm) long, with a sub-orbicular widely spreading standard.
**Size** 4–12 ins (10–30 cm).
**Flowering period** June–August.
**Ecology and distribution** Pastures, grassy places and detritus, from 4,595 to 8,200 ft (1,400–2,500 m). Exclusive to the French and Spanish Pyrenees and southern French Alps, but quite rare.

---

### 294 VIOLA BIFLORA L.
Yellow Wood Violet

**Family** *Violaceae*
**Description** A fragile, tufted, sub-acaulescent perennial, with a short rhizome from which emerges a slender epigeal, simple or slightly branched stem. Leaves 2–4, mostly in a basal rosette, kidney-shaped, crenate, on long petioles. Flowers 2–3, yellow, apical on long peduncles. Calyx 5 lanceolate sepals, with appendages at the base. Corolla irregular, ⅝ in (1.5 cm) wide, with 5 petals, 4 of which are sub-equal to each other and the fifth oblong-rhomboid, with 4–6 brown lines and a short straight spur. Stamens enclosed within the corolla.
**Size** 2–4 ins (5–10 cm).
**Flowering period** (May–)June–August.
**Ecology and distribution** Moist stony places, stabilized rubble, rock crevices and woods, from (1,640–)3,280 to 8,860(–9,840) ft ((500–)1,000–2,700(–3,000) m). Frequent in the Pyrenees, Alps, Apennines, Caucasus, in the mountains of Corsica and Scandinavia, central Asia and the Arctic regions of Eurasia and North America.

**295  VIOLA CALCARATA**  L.
Long-spurred Pansy

**Family**  *Violaceae*
**Description**  A sub-acaulescent, more or less tufted, herbaceous perennial, very variable in size and morphology. Rhizome short, vertical, from which emerge one or two leafless, flowering stems, sometimes almost creeping. Basal leaves mostly in rosette-form, ovate or lanceolate, crenate-serrate, ½–1½ in (1–4 cm) long on a short petiole; stipules oblong, the lower ones entire or dentate, the upper trifid, ¼–⅝ in (0.5–1.5 cm) long. Flowers varying from violet to red, yellow, white or bicoloured, ¾–1½ ins (2–4 cm) long and ¾–1¼ ins (2–3 cm) wide, solitary at the apex of short leafless flower stalks or with two short, opposite, linear bracts. Calyx with serrate, lanceolate lobes. Corolla with 5 slightly unequal petals of which two are superior, two lateral and one inferior, the latter rather different from the others, being broadly obovate or spatulate with a spur ⅓–⅝ in (8–15 mm) long, straight or slightly recurved upwards, sub-equal to the petals.
**Size**  1¼–3¼(–4) ins (3–8(–10) cm).
**Flowering period**  May–August(–September).

**Ecology and distribution**  Very common in high altitude meadows and pastures where, in the summer, extensive areas can be seen covered with yellow and violet-coloured blooms mixed with flowers of other colours. It is also common in smaller sizes in stabilized rubble and detritus of the lower slopes. It will grow on any type of subsoil although with a preference for limestone, from (3,280–)4,920 to 7,875 ft ((1,000–)1,500–2,400 m); in exceptional cases it may even be found up to 9,185 to 10,500 ft (2,800–3,200 m). Very frequent in the western and central Alps, and in the Jura.

**Notes**  Because of its variability, numerous subspecies have been identified, sometimes even as separate species, e.g. *V. zoysii*, *V. villarsiana*. These are distributed in the western and eastern Alps, in the Dinaric Alps and the western Balkan peninsula. Similar species to *V. calcarata* are *V. eugeniae*, found in the Apennines (see entry 297), *V. bertolonii*, in the Alpes Maritimes, Apennines and in Sicily, and *V. graeca*, in the mountains of Albania and Greece.

## 296 VIOLA CORNUTA L.
Horned Pansy

**Family** *Violaceae*
**Description** A tufted perennial, with a slender rhizome. Stems epigeal, slender, slightly branched, ascending. Leaves ovate, acute, ¾–2 ins (2–5 cm) long, pilose on the underside. Stipule ovate-triangular, palmate-incise, ¼–⅝ in (0.5–1.5 cm) long. Flowers solitary flowering, large, fragrant, sky-blue or violet-blue, ¾–1½ ins (2–4 cm) wide. Calyx, 5 sepals with basal appendages. Petals 5, slightly unequal, oblanceolate or obovate, distant, the lower one broadly obovate with a long spur, ½–⅝ in (10–15 mm) long, straight or slightly recurved, often longer than the petals.
**Size** 2–12 ins (5–30 cm).
**Flowering period** June–August.
**Ecology and distribution** Meadows, pastures, woodland clearings and stony places, usually on a calcareous subsoil, from (2,295–)3,280 to 8,200 ft ((700–)1,000–2,500 m). Endemic to the Pyrenees.
**Notes** Frequently grown as a garden plant, but sometimes reverts to its wild state, for example, in central Europe.

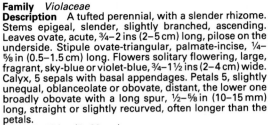

## 297 VIOLA EUGENIAE Parl

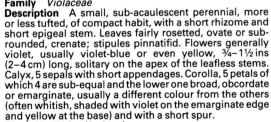

**Family** *Violaceae*
**Description** A small, sub-acaulescent perennial, more or less tufted, of compact habit, with a short rhizome and short epigeal stem. Leaves fairly rosetted, ovate or sub-rounded, crenate; stipules pinnatifid. Flowers generally violet, usually violet-blue or even yellow, ¾–1½ ins (2–4 cm) long, solitary on the apex of the leafless stems. Calyx, 5 sepals with short appendages. Corolla, 5 petals of which 4 are sub-equal and the lower one broad, obcordate or emarginate, usually a different colour from the others (often whitish, shaded with violet on the emarginate edge and yellow at the base) and with a short spur.
**Size** ¾–1½ ins (2–4 cm).
**Flowering period** May–July.
**Ecology and distribution** Pastures and open stony places, preferably on calcareous soil, from (3,935–)4,595 to 7,220(–8,200) ft ((1,200–)1,400–2,200(–2,500)m). Endemic to the Apennines where it is quite common, from Tuscany-Romagna to Calabria.
**Notes** In the past it was regarded as a variety of *Viola calcarata* but the shape of its petals and pinnatifid stipules (in *V. calcarata* they are trifid), distinguish it as a species in its own right; limited to the Apennines.

**298  VITALIANA PRIMULIFLORA**  Bertol.
*Douglasia vitaliana* (L.) Pax; *Gregoria vitaliana* (L.) Duby

**Family**  *Primulaceae*
**Description**  A prostrate, herbaceous perennial, with creeping, very branched stems forming loose mats. Leaves in dense rosettes at the end of the ascending branches, linear, entire, ¼ in (5 mm) long, green or greyish-green. Flowers bright yellow, sub-sessile, in groups of 1–5, apical on the branches in the centre of the rosettes. Calyx sub-cylindrical, divided into 5 linear lobes. Corolla about ½ in (1 cm) wide, with a long cylindrical tube, narrow, and an expanded limb formed of 5 oblong lobes, often almost convergent.
**Size**  ¾–1¼ ins (2–3 cm).
**Flowering period**  May–July(–August).
**Ecology and distribution**  Stony places, rocks, stabilized detritus and rocky ridges, often on an acid subsoil, from 5,575 to 9,840(–11,155) ft (1,700–3,000(–3,400) m). Quite frequent in the mountains of south-western Europe (the Iberian Mountains, Pyrenees, Alps and central Apennines).
**Notes**  Numerous subspecies have been identified, each with a very limited distribution area, and differing in their hairiness, leaves and corolla.

---

**299  WALDSTEINIA FRAGARIOIDES**  (Michx.) Tratt.

**Family**  *Rosaceae*
**Description**  A more or less stemless perennial with a creeping rhizome. Basal leaves trifoliate, on long petioles; leaflets obovate, broadly cuneate and entire near the base, dentate or crenate in the upper half, often deeply incised, 1–2½ ins (2.5–6 cm) long. Flower stem delicate, erect or spreading, with a lax corymb of 3–8 flowers on long peduncles from the axils of short lanceolate bracts. Flowers yellow, ¼–½ in (6–14 mm) long. Calyx campanulate with 5 lobes, ovate-lanceolate, acute. Corolla, 5 obovate or elliptical petals, twice the length of the calyx lobes.
**Size**  5–8 ins (12–20 cm).
**Flowering period**  May–June.
**Ecology and distribution**  Montane woods and shady hillside sites, from 1,640 to 6,560 ft (500–2,000 m). Widespread in south-eastern Canada and through the eastern states of North America, from New Brunswick to Michigan, Indiana and Georgia.
**Notes**  The specific name derives from the resemblance to the strawberry plant (*Fragaria vesca*), although it is easily recognizable by its yellow flowers which in the strawberry are white.

## 300 WULFENIA CARINTHIACA Jacq.

**Family** *Scrophulariaceae*
**Description** A sub-acaulescent, herbaceous perennial, with a short rhizome and erect stem emerging from a basal rosette of oblong-spatulate leaves, attenuate at the base into a short petiole, large, puckered-undulate, marginally crenate. Flower stems with small, alternate, sessile, lanceolate-acute, distant leaves. Flowers violet-blue, in a dense terminal spike, 1½–2½ ins (4–6 cm) long. Calyx shortly campanulate, with a short tube and five-lobed limb. Corolla tubular, irregular, sky-blue and lighter inside; a short bilabiate limb, upper lip with 2 lips and lower lip three-lobed. Stamens 2, within the corolla tube; style lengthily protruding.
**Size** 6–10(–16) ins (15–25(–40) cm).
**Flowering period** July–August.
**Ecology and distribution** Wet pastures and damp grassy places, from 4,920 to 6,560 ft (1,500–2,000m). Endemic to the Carnic Alps and to the region of Montenegro in the southern Dinaric Alps.
**Notes** Strictly protected because of its rarity.

---

## 301 ZIGADENUS ELEGANS Pursh

**Family** *Liliaceae*
**Description** A bulbous, acaulescent or more or less stemless, herbaceous plant, with a basal tuft of linear, acuminate leaves, 6–10 ins (15–25 cm) long. Flower stems 1–3 per plant, each with a lax terminal inflorescence of 3–10 shortly pedunculate flowers, in the axil of small lanceolate bracts. Flowers greenish-white, 1–1¼ ins (2.5–3 cm), composed of 6 oval tepals, obtuse or slightly small-toothed at the apex, with a transverse dark green mark near the base. Stamens 6, short.
**Size** 10–24 ins (25–60 cm).
**Flowering period** June–August.
**Ecology and distribution** Damp meadows, along the banks of streams, in moist woods and open grassy places, 5,905 to 11,810 ft (1,800–3,600 m). Widespread in the Rocky Mountains and neighbouring ranges, from Alaska to Nevada and New Mexico, and spreading east as far as Minnesota.

# GLOSSARY

**acaulescent/acauline/acaulose**  stemless or nearly so.
**achene**  indehiscent dry fruit with one seed only.
**acuminate**  narrowing to a point.
**acute**  ending in a point.
**alternate leaves**  arranged at different heights on the stem, with one leaf at each node.
**amplexicaul**  a sessile leaf whose base clasps the stem horizontally.
**anther**  the fertile part of a stamen which produces pollen.
**aphyllous/aphylly**  without leaves.
**apical/apiculate**  ending in a short, sharp point.
**appressed/addressed leaves**  closely flattened; compacted but not joined.
**arachnoid**  covered with long, fine hairs or fibres which intertwine and cover the flower or leaf like a spider's web.
**aristate/awned/bearded**  equipped at the apex with a long, narrow point.
**ascending**  said of a stem or branch which grows more or less horizontally at first and then gradually becomes erect.
**attenuate leaf**  tapering gradually towards its base.
**auriculate**  having two ear-like appendages at the base.
**awn/arista**  a thread-like outgrowth found at the apex of some types of sepal or bract.
**axil**  the angle formed between a leaf and the stem at its point of attachment to the node.
**basal leaves**  leaves growing from the base of a plant, as distinct from stem leaves.
**basophilous**  describes a plant that thrives best in alkaline soil.
**berry**  a fleshy fruit with a high water content and numerous cartilaginous seeds.
**bifid petal**  divided into two laciniae by a deep cleft.
**bilabiate corolla**  formed by an upper and lower lip.
**bilobed petal**  divided into two lobes.
**bilocular ovary**  divided into two cavities or chambers.
**bipinnate**  a compound leaf with main segments pinnately divided.
**bract**  a type of modified leaf at the base of a flower or inflorescence.
**bracteole**  a small leaf on a flower stalk.
**bulb**  an ovoid, underground organ consisting of a small, compressed stem surrounded by several overlapping scales, papery on the outside (tunics) and fleshy inside.
**bulbil**  a small aerial bulb produced at the axil of the leaves or among the flowers.
**bullate**  puckered (as primrose leaf).
**calcicole**  lime-loving.
**calyx**  external whorl consisting of sepals, usually green, which protect the flower when in bud.
**campanulate corolla**  bell-shaped.
**capitate inflorescence**  like a capitulum.
**capitulum**  an inflorescence consisting of numerous sessile flowers arranged at the apex of the peduncle on the receptacle, all on the same level, and surrounded by a corona of bracts.
**capsule**  a dry, ovoid or globose fruit that opens on ripening by a parting of its valves.

**carinate leaf** with the central vein angled, like the keel of a boat.

**cespitose plant** growing in tufts; a plant that sends up a number of branches, fairly close together, from its base.

**ciliate** having margins fringed with hairs.

**cinerous** covered with short, thick, ash-grey hairs.

**claviform calyx** club-shaped.

**claw** the narrowed base of a petal.

**compound-ternate** a trifoliate leaf with ramified leaflets.

**cordate** in the shape of a reversed heart, with the point at the top.

**corolla or calyx tube** the basal part of the gamopetalous corolla or of the gamopetalous calyx.

**corymb** an elongated inflorescence of pedunculate flowers that spring from different points of the primary axis but all reaching the same height.

**crenate** with a notched edge or small, rounded teeth.

**cristate/cristatus petal** having a narrow band of hairs running centrally like a crest.

**cuneate/cuneiform leaf** wedge-shaped, narrowing down to a point.

**cyme** a determinate inflorescence in which the terminal flower of the primary axis opens first.

**deciduous** losing its leaves at the end of each vegetative season.

**decumbent branches** lying along the ground but turning upwards at the tip.

**decurrent leaf** of which the base extends down the stem like two wings.

**dentate** a margin with sharp, tooth-like notches.

**dialypetalous corolla** with separate petals.

**dialysepalous calyx** with separate sepals.

**diffuse plant or stem** almost prostrate, branching out in all directions.

**digitate leaf** divided into lobes like the fingers of a hand.

**dioecious** having male and female sex organs on separate individuals.

**drupe** a fleshy fruit with a pulpous pericarp and a single seed contained in a woody involucre.

**elliptical** narrow, tapering at each end like an ellipse.

**emarginate** having a deep cut at the tip.

**endemic** said of a plant with a very restricted distribution area; limited to a relatively small territory.

**epigeal** growing above ground.

**equitant leaves** folded lengthwise from the base, one within the other.

**erect-patent** a leaf positioned at an acute angle of about 45° to the stem.

**falcate/falciform** curved, like a sickle.

**fasciculate** in bundles, all being of the same kind, e.g. leaves.

**filament** the stalk of a stamen with an anther at its apex.

**fistulose/fistular stem** hollow, like a pipe.

**flabellate/flabelliform** spread out in the shape of a fan.

**floccose** covered with long, tangled white hairs.

**floral involucre** a group of bracts surrounding a flower or inflorescence.

**foliar rosette**   a group of leaves arranged at the base of a short stem, lying close together on or near the ground.
**foliar segments**   the portions of the lamina of a leaf when deeply lobed but not divided into leaflets.
**follicle**   an elongate, dry fruit that splits open longitudinally on maturity to release its many seeds.
**gamopetalous/monopetalous/sympetalous corolla**   petals partly or entirely fused together; tubular.
**gamosepalous/monosepalous calyx**   sepals partly or entirely fused together; tubular.
**glandulous/glandular**   covered with hairs that emit a viscous fluid when touched.
**glaucous/glaucescent**   covered with a waxy, sea-green bloom.
**gramineous**   similar to the linear leaves of the grass family; grass-like.
**hirsute**   covered with long, but not stiff, hairs.
**hispid**   covered with rough, bristly hairs.
**hyaline**   the very fine, translucent white margin of a leaf or bract.
**imparipinnate**   a compound-pinnate leaf with a terminal leaflet.
**indehiscent**   not opening at maturity; a seedpod, for example.
**inferior ovary**   positioned below the insertion of the perianth.
**labellum**   the lower tepal of an orchid bloom, usually very showy and colourful.
**laciniae**   the parts into which some types of corolla or leaf blade are divided.
**laciniate**   divided into deep, narrow segments (laciniae).
**lamina or blade**   the broad part of a leaf.
**lanceolate**   lance-shaped, tapering to a pointed apex.
**leaflets**   the separate portions of a compound-pinnate leaf.
**legume**   an elongate, dry fruit that splits open by two longitudinal sutures on maturity, e.g. a pea-pod.
**ligulate/liguliform**   strap-shaped, as the ray-florets of many Composites e.g. Daisy, Chicory, etc.
**limb of a petal**   the distal part of a petal.
**linear**   narrow and long.
**lip**   part of the limb of a bilabiate gamopetalous corolla.
**lobes**   the parts into which a leaf, calyx or corolla are cut.
**lyrate**   lyre-shaped; a lobed leaf with a broad terminal lobe and smaller lateral lobes that decrease in size towards the leaf base.
**mucronate**   a leaf which is tipped with a short, sharp, stiff point.
**nectary**   a gland in some flowers, the purpose of which is to attract pollinating insects.
**nitrophilous**   referring to plants characteristic of sites with a high concentration of nitrogen compounds.
**obconic/obconical calyx**   reverse cone-shape.
**obcordate**   heart-shaped, with the point at the base.
**oblanceolate**   shaped like a lance in reverse.
**oblong leaf**   an elongate leaf, with margins almost parallel.
**obovate**   shaped like an upside-down egg, i.e. point at the base.
**obtuse**   having a blunted apex.
**orbicular/orbiculate**   circular, round.
**outer calyx**   an involucre of bracts at the base of the calyx.
**ovary**   the female part of a flower which contains the ovules.
**ovate**   egg-shaped.

**palmatifid**   a palmate leaf whose margin is cut into by at least two-thirds.

**palmatinervis/palmatinerved**   a leaf with venation arranged like the fingers of a hand.

**palmatisect**   a palmate leaf whose margin is deeply cut almost to the centre.

**panicle**   a branched, elongate inflorescence with pedunculate flowers positioned at various heights.

**papillose**   covered with very small protuberances (papillae).

**pappus**   a ring of fine hairs or scales developed from the calyx to aid wind-dispersal.

**parallel-veined**   a leaf in which the main veins run parallel to each other.

**paripinnate**   a compound-pinnate leaf with two terminal leaflets.

**patent**   a leaf that is set at an angle of about 90° to the stem; spreading.

**pedicel**   the stalk of each individual flower of an inflorescence.

**peduncle**   the stalk supporting a flower or inflorescence.

**peltate**   a leaf in which the petiole is attached to the centre of the blade, like an umbrella.

**perfoliate**   a leaf base which surrounds the stem on which it is growing so completely that it appears to be perforated by it.

**perianth**   a floral involucre formed by sterile floral leaves.

**perule/leaf-bud scale**   a small leaf found at the base of a shoot when in its bud state.

**petals**   floral leaves which form the corolla.

**petiole**   the stalk of a leaf at the base of the blade.

**pinnate-lobed**   a pinnate-leaf in which the margin is slightly cut.

**pinnate-parted**   a leaf in which the margin is cut about one-third towards the mid-rib into pinnately arranged lobes.

**pinnately veined**   a leaf in which the venation is arranged like a bird's feathers.

**pinnatifid**   a leaf in which the margin is cut at least two-thirds towards the mid-rib into pinnately arranged lobes.

**pinnatisect**   a leaf in which the margin is cut right down to the mid-rib into pinnately arranged lobes.

**prostrate/procumbent**   a stem or plant with a creeping habit.

**raceme**   an elongate inflorescence with pedunculate flowers produced in succession from the base of the stem upwards.

**reflexed**   abruptly turned back and downwards.

**retuse**   having a small notch at the apex.

**revolute**   with the margin rolled back, usually downwards.

**rhizome**   an elongated underground stem with a bud at one end from which develop one or more branches above ground bearing leaves and flowers.

**rosulate plant**   equipped with a basal rosette of leaves.

**rotate corolla**   spreading out like a wheel; flattened-circular.

**saccate**   a petal or sepal that bulges out at its base like a small bag.

**scabrous**   having a rough surface.

**scape**   a flower-stalk equipped only with basal leaves.

**scapiform stem**   similar to a scape.

**scarious/scariose**   having a whitish, thin edge to the margin.

**scorpioid cyme**   a definitive inflorescence which is curled round like the tail of a scorpion.

**sepals**   floral leaves forming the calyx of a flower.

**sericerous**   covered with short, soft hairs; silky.

**serrate**   having a toothed margin like the teeth of a saw.

**sessile**   with either a petiole or a peduncle.

**setaceous leaf**   shaped like a bristle.

**setose**   bristly.

**sheath**   the basal part of some leaves enveloping a stem.

**silicle**   the fruit of the Cruciferae family formed in two parts that split open on maturity, leaving the seeds exposed on a central septum.

**spadix**   a spiky inflorescence with a thickened, fleshy axis, enclosed in a spathe.

**spathe**   a large, coloured bract enclosing a spadix-type of inflorescence.

**spatulate**   spatula-shaped, i.e. narrow at the base and broadening at the top.

**spicate**   spike-shaped.

**spiciform**   a spike-like inflorescence.

**spike**   an elongate inflorescence of sessile flowers arranged at different levels on the axis.

**spur**   an extension of the petal or sepal to be seen in some types of flower.

**stem**   the axis of a plant bearing its leaves; it acts both as support and conductor of nutriments.

**stigma**   the terminal part of the female organ of the flower which is designed to receive the pollen.

**stipules**   small appendages arranged in pairs at the base of some types of leaves.

**stolon**   a long, creeping stem that puts out roots from its nodes and leaves.

**style**   the axis linking the ovary to the stigma.

**sub-acaulescent**   almost acaulescent, i.e. with very few leaves on the stem but having a basal rosette.

**subulate**   awl-shaped; sub-cylindrical.

**suffrutescent/suffruticose**   small woody plant with herbaceous branches shooting out from the base; usually less than 20 ins (50 cm) in height.

**superior ovary**   positioned above the point of attachment of the perianth.

**tap-root**   a thick, cylindrical root directed vertically downwards and tapering away.

**tepal**   a floral leaf; a segment of the perianth.

**ternate**   a leaf divided into three fairly deeply-cut parts.

**tomentose**   covered with felt-like, whitish hairs.

**tomentum**   a covering of cotton-like hairs.

**trifid**   divided about half-way down into three parts.

**trifoliate**   a compound palmate leaf with three leaflets.

**tripartite**   a leaf divided nearly to the base into three parts.

**tripinnate**   a pinnately compound leaf with pinnately divided leaflets which are themselves pinnately divided.

**tubular**   elongate and cylindrically-shaped capitulum flowers.

**umbel**   an inflorescence of pedunculate flowers that all spring from the same point and all reach the same height.

**umbilicate calyx**   hemispherical but embedded into the point of attachment of the peduncle.

**uncinate/uncate**   equipped with a hook-shaped point.
**uniflorous/unifloral**   producing only one flower.
**uninervate leaf**   having only one vein.
**valves**   the parts into which a dry fruit divides when it opens.
**villose**   covered with long, wavy hairs.
**whorl/verticel**   a group of normal or floral leaves arranged around the same node to form a corona.
**xerophilous**   able to tolerate a dry habitat.
**zygomorphic/zygomorphous flower**   having bilateral symmetry; divisible into similar halves by only one plane.

## ACKNOWLEDGMENTS

The Publisher gratefully acknowledges the co-operation of the following: Giardino Botanico Alpino 'Paradisia', Ente Parco Nazionale, Gran Paradiso, Cogne (Italy); Jardin d'Altitude du Haut-Chitelet, Col de la Schlucht, Hautes Vosges (France); Giardino Botanico Alpino delle Viotte, Monte Bondone (Italy); Egidio Anchisi of the Jardin Alpin 'Flore-Alpe', foundation Jean-Marcel Aubert, Champex-Lax, Valais (Switzerland); Jardin Botanique de l'Université et de la Ville de Lausanne (Switzerland); Jardin Alpin 'La Thomasia', Pont-de-Nant sur Bex (Switzerland); Orto Botanico 'Chanousia', Piccolo San Bernardo (France–Italy); Conservatoire et Jardin Botaniques de la Ville de Genève (Switzerland); Garden Club, Monaco (Principality of Monaco); Marcel Kroenlein of the Jardin Exotique, Monaco (Principality of Monaco); Jardin Alpin 'La Rambertia', Rochers-de-Naye (France); Funivie di Val Veny, Courmayeur (Italy); Jardin Botanique et Station d'Ecologie Végétale 'La Jaysiniia', Samoëns (France); Réserve Naturelle des Aiguilles Rouges, Argentière (France); Royal Botanic Gardens, Kew (England).

## PICTURE CREDITS

All photographs are by Giuseppe Mazza, Monte Carlo, with the exception of the following: p. 10, Erwin A. Bauer; p. 45 and plant species entries 158 and 265, Benedetto Lanza, Florence; plant species entry 216, Marcello Tardelli, Florence.
*Diagrams and maps:* pp. 11, 14–15, 18, 19, Andrea Corbella, Milan.

# INDEX